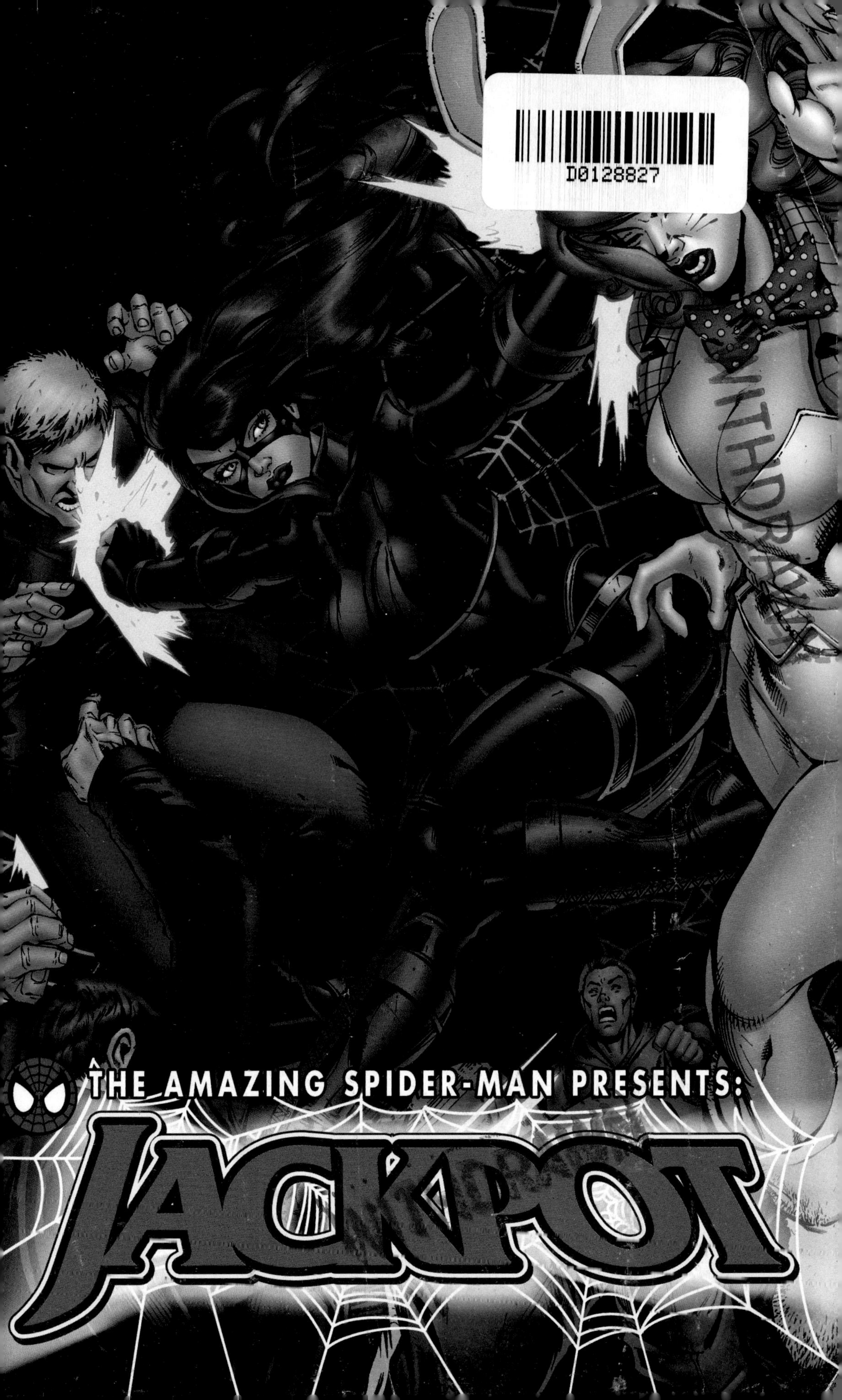
THE AMAZING SPIDER-MAN PRESENTS:
JACKPOT

THE AMAZING SPIDER-MAN PRESENTS:

JACKPOT

Writer: **MARC GUGGENHEIM**
Penciler: **ADRIANA MELO** • Inker: **MARIAH BENES**
Colorist: **ANDREW DALHOUSE** • Letterer: **VC'S JOE CARAMAGNA**
Cover artists: **DAVID YARDIN & FRANK D'ARMATA;**
ADRIANA MELO, MARIAH BENES & CHRISTOPHER SOTOMAYOR;
MIRCO PIERFEDERICI; PAULO SIQUEIRA & RAIN BEREDO

"EXIT INTERVIEW"

Writer: **BRIAN REED** • Penciler: **TIM LEVINS**
Inkers: **VICTOR OLAZABA & WALDEN WONG**
Colorist: **CHRISTOPHER SOTOMAYOR**
Letterer: **DAVE SHARPE**

Assistant Editor: **TOM BRENNAN**
Editor: **STEVE WACKER**
Executive Editor: **TOM BREVOORT**

Collection Editor: **NICOLE BOOSE** • Assistant Editor: **ALEX STARBUCK**
Associate Editor: **JOHN DENNING**
Editors, Special Projects: **JENNIFER GRÜNWALD & MARK D. BEAZLEY**
Senior Editor, Special Projects: **JEFF YOUNGQUIST**
Senior Vice President of Sales: **DAVID GABRIEL**

Editor in Chief: **JOE QUESADA**
Publisher: **DAN BUCKLEY**
Executive Producer: **ALAN FINE**

SPECIAL THANKS TO BETH SCORZATO

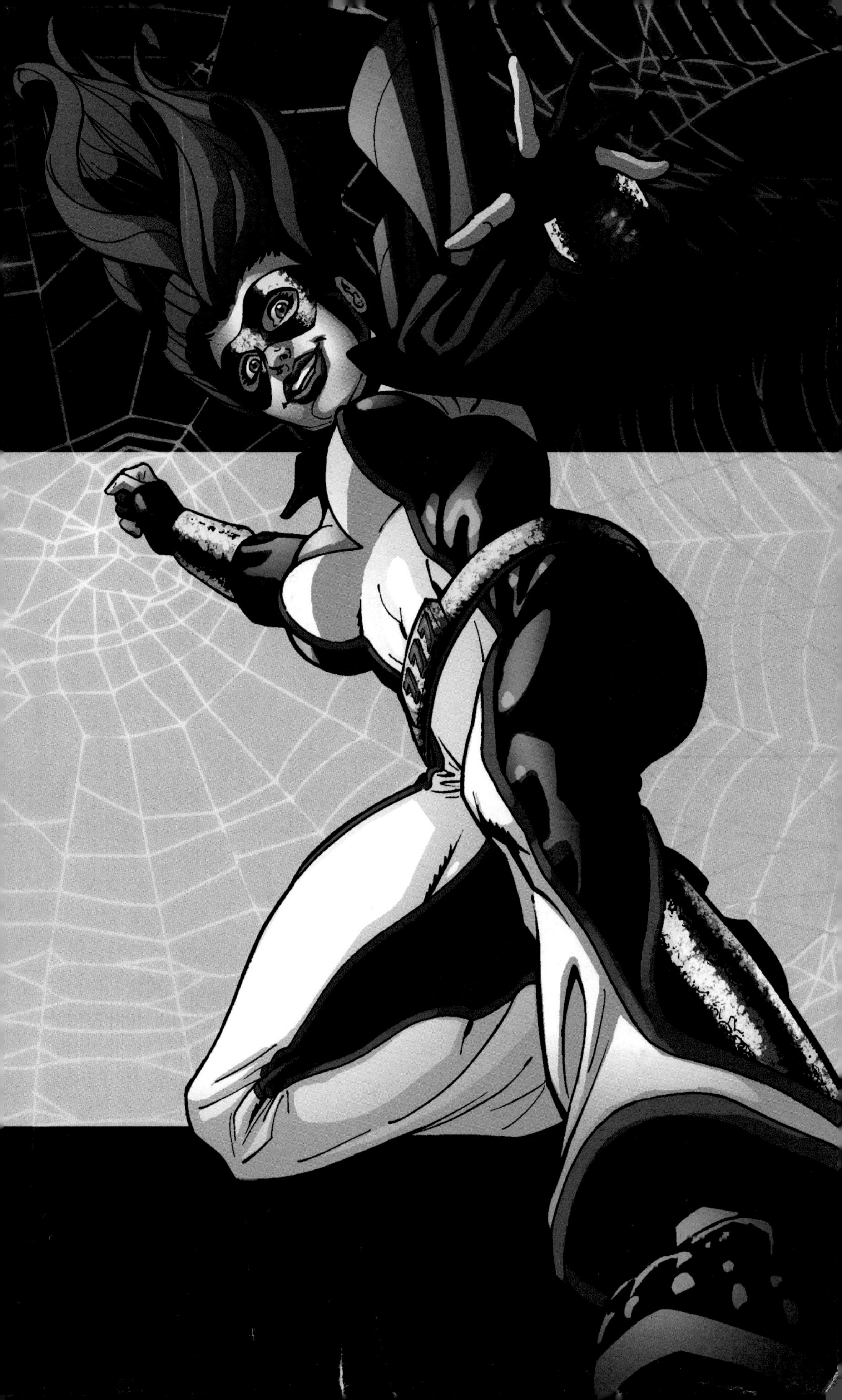

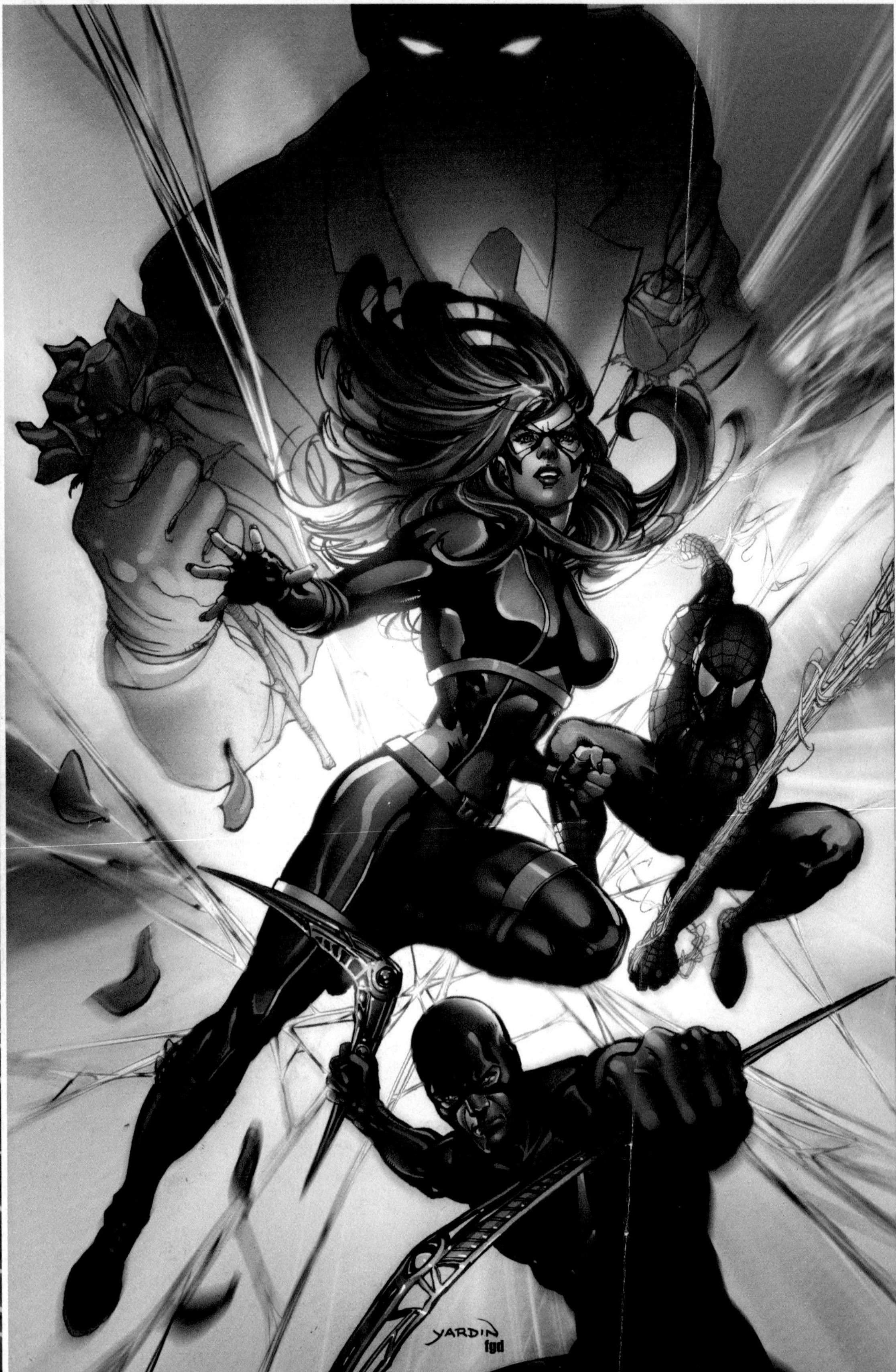
YARDIN
fgd

AMAZING SPIDER-MAN PRESENTS: JACKPOT #1

SARA EHRET – THE *ORIGINAL* JACKPOT
– What's her real
life like?!   more…

SUPER-MOURNING?
Reed Richards talks
about the life expectancy
rate on superhumans in
today's world… more…

**WHATEVER HAPPENED
TO THIS GUY?**
Boomerang goes
off-radar…more…

Who is Jackpot?! This question consumed Spider-Man's life for the better part of a year when he first ran across the red-headed super heroine who reminded him of his erstwhile ex, Mary Jane Watson. But when he discovered she was Alana Jobson, a would-be heroine taking the power enhancing Mutant Growth Hormone pills, he tried to put a stop to her efforts – only to watch her die from poisons the drug had introduced into her body.

But Alana wasn't the first Jackpot…she'd bought the name from Sara Ehret, a woman with super-powers but no impetus to use them. Sara didn't want to fight crime, she wanted a normal life. When Spider-Man confronted Sara over leaving the great responsibility entrusted in her to someone else's care, Sara became defiant and ordered Spider-Man out of her home. But Spider-Man left her Jackpot's costume… and a reminder that she owed the world a hero.

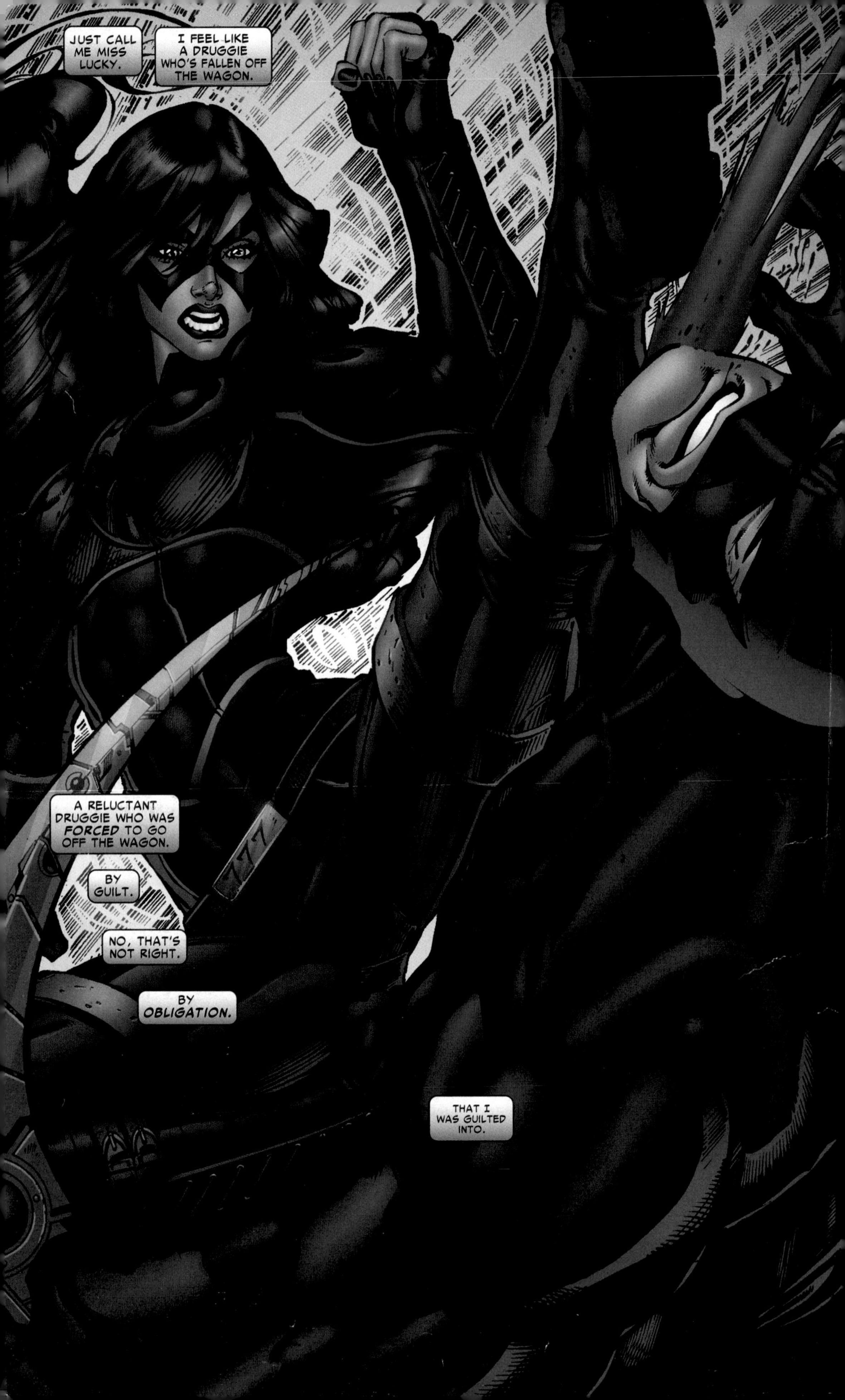
JUST CALL ME MISS LUCKY.
I FEEL LIKE A DRUGGIE WHO'S FALLEN OFF THE WAGON.
A RELUCTANT DRUGGIE WHO WAS *FORCED* TO GO OFF THE WAGON.
BY GUILT.
NO, THAT'S NOT RIGHT.
BY *OBLIGATION.*
THAT I WAS GUILTED INTO.

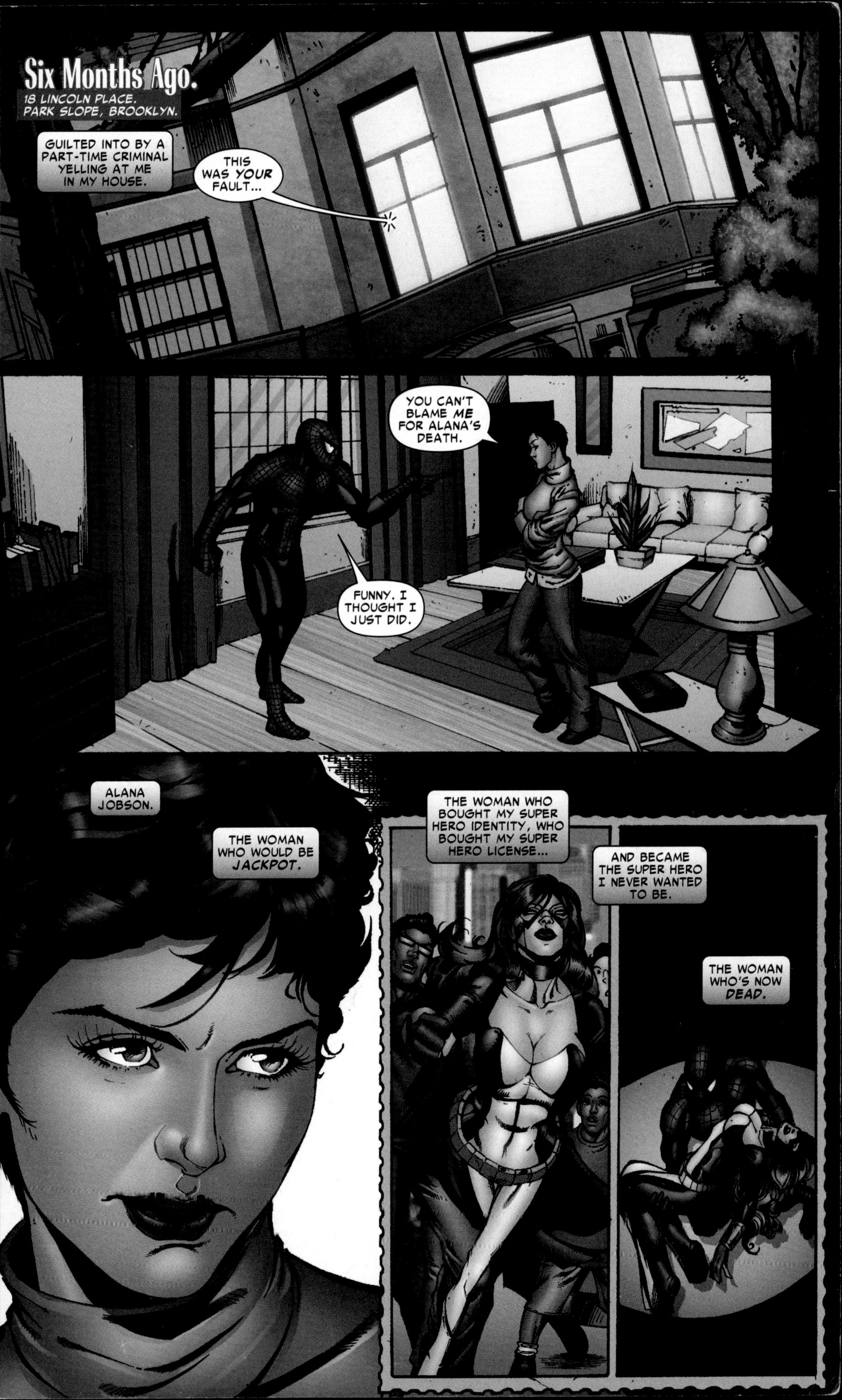
Six Months Ago.
18 LINCOLN PLACE.
PARK SLOPE, BROOKLYN.
GUILTED INTO BY A PART-TIME CRIMINAL YELLING AT ME IN MY HOUSE.
THIS WAS YOUR FAULT...
YOU CAN'T BLAME ME FOR ALANA'S DEATH.
FUNNY. I THOUGHT I JUST DID.
ALANA JOBSON.
THE WOMAN WHO WOULD BE JACKPOT.
THE WOMAN WHO BOUGHT MY SUPER HERO IDENTITY, WHO BOUGHT MY SUPER HERO LICENSE...
AND BECAME THE SUPER HERO I NEVER WANTED TO BE.
THE WOMAN WHO'S NOW DEAD.

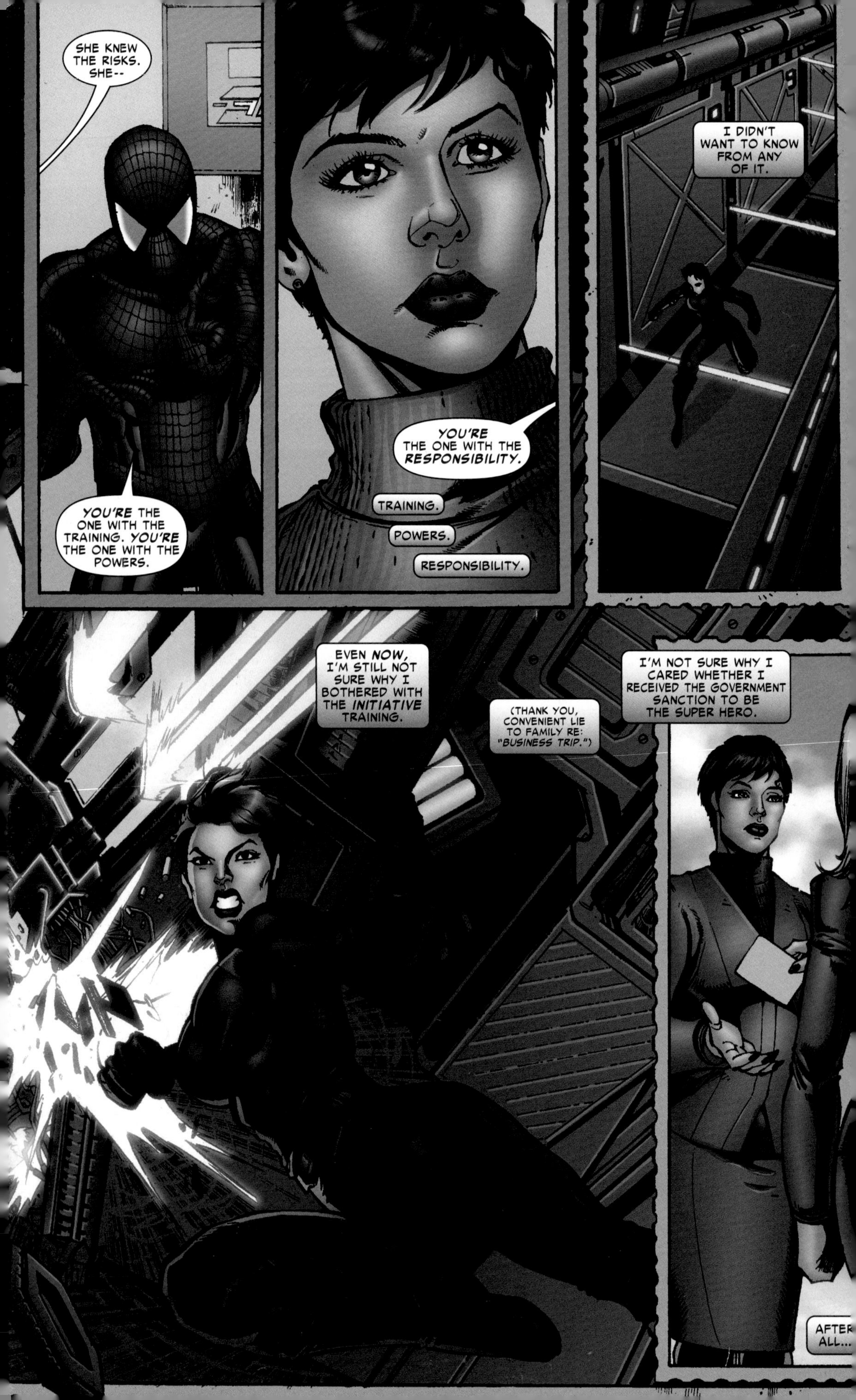
SHE KNEW THE RISKS. SHE--
YOU'RE THE ONE WITH THE TRAINING. YOU'RE THE ONE WITH THE POWERS.
YOU'RE THE ONE WITH THE RESPONSIBILITY.
TRAINING.
POWERS.
RESPONSIBILITY.
I DIDN'T WANT TO KNOW FROM ANY OF IT.
EVEN NOW, I'M STILL NOT SURE WHY I BOTHERED WITH THE INITIATIVE TRAINING.
(THANK YOU, CONVENIENT LIE TO FAMILY RE: "BUSINESS TRIP.")
I'M NOT SURE WHY I CARED WHETHER I RECEIVED THE GOVERNMENT SANCTION TO BE THE SUPER HERO.
AFTER ALL...

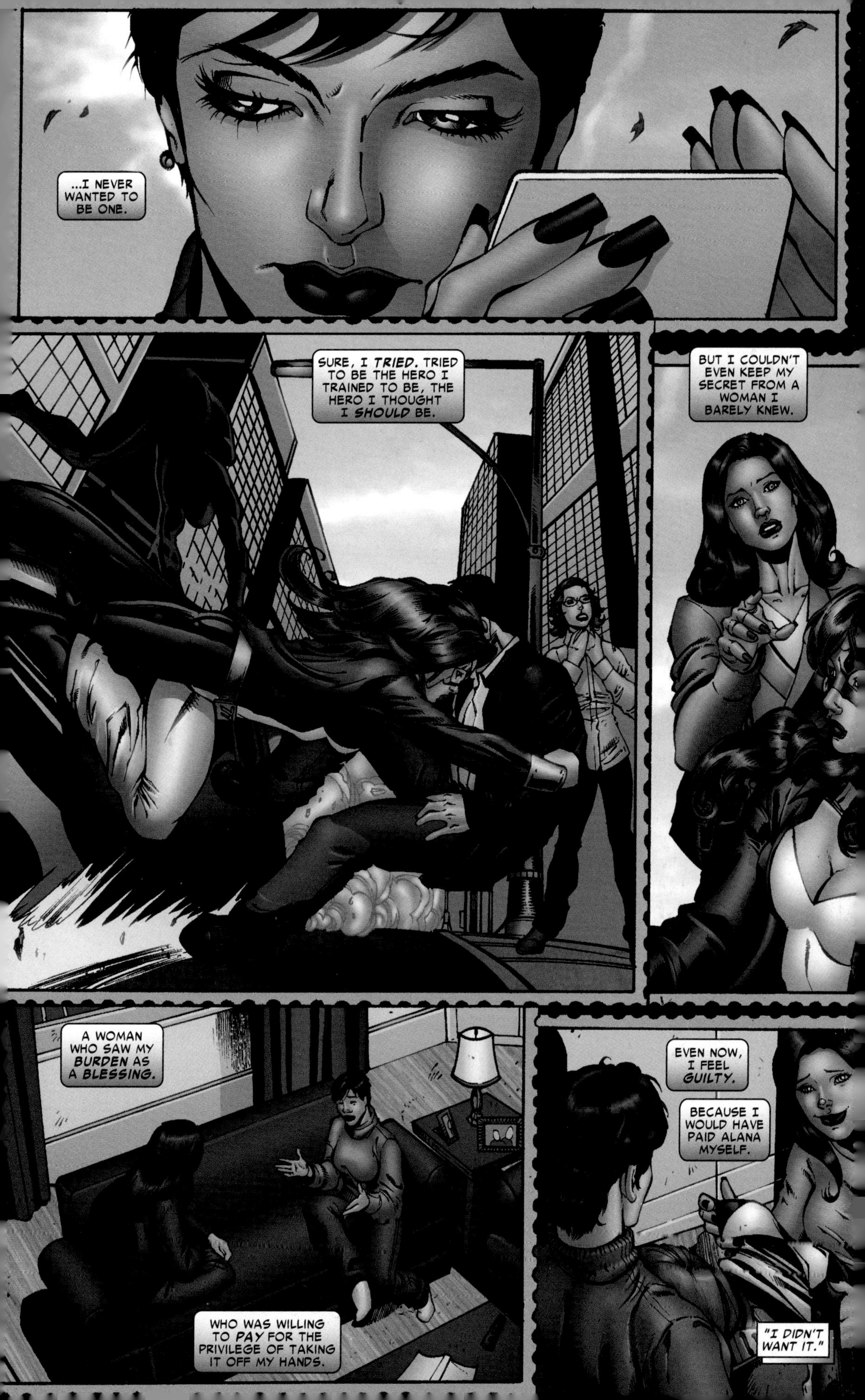
...I NEVER WANTED TO BE ONE.
SURE, I TRIED. TRIED TO BE THE HERO I TRAINED TO BE, THE HERO I THOUGHT I SHOULD BE.
BUT I COULDN'T EVEN KEEP MY SECRET FROM A WOMAN I BARELY KNEW.
A WOMAN WHO SAW MY BURDEN AS A BLESSING.
WHO WAS WILLING TO PAY FOR THE PRIVILEGE OF TAKING IT OFF MY HANDS.
EVEN NOW, I FEEL GUILTY.
BECAUSE I WOULD HAVE PAID ALANA MYSELF.
"I DIDN'T WANT IT."

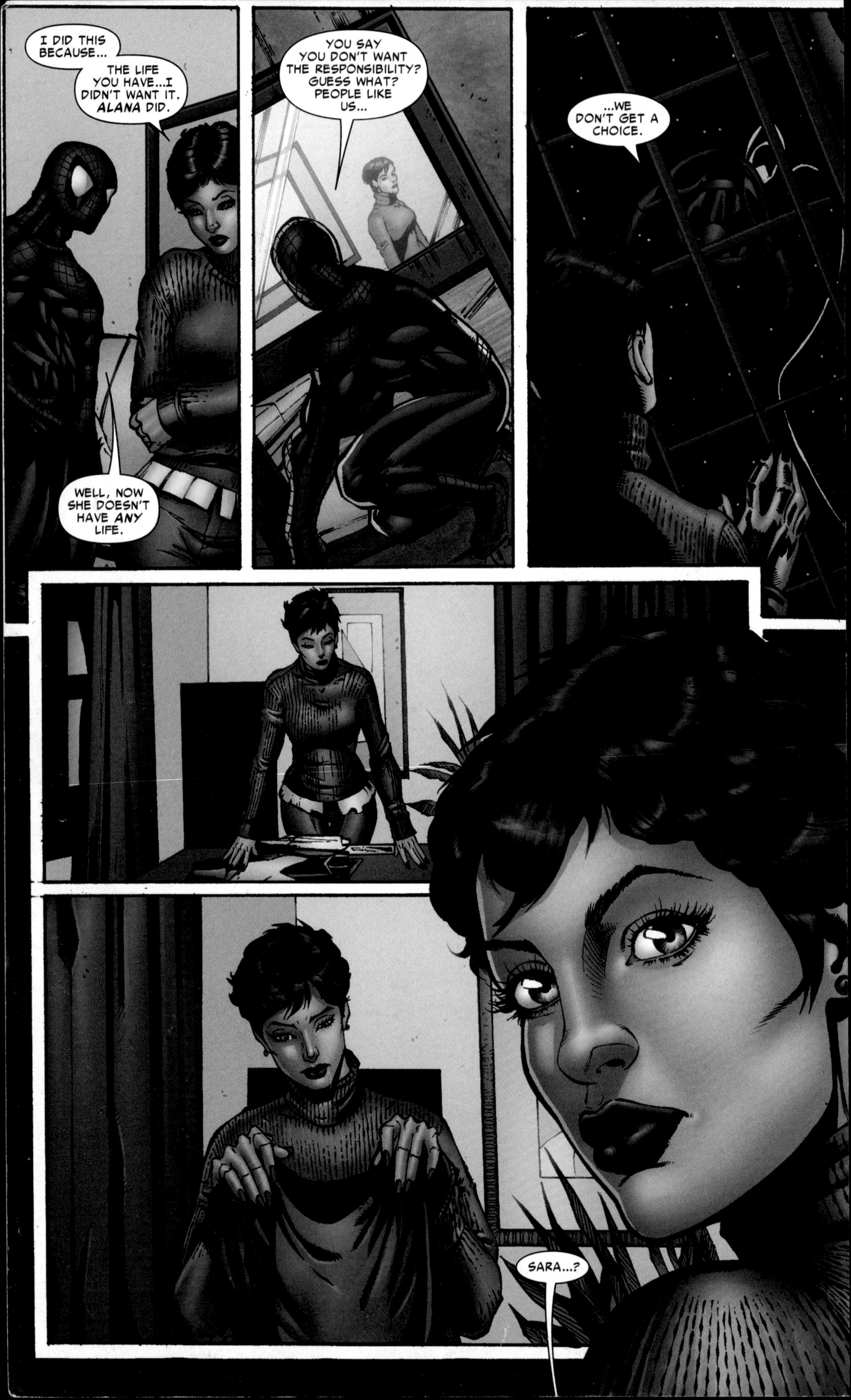
I DID THIS BECAUSE...
THE LIFE YOU HAVE...I DIDN'T WANT IT. ALANA DID.
WELL, NOW SHE DOESN'T HAVE ANY LIFE.
YOU SAY YOU DON'T WANT THE RESPONSIBILITY? GUESS WHAT? PEOPLE LIKE US...
...WE DON'T GET A CHOICE.
SARA...?

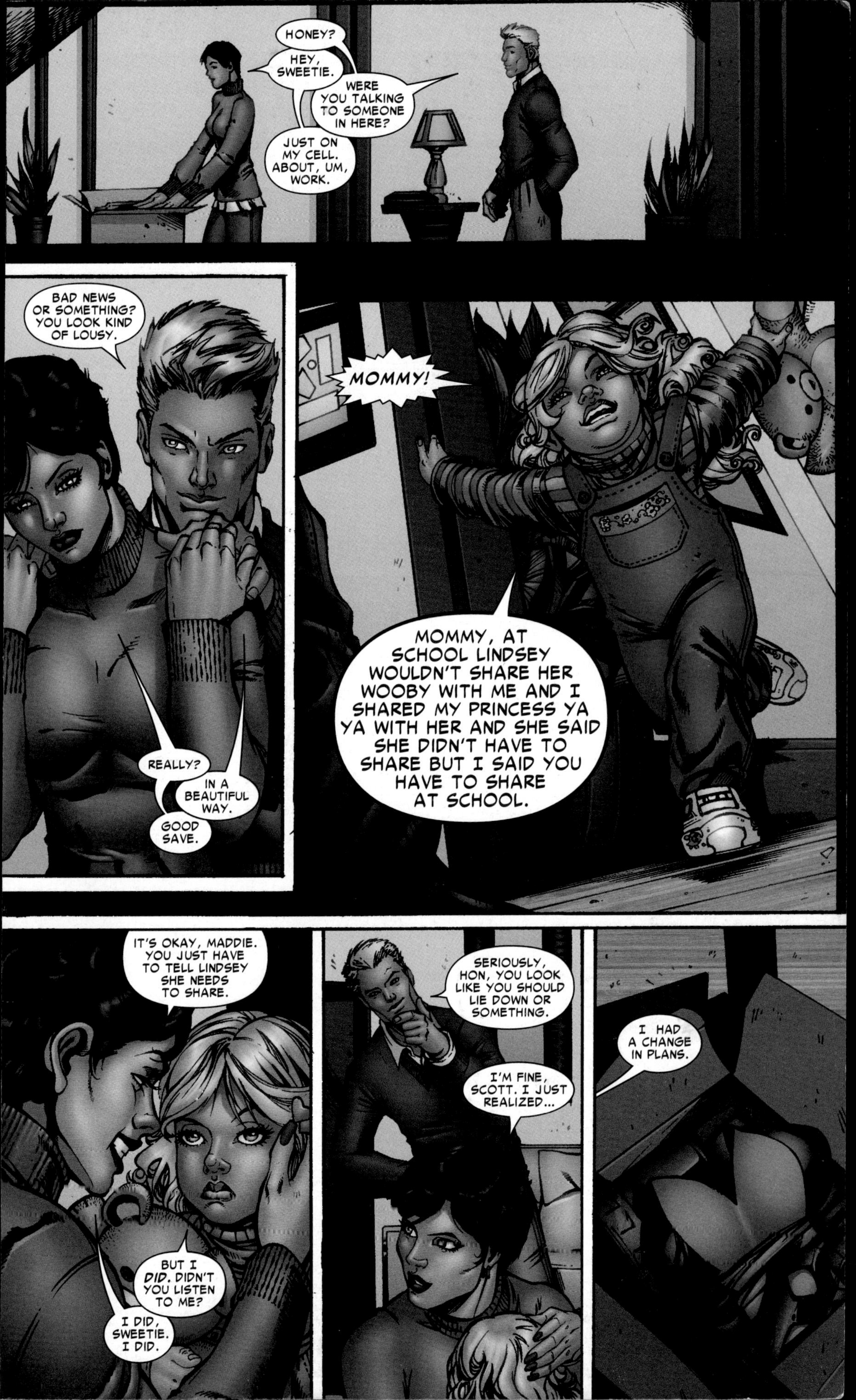
HONEY?
HEY, SWEETIE.
WERE YOU TALKING TO SOMEONE IN HERE?
JUST ON MY CELL. ABOUT, UM, WORK.
BAD NEWS OR SOMETHING? YOU LOOK KIND OF LOUSY.
REALLY?
IN A BEAUTIFUL WAY.
GOOD SAVE.
MOMMY!
MOMMY, AT SCHOOL LINDSEY WOULDN'T SHARE HER WOOBY WITH ME AND I SHARED MY PRINCESS YA YA WITH HER AND SHE SAID SHE DIDN'T HAVE TO SHARE BUT I SAID YOU HAVE TO SHARE AT SCHOOL.
IT'S OKAY, MADDIE. YOU JUST HAVE TO TELL LINDSEY SHE NEEDS TO SHARE.
BUT I *DID*. DIDN'T YOU LISTEN TO ME?
I DID, SWEETIE. I DID.
SERIOUSLY, HON, YOU LOOK LIKE YOU SHOULD LIE DOWN OR SOMETHING.
I'M FINE, SCOTT. I JUST REALIZED...
I HAD A CHANGE IN PLANS.

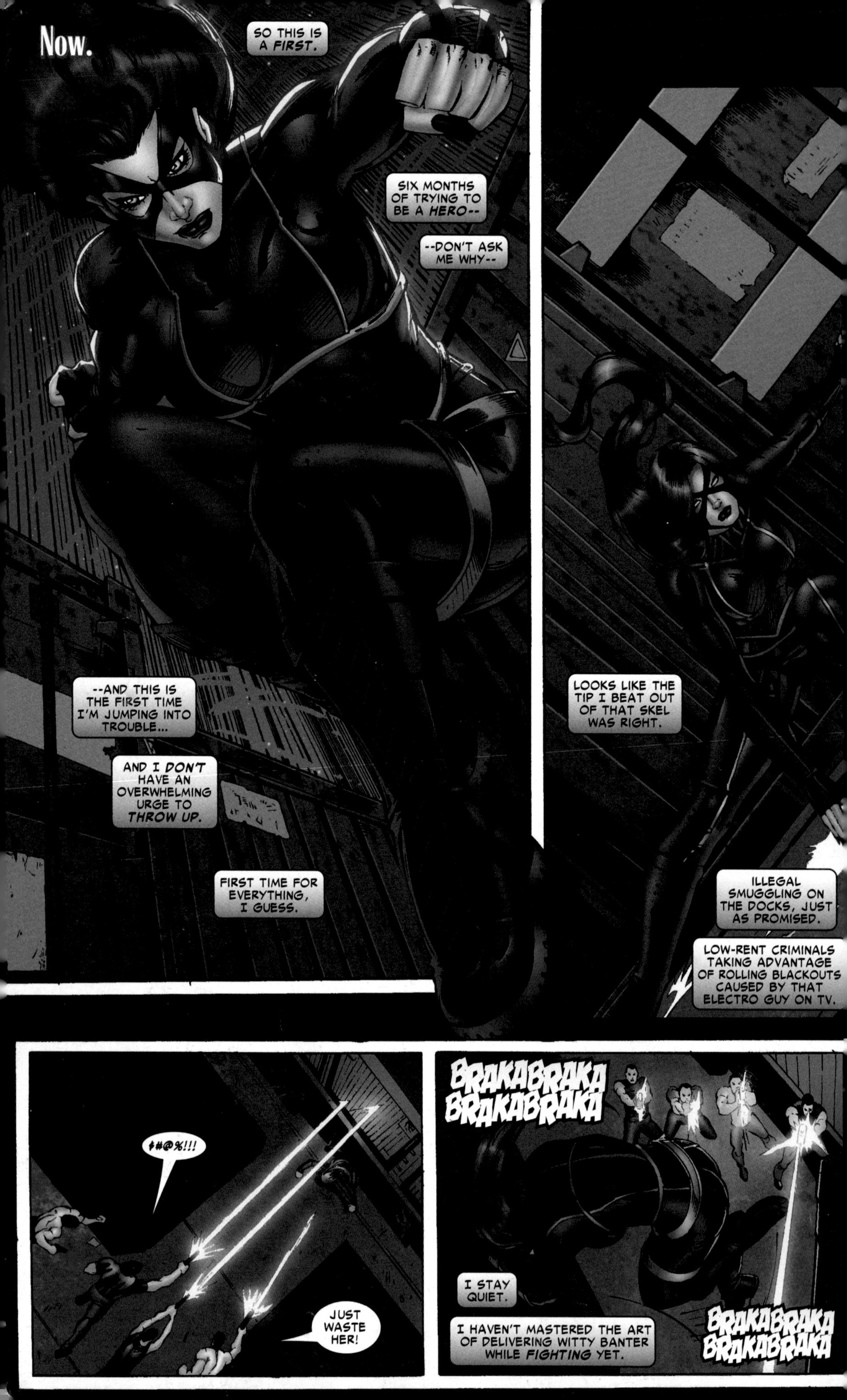
Now.
SO THIS IS A *FIRST*.
SIX MONTHS OF TRYING TO BE A *HERO*--
--DON'T ASK ME WHY--
--AND THIS IS THE FIRST TIME I'M JUMPING INTO TROUBLE...
AND I *DON'T* HAVE AN OVERWHELMING URGE TO *THROW UP*.
FIRST TIME FOR EVERYTHING, I GUESS.
LOOKS LIKE THE TIP I BEAT OUT OF THAT SKEL WAS RIGHT.
ILLEGAL SMUGGLING ON THE DOCKS, JUST AS PROMISED.
LOW-RENT CRIMINALS TAKING ADVANTAGE OF ROLLING BLACKOUTS CAUSED BY THAT ELECTRO GUY ON TV.
$#@%!!!
JUST WASTE HER!
BRAKABRAKA BRAKABRAKA
I STAY QUIET.
I HAVEN'T MASTERED THE ART OF DELIVERING WITTY BANTER WHILE *FIGHTING* YET.
BRAKABRAKA BRAKABRAKA

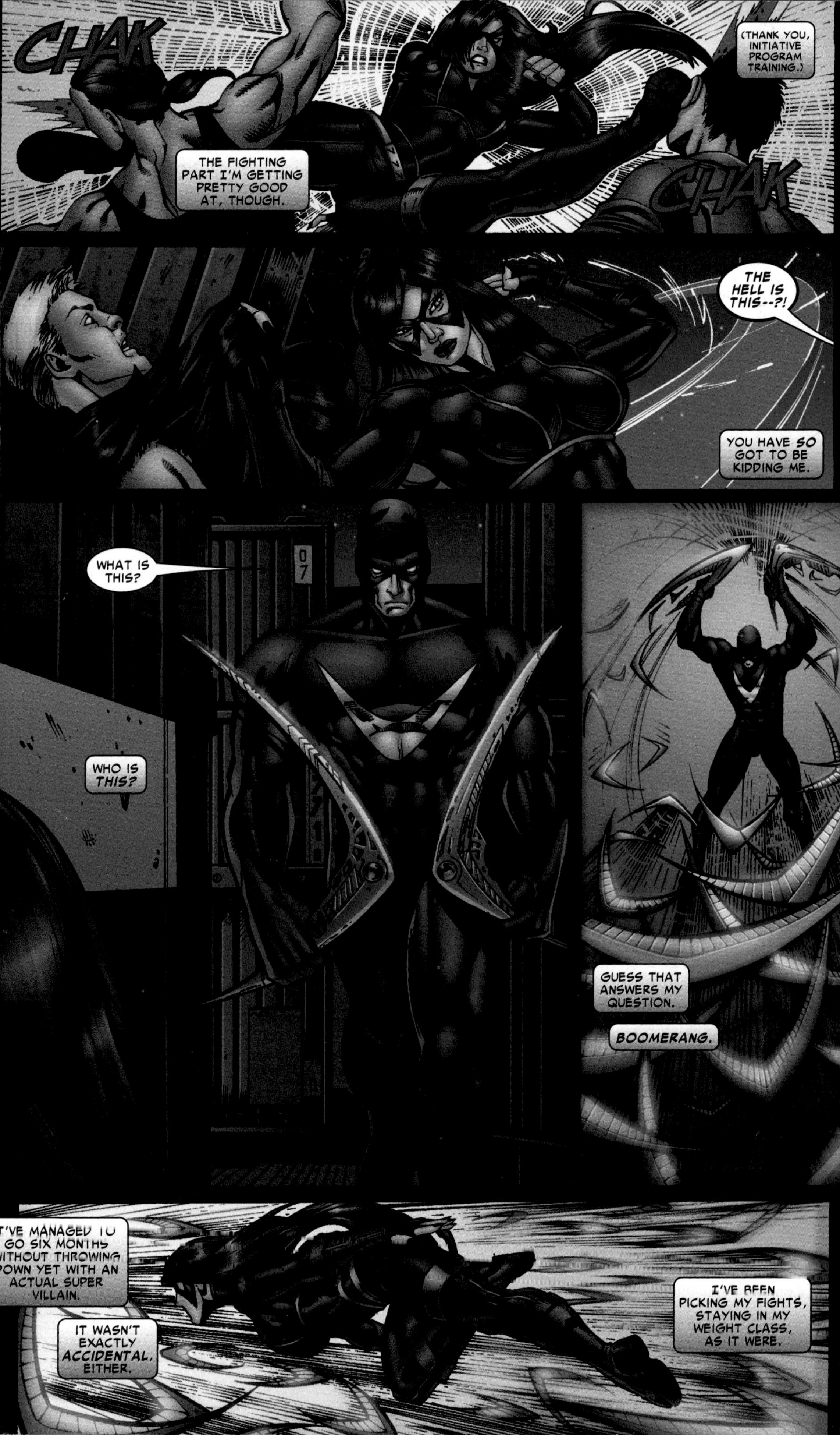
CHAK
THE FIGHTING PART I'M GETTING PRETTY GOOD AT, THOUGH.
(THANK YOU, INITIATIVE PROGRAM TRAINING.)
CHAK
THE HELL IS THIS--?!
YOU HAVE SO GOT TO BE KIDDING ME.
WHAT IS THIS?
WHO IS THIS?
GUESS THAT ANSWERS MY QUESTION.
BOOMERANG.
'VE MANAGED TO GO SIX MONTHS WITHOUT THROWING DOWN YET WITH AN ACTUAL SUPER VILLAIN.
IT WASN'T EXACTLY ACCIDENTAL, EITHER.
I'VE BEEN PICKING MY FIGHTS, STAYING IN MY WEIGHT CLASS, AS IT WERE.

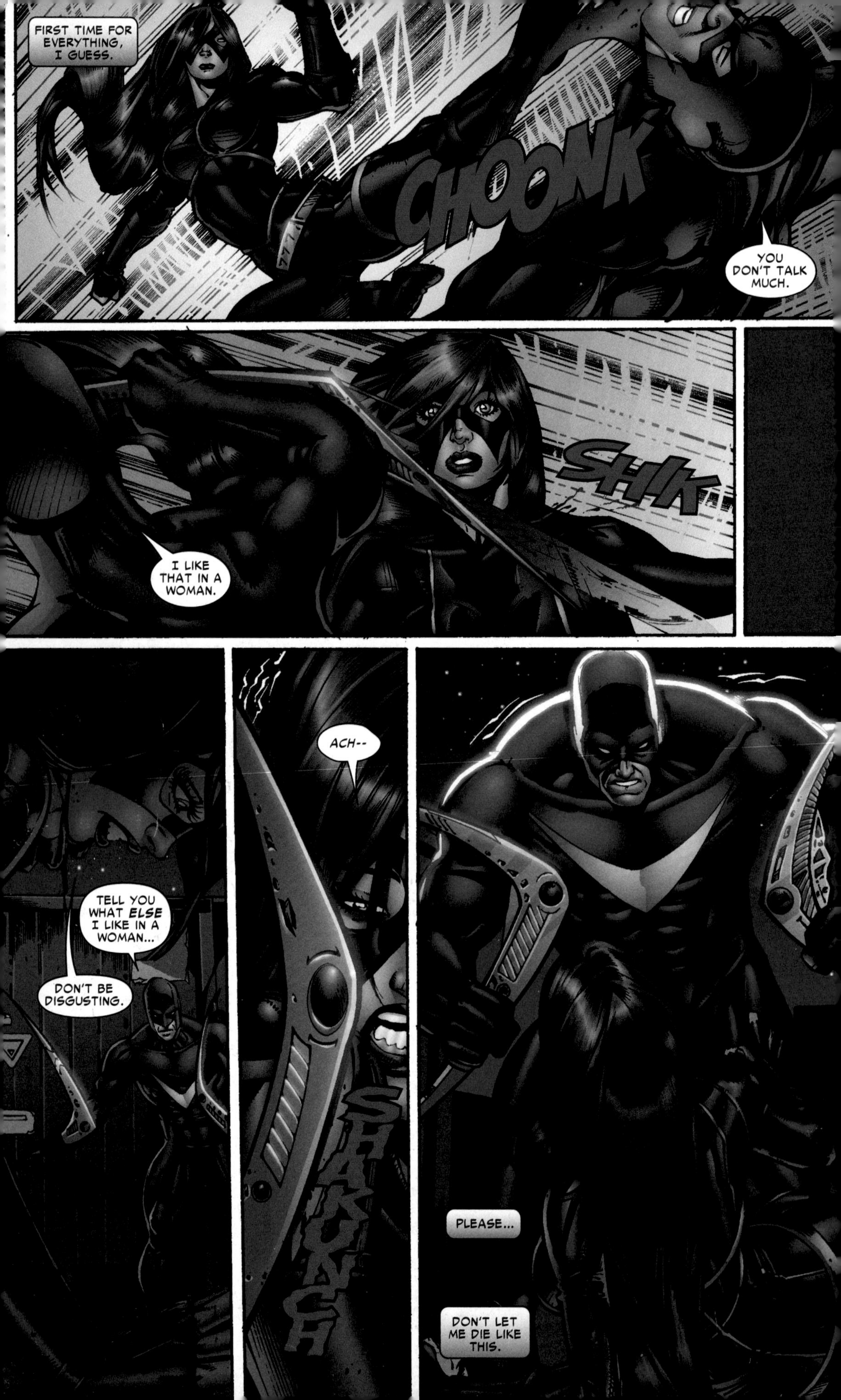

FIRST TIME FOR EVERYTHING, I GUESS.
CHOONK
YOU DON'T TALK MUCH.
SHIK
I LIKE THAT IN A WOMAN.
TELL YOU WHAT *ELSE* I LIKE IN A WOMAN...
DON'T BE DISGUSTING.
ACH--
SHAKUNCH
PLEASE...
DON'T LET ME DIE LIKE THIS.

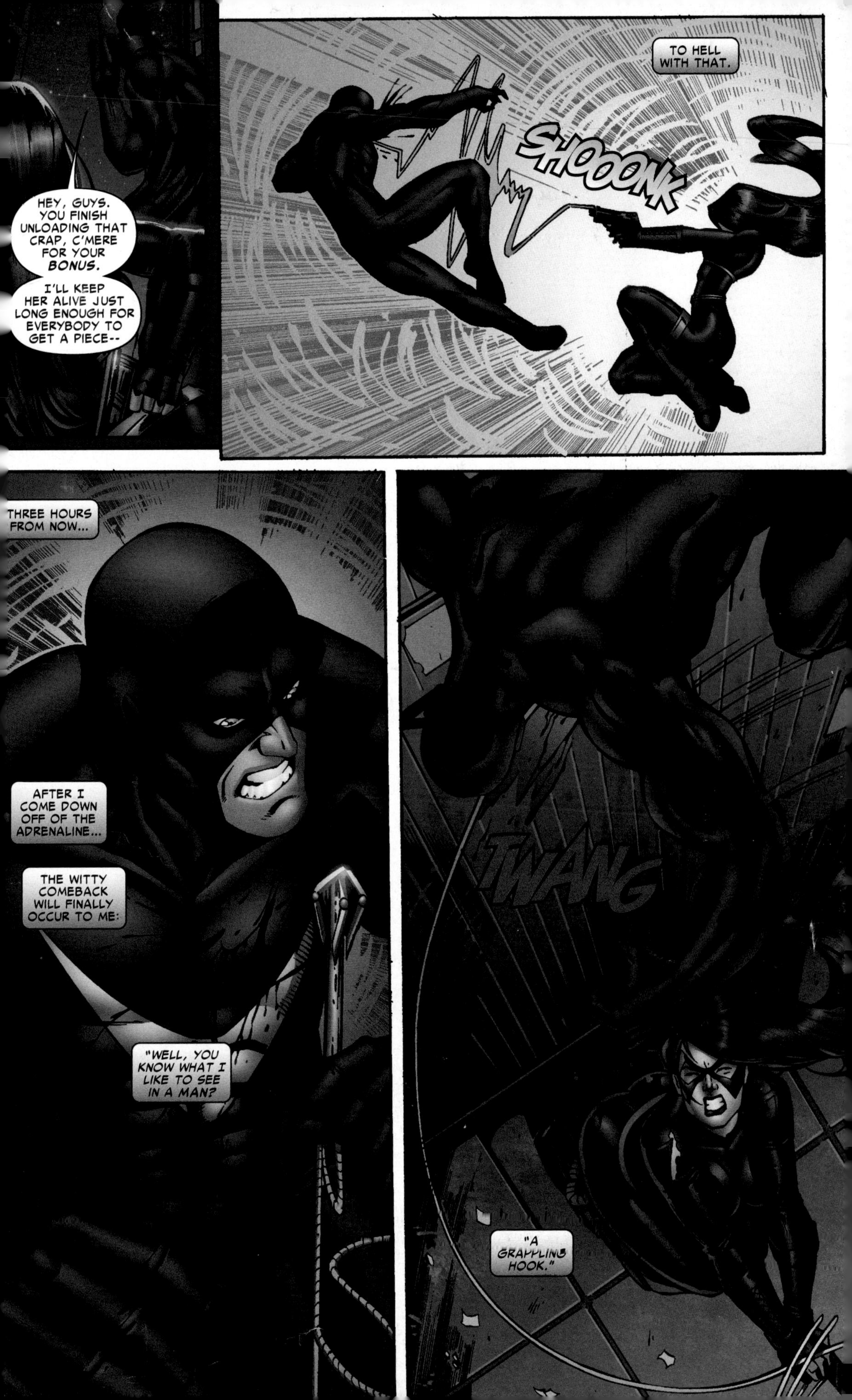
HEY, GUYS. YOU FINISH UNLOADING THAT CRAP, C'MERE FOR YOUR BONUS.
I'LL KEEP HER ALIVE JUST LONG ENOUGH FOR EVERYBODY TO GET A PIECE--
TO HELL WITH THAT.
SHOOOONK
THREE HOURS FROM NOW...
AFTER I COME DOWN OFF OF THE ADRENALINE...
THE WITTY COMEBACK WILL FINALLY OCCUR TO ME:
"WELL, YOU KNOW WHAT I LIKE TO SEE IN A MAN?
TWANG
"A GRAPPLING HOOK."

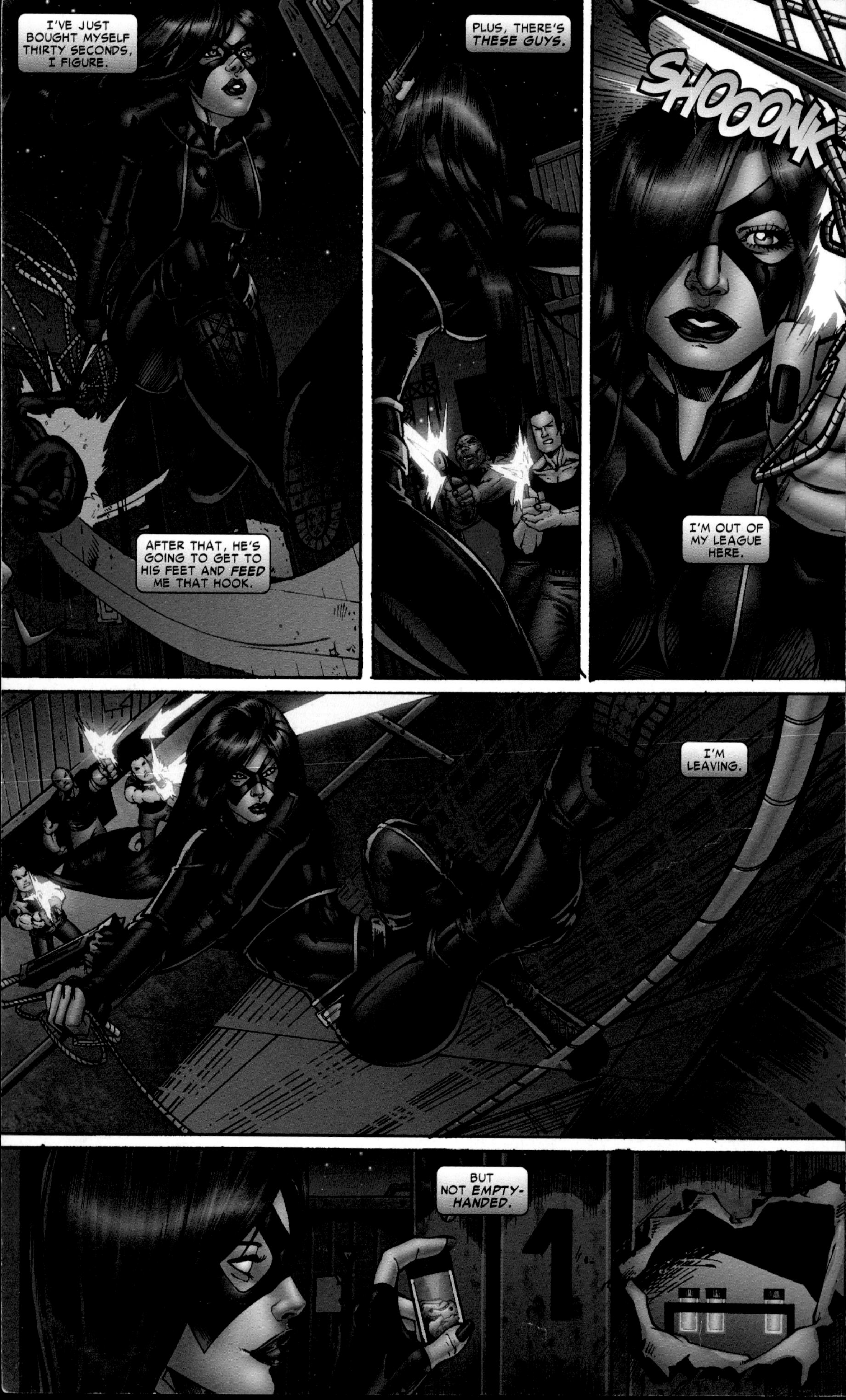
I'VE JUST BOUGHT MYSELF THIRTY SECONDS, I FIGURE.
AFTER THAT, HE'S GOING TO GET TO HIS FEET AND FEED ME THAT HOOK.
PLUS, THERE'S THESE GUYS.
SHOOOONK
I'M OUT OF MY LEAGUE HERE.
I'M LEAVING.
BUT NOT EMPTY-HANDED.
1

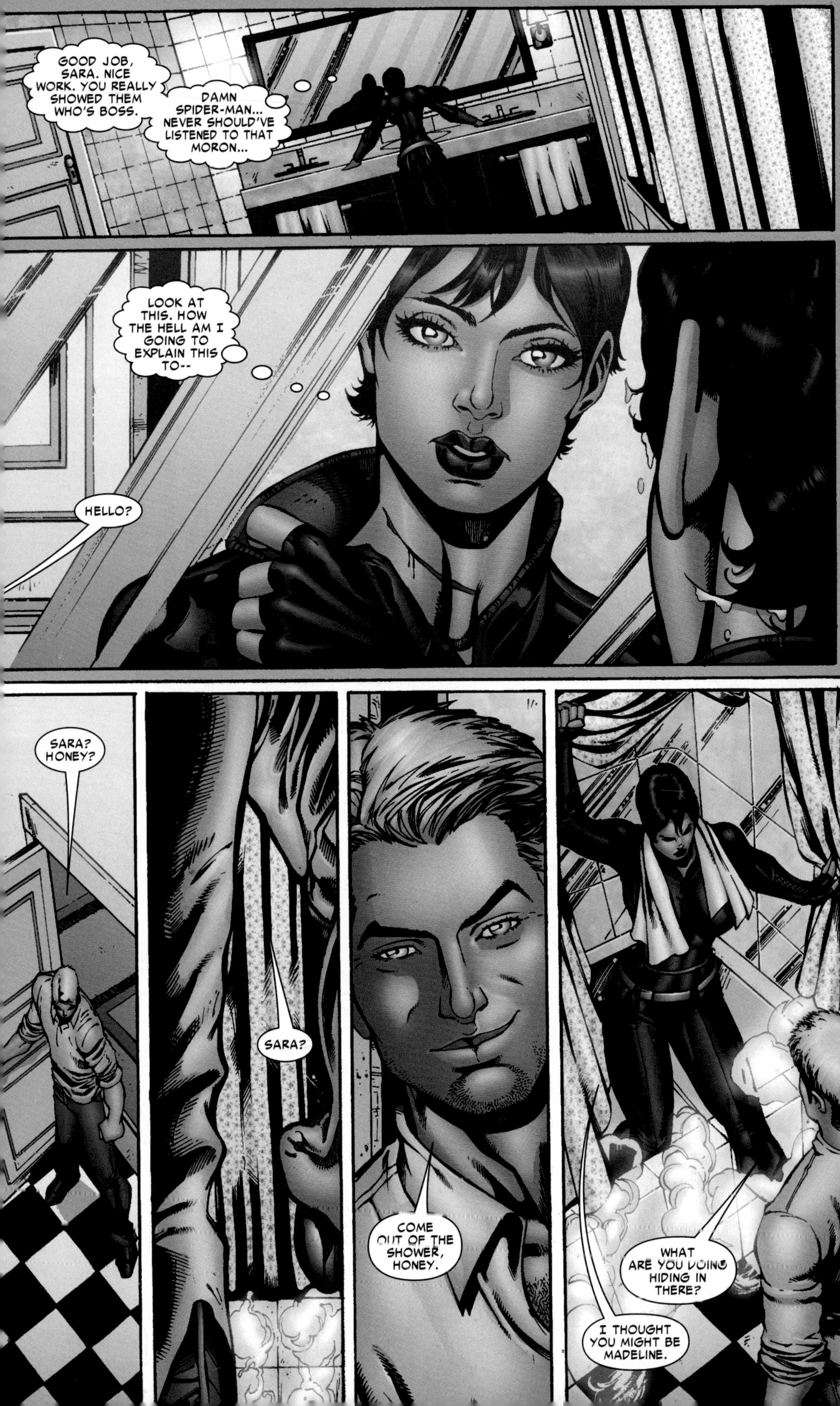
GOOD JOB, SARA. NICE WORK. YOU REALLY SHOWED THEM WHO'S BOSS.
DAMN SPIDER-MAN... NEVER SHOULD'VE LISTENED TO THAT MORON...
LOOK AT THIS. HOW THE HELL AM I GOING TO EXPLAIN THIS TO--
HELLO?
SARA? HONEY?
SARA?
COME OUT OF THE SHOWER, HONEY.
WHAT ARE YOU DOING HIDING IN THERE?
I THOUGHT YOU MIGHT BE MADELINE.

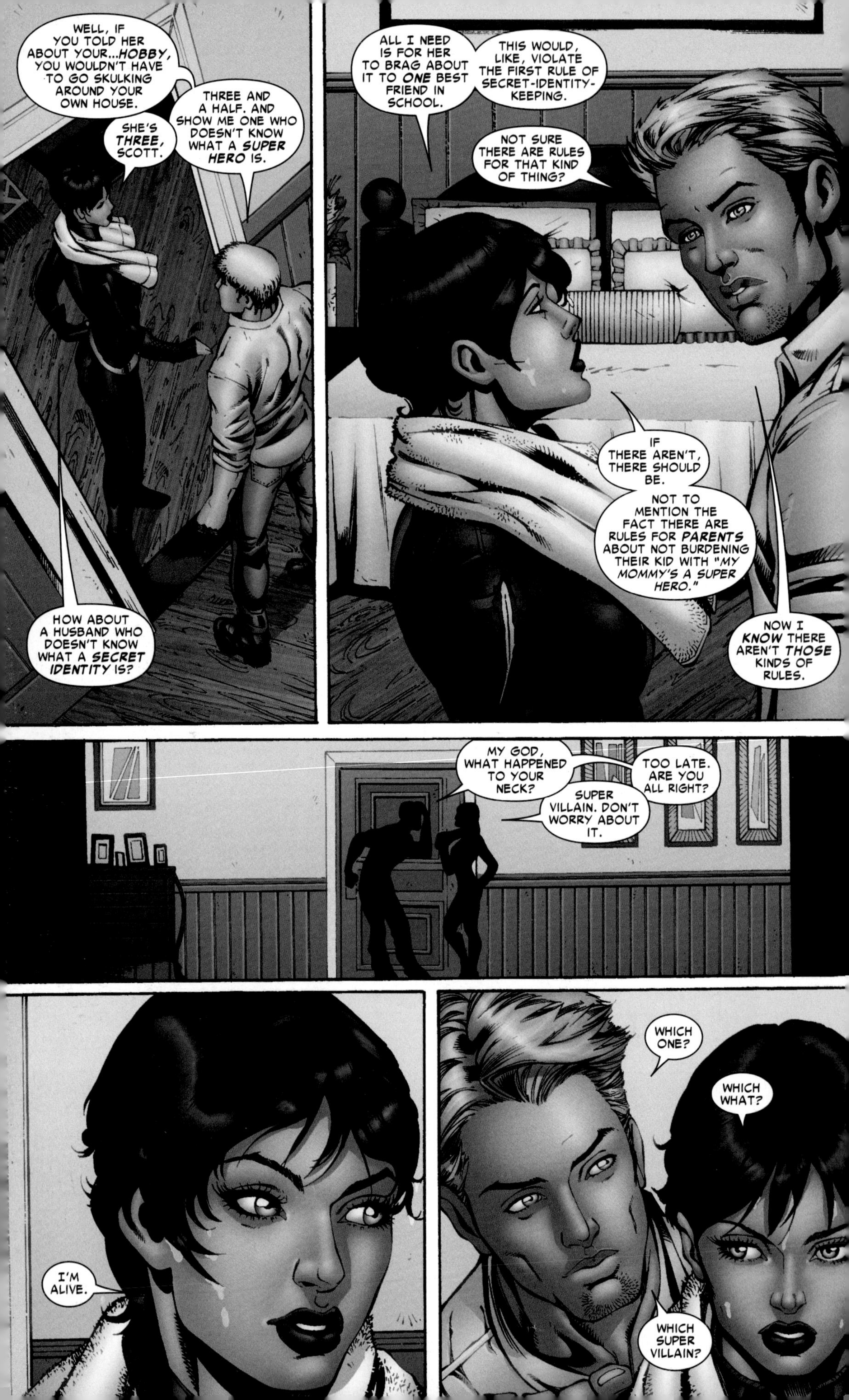
WELL, IF YOU TOLD HER ABOUT YOUR...HOBBY, YOU WOULDN'T HAVE TO GO SKULKING AROUND YOUR OWN HOUSE.
SHE'S THREE, SCOTT.
THREE AND A HALF. AND SHOW ME ONE WHO DOESN'T KNOW WHAT A SUPER HERO IS.
HOW ABOUT A HUSBAND WHO DOESN'T KNOW WHAT A SECRET IDENTITY IS?
ALL I NEED IS FOR HER TO BRAG ABOUT IT TO ONE BEST FRIEND IN SCHOOL.
THIS WOULD, LIKE, VIOLATE THE FIRST RULE OF SECRET-IDENTITY-KEEPING.
NOT SURE THERE ARE RULES FOR THAT KIND OF THING?
IF THERE AREN'T, THERE SHOULD BE.
NOT TO MENTION THE FACT THERE ARE RULES FOR PARENTS ABOUT NOT BURDENING THEIR KID WITH "MY MOMMY'S A SUPER HERO."
NOW I KNOW THERE AREN'T THOSE KINDS OF RULES.
MY GOD, WHAT HAPPENED TO YOUR NECK?
TOO LATE. ARE YOU ALL RIGHT?
SUPER VILLAIN. DON'T WORRY ABOUT IT.
I'M ALIVE.
WHICH ONE?
WHICH WHAT?
WHICH SUPER VILLAIN?

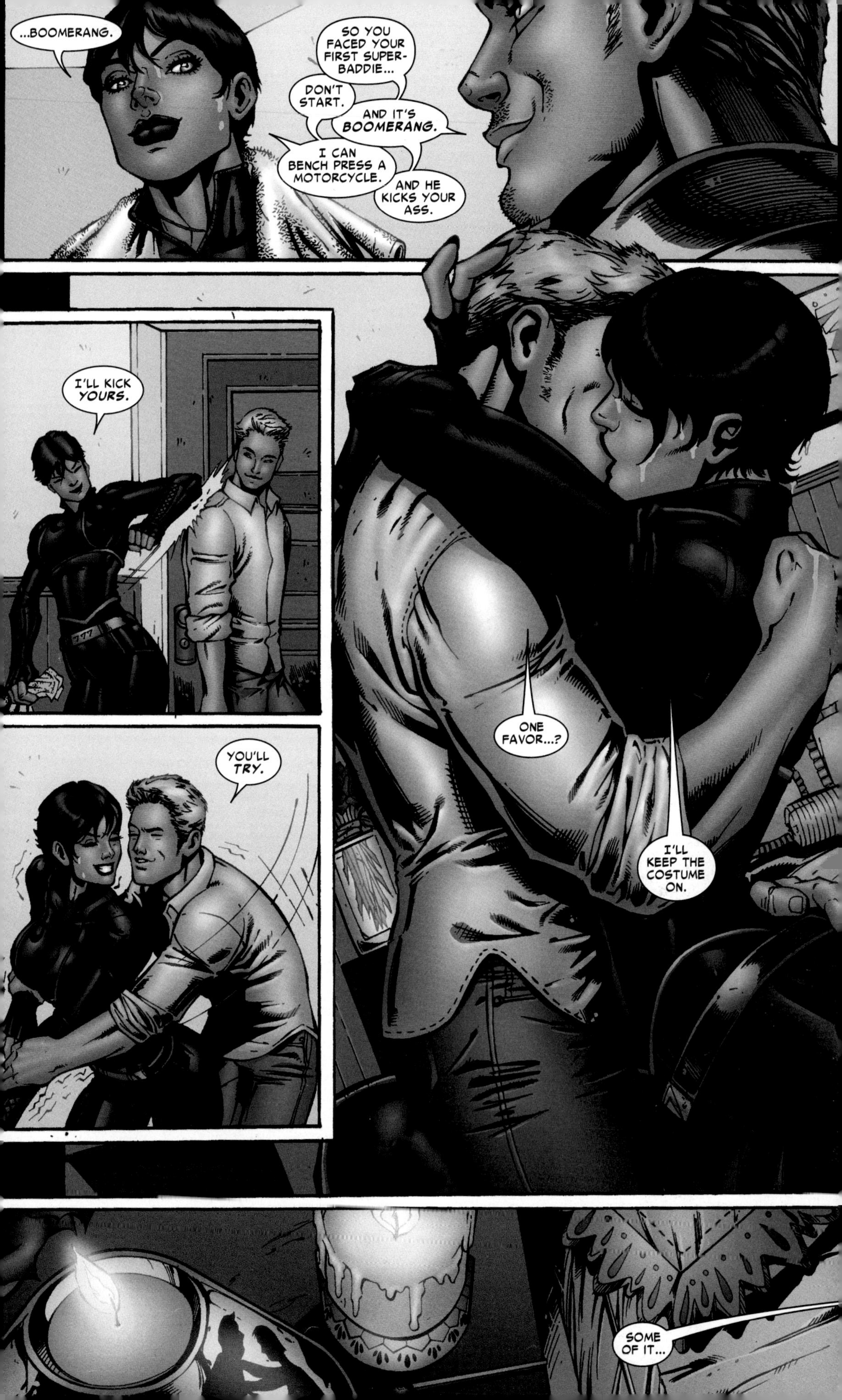
...BOOMERANG.
SO YOU FACED YOUR FIRST SUPER-BADDIE...
DON'T START.
AND IT'S BOOMERANG.
I CAN BENCH PRESS A MOTORCYCLE.
AND HE KICKS YOUR ASS.
I'LL KICK YOURS.
YOU'LL TRY.
ONE FAVOR...?
I'LL KEEP THE COSTUME ON.
SOME OF IT...

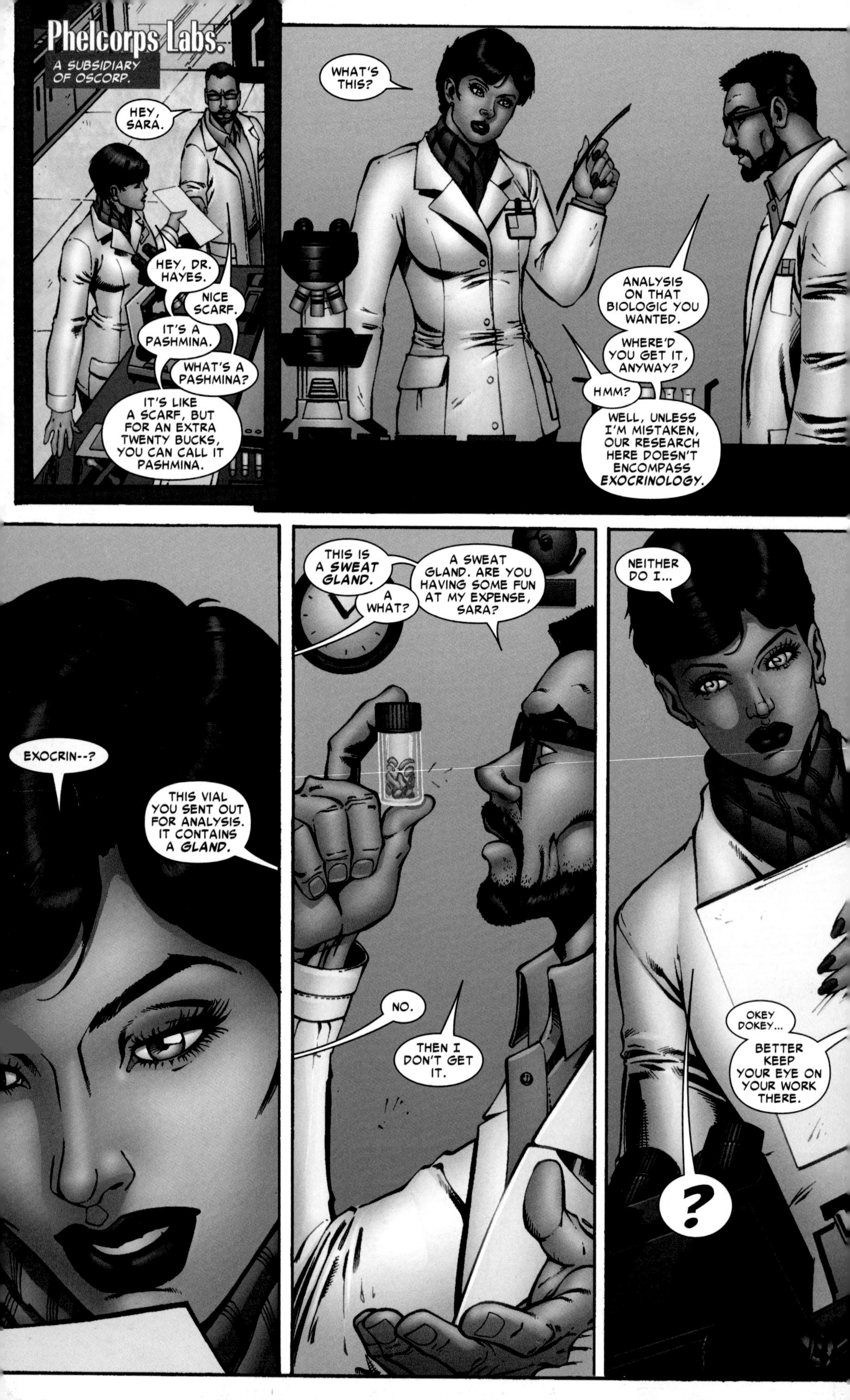
Phelcorps Labs.
A SUBSIDIARY OF OSCORP.
HEY, SARA.
HEY, DR. HAYES.
NICE SCARF.
IT'S A PASHMINA.
WHAT'S A PASHMINA?
IT'S LIKE A SCARF, BUT FOR AN EXTRA TWENTY BUCKS, YOU CAN CALL IT PASHMINA.
WHAT'S THIS?
ANALYSIS ON THAT BIOLOGIC YOU WANTED.
WHERE'D YOU GET IT, ANYWAY?
HMM?
WELL, UNLESS I'M MISTAKEN, OUR RESEARCH HERE DOESN'T ENCOMPASS EXOCRINOLOGY.
EXOCRIN--?
THIS VIAL YOU SENT OUT FOR ANALYSIS. IT CONTAINS A GLAND.
THIS IS A SWEAT GLAND.
A WHAT?
A SWEAT GLAND. ARE YOU HAVING SOME FUN AT MY EXPENSE, SARA?
NO.
THEN I DON'T GET IT.
NEITHER DO I...
OKEY DOKEY...
BETTER KEEP YOUR EYE ON YOUR WORK THERE.
?

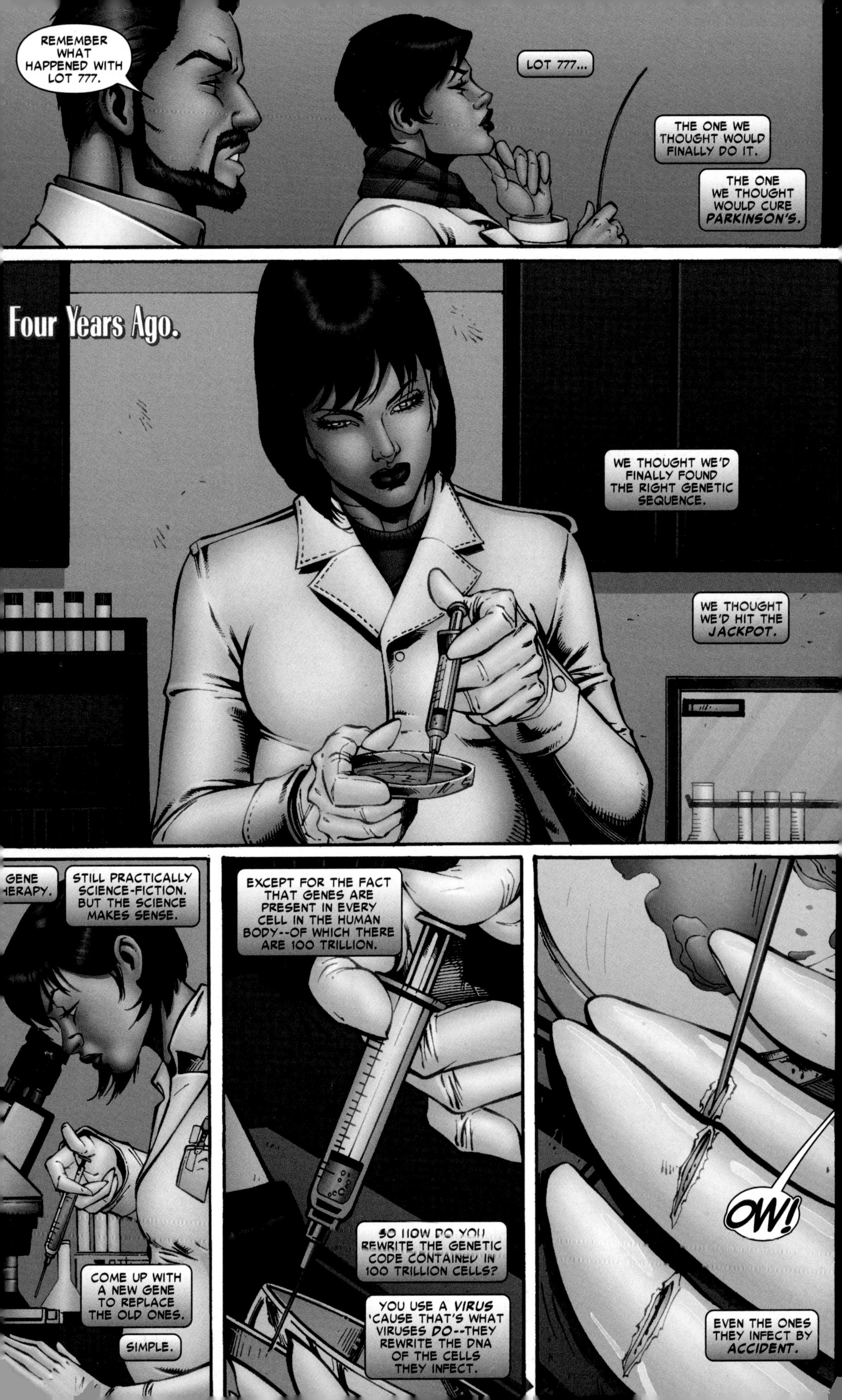
REMEMBER WHAT HAPPENED WITH LOT 777.
LOT 777...
THE ONE WE THOUGHT WOULD FINALLY DO IT.
THE ONE WE THOUGHT WOULD CURE PARKINSON'S.
Four Years Ago.
WE THOUGHT WE'D FINALLY FOUND THE RIGHT GENETIC SEQUENCE.
WE THOUGHT WE'D HIT THE JACKPOT.
GENE HERAPY.
STILL PRACTICALLY SCIENCE-FICTION. BUT THE SCIENCE MAKES SENSE.
COME UP WITH A NEW GENE TO REPLACE THE OLD ONES.
SIMPLE.
EXCEPT FOR THE FACT THAT GENES ARE PRESENT IN EVERY CELL IN THE HUMAN BODY--OF WHICH THERE ARE 100 TRILLION.
SO HOW DO YOU REWRITE THE GENETIC CODE CONTAINED IN 100 TRILLION CELLS?
YOU USE A VIRUS 'CAUSE THAT'S WHAT VIRUSES DO--THEY REWRITE THE DNA OF THE CELLS THEY INFECT.
OW!
EVEN THE ONES THEY INFECT BY ACCIDENT.

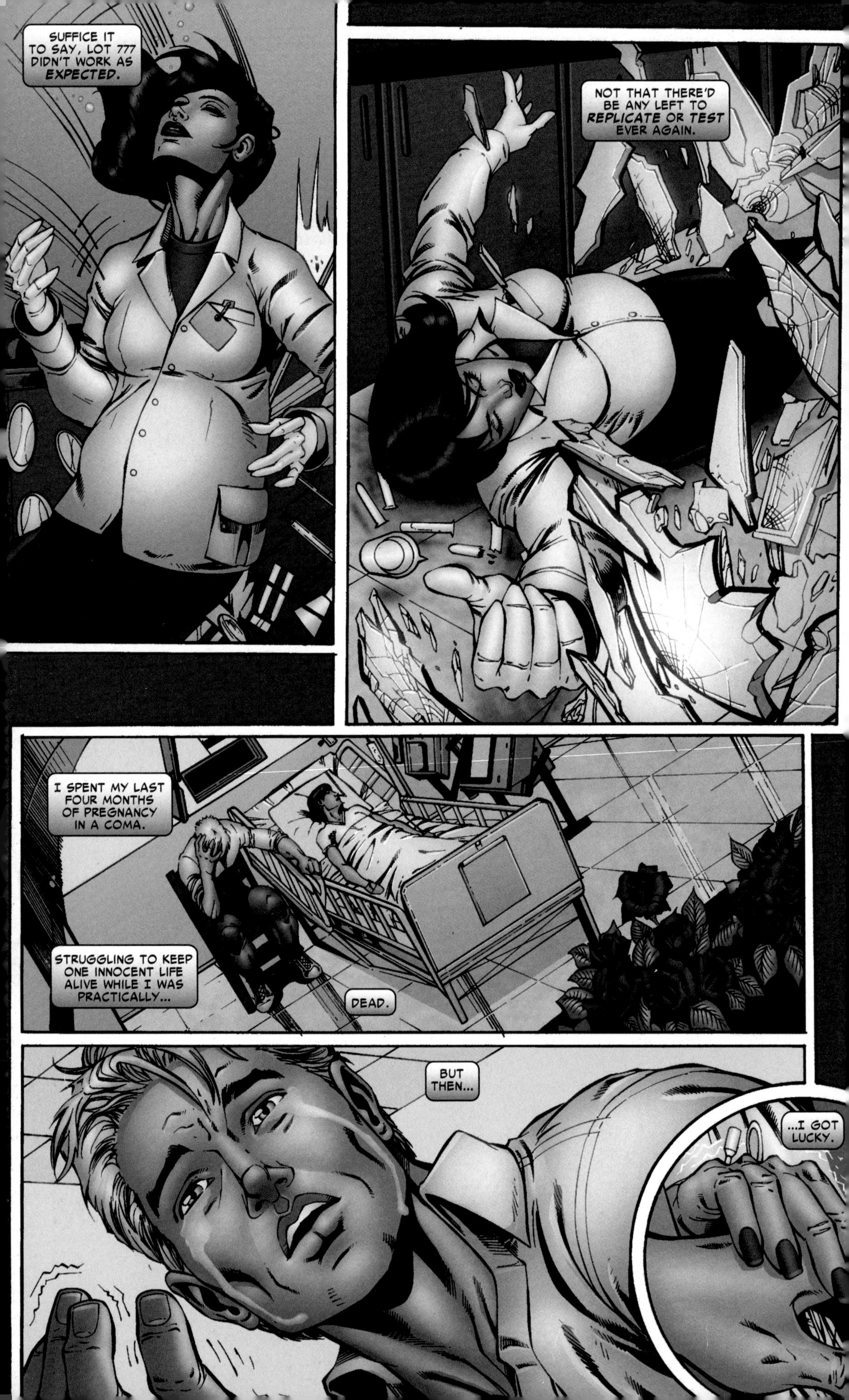
SUFFICE IT TO SAY, LOT 777 DIDN'T WORK AS EXPECTED.
NOT THAT THERE'D BE ANY LEFT TO REPLICATE OR TEST EVER AGAIN.
I SPENT MY LAST FOUR MONTHS OF PREGNANCY IN A COMA.
STRUGGLING TO KEEP ONE INNOCENT LIFE ALIVE WHILE I WAS PRACTICALLY...
DEAD.
BUT THEN...
...I GOT LUCKY.

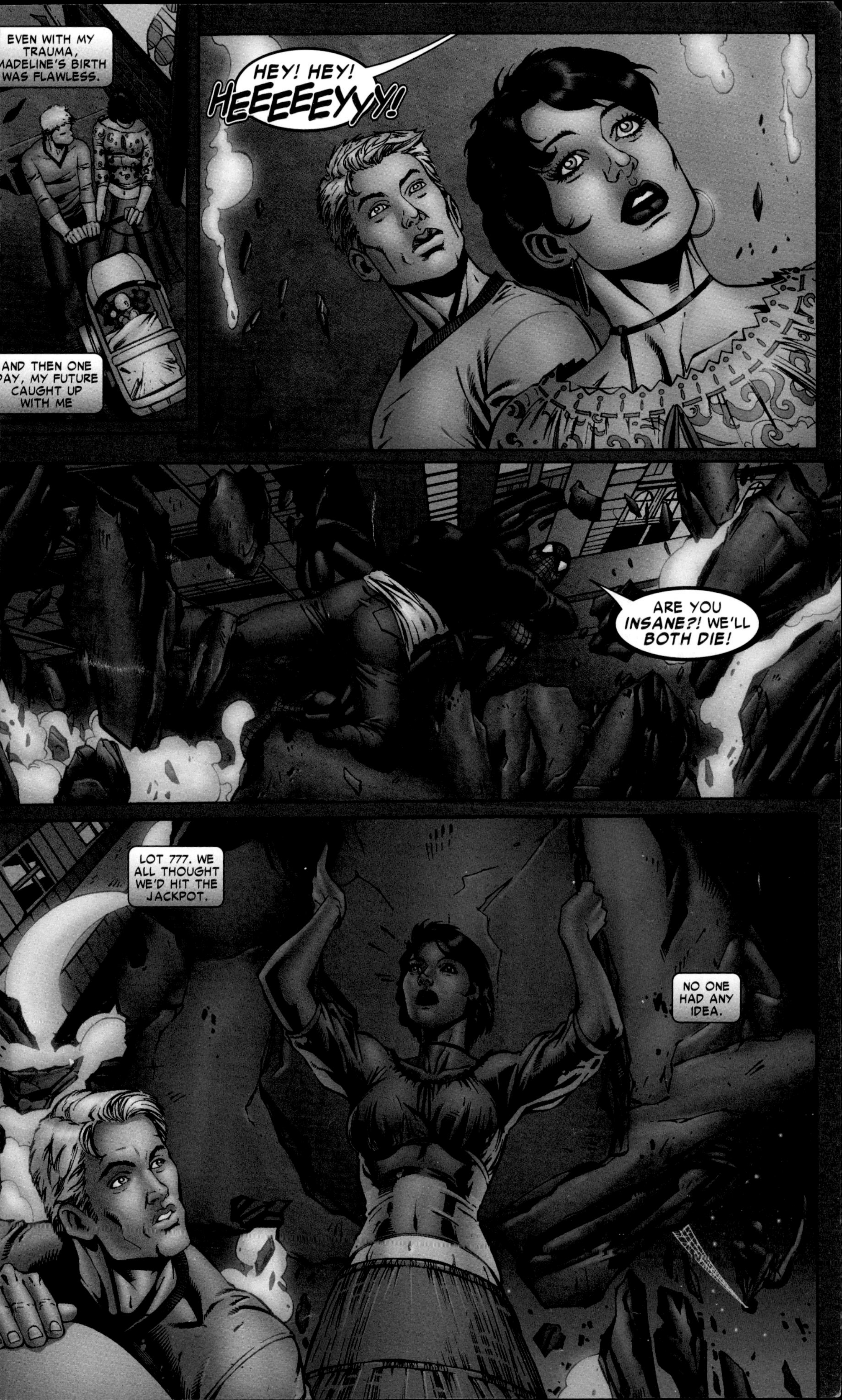
EVEN WITH MY TRAUMA, MADELINE'S BIRTH WAS FLAWLESS.
AND THEN ONE DAY, MY FUTURE CAUGHT UP WITH ME
HEY! HEY! HEEEEEYYYY!
ARE YOU INSANE?! WE'LL BOTH DIE!
LOT 777. WE ALL THOUGHT WE'D HIT THE JACKPOT.
NO ONE HAD ANY IDEA.

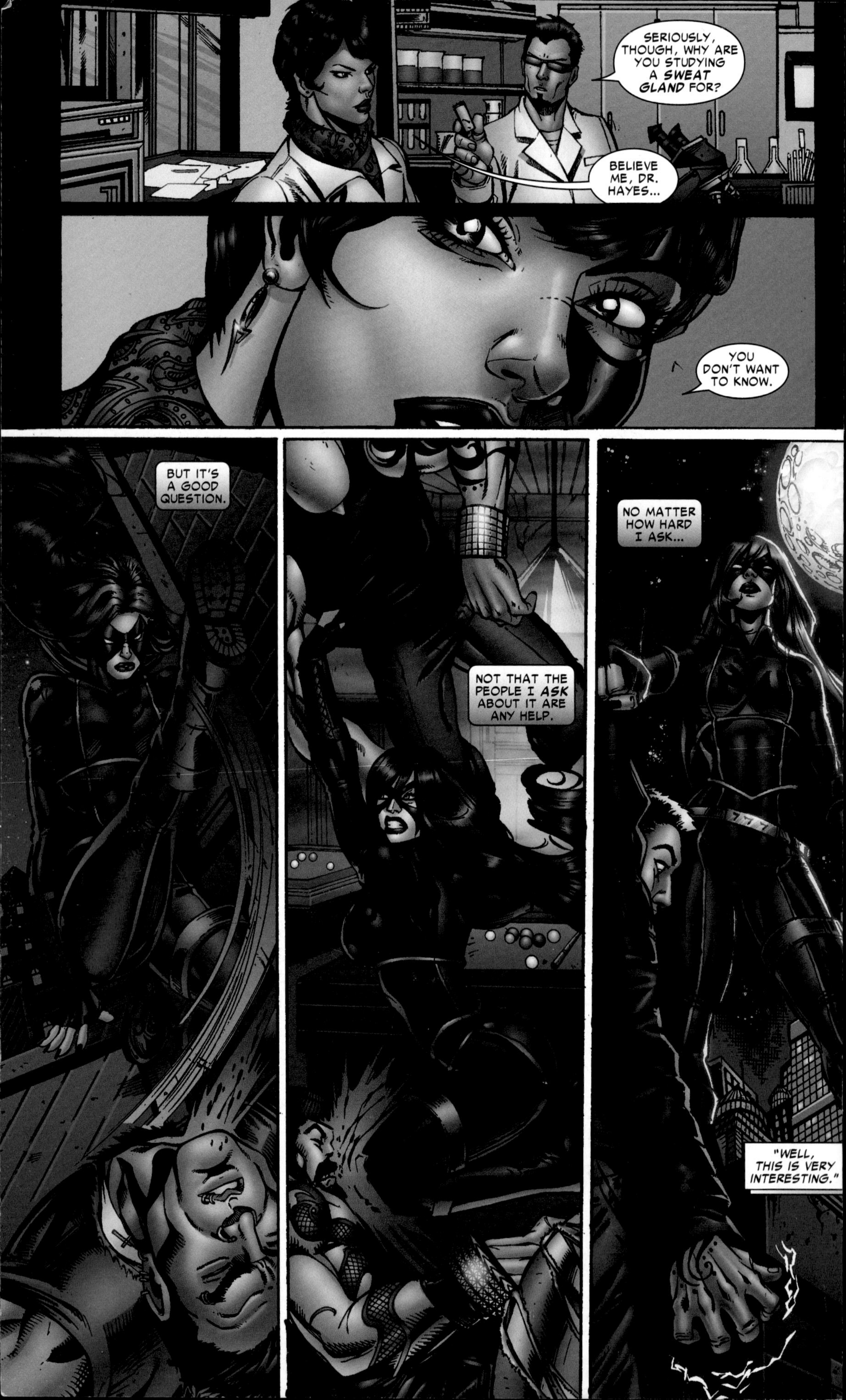
SERIOUSLY, THOUGH, WHY ARE YOU STUDYING A SWEAT GLAND FOR?
BELIEVE ME, DR. HAYES...
YOU DON'T WANT TO KNOW.
BUT IT'S A GOOD QUESTION.
NOT THAT THE PEOPLE I ASK ABOUT IT ARE ANY HELP.
NO MATTER HOW HARD I ASK...
"WELL, THIS IS VERY INTERESTING."

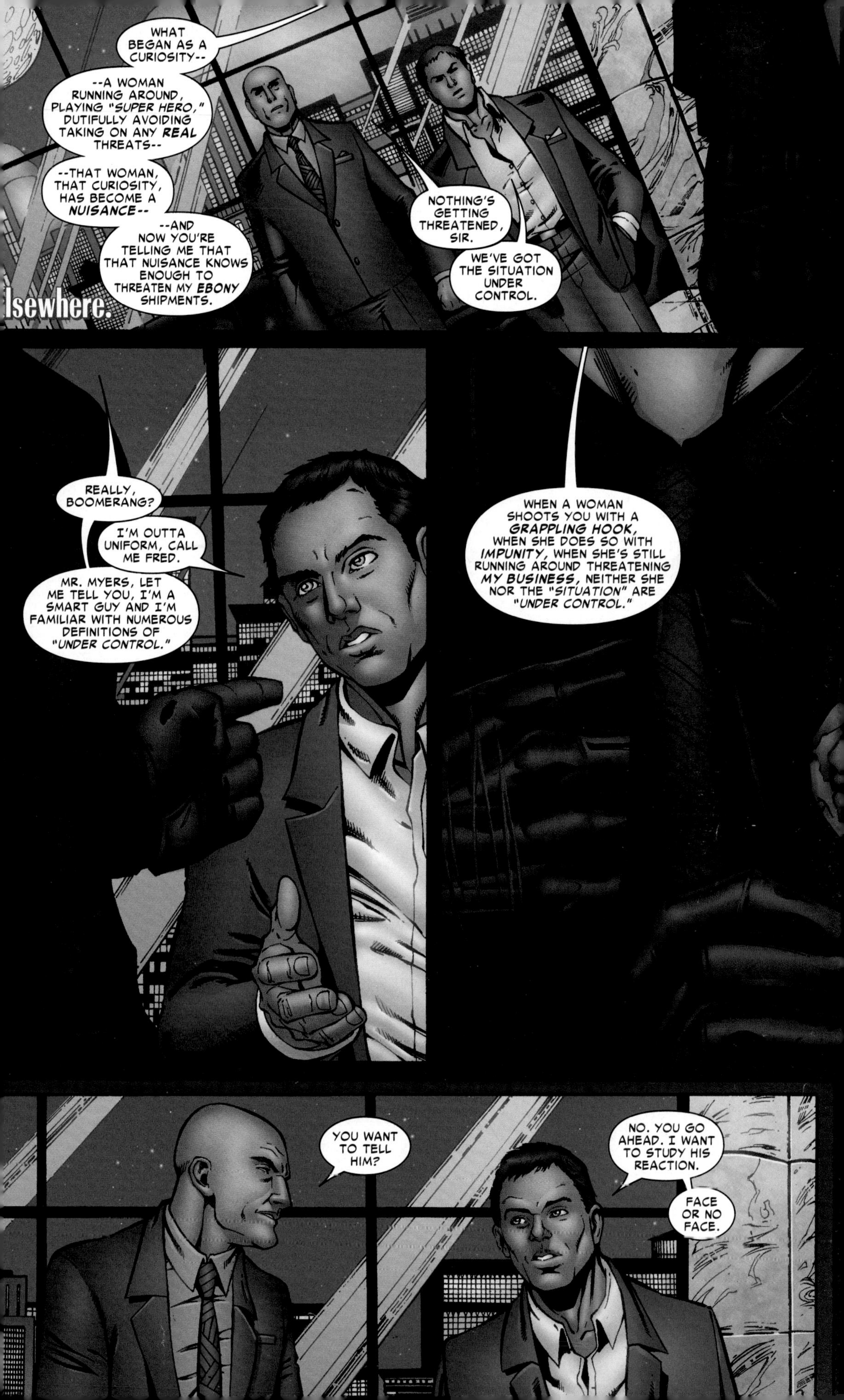
lsewhere.
WHAT BEGAN AS A CURIOSITY--
--A WOMAN RUNNING AROUND, PLAYING "SUPER HERO," DUTIFULLY AVOIDING TAKING ON ANY REAL THREATS--
--THAT WOMAN, THAT CURIOSITY, HAS BECOME A NUISANCE--
--AND NOW YOU'RE TELLING ME THAT THAT NUISANCE KNOWS ENOUGH TO THREATEN MY EBONY SHIPMENTS.
NOTHING'S GETTING THREATENED, SIR.
WE'VE GOT THE SITUATION UNDER CONTROL.
REALLY, BOOMERANG?
I'M OUTTA UNIFORM, CALL ME FRED.
MR. MYERS, LET ME TELL YOU, I'M A SMART GUY AND I'M FAMILIAR WITH NUMEROUS DEFINITIONS OF "UNDER CONTROL."
WHEN A WOMAN SHOOTS YOU WITH A GRAPPLING HOOK, WHEN SHE DOES SO WITH IMPUNITY, WHEN SHE'S STILL RUNNING AROUND THREATENING MY BUSINESS, NEITHER SHE NOR THE "SITUATION" ARE "UNDER CONTROL."
YOU WANT TO TELL HIM?
NO. YOU GO AHEAD. I WANT TO STUDY HIS REACTION.
FACE OR NO FACE.

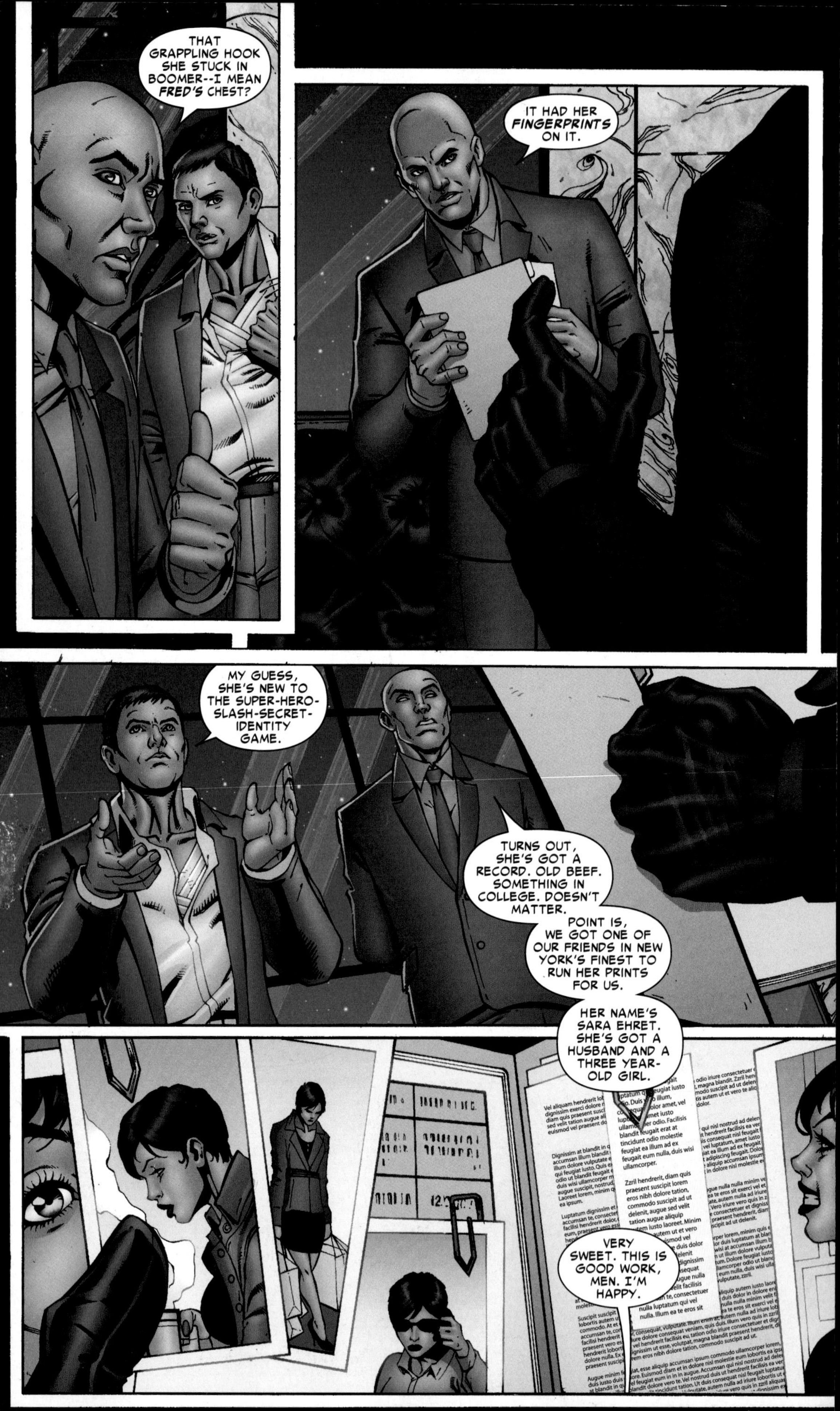
THAT GRAPPLING HOOK SHE STUCK IN BOOMER--I MEAN FRED'S CHEST?
IT HAD HER FINGERPRINTS ON IT.
MY GUESS, SHE'S NEW TO THE SUPER-HERO-SLASH-SECRET-IDENTITY GAME.
TURNS OUT, SHE'S GOT A RECORD. OLD BEEF. SOMETHING IN COLLEGE. DOESN'T MATTER.
POINT IS, WE GOT ONE OF OUR FRIENDS IN NEW YORK'S FINEST TO RUN HER PRINTS FOR US.
HER NAME'S SARA EHRET. SHE'S GOT A HUSBAND AND A THREE YEAR-OLD GIRL.
VERY SWEET. THIS IS GOOD WORK, MEN. I'M HAPPY.

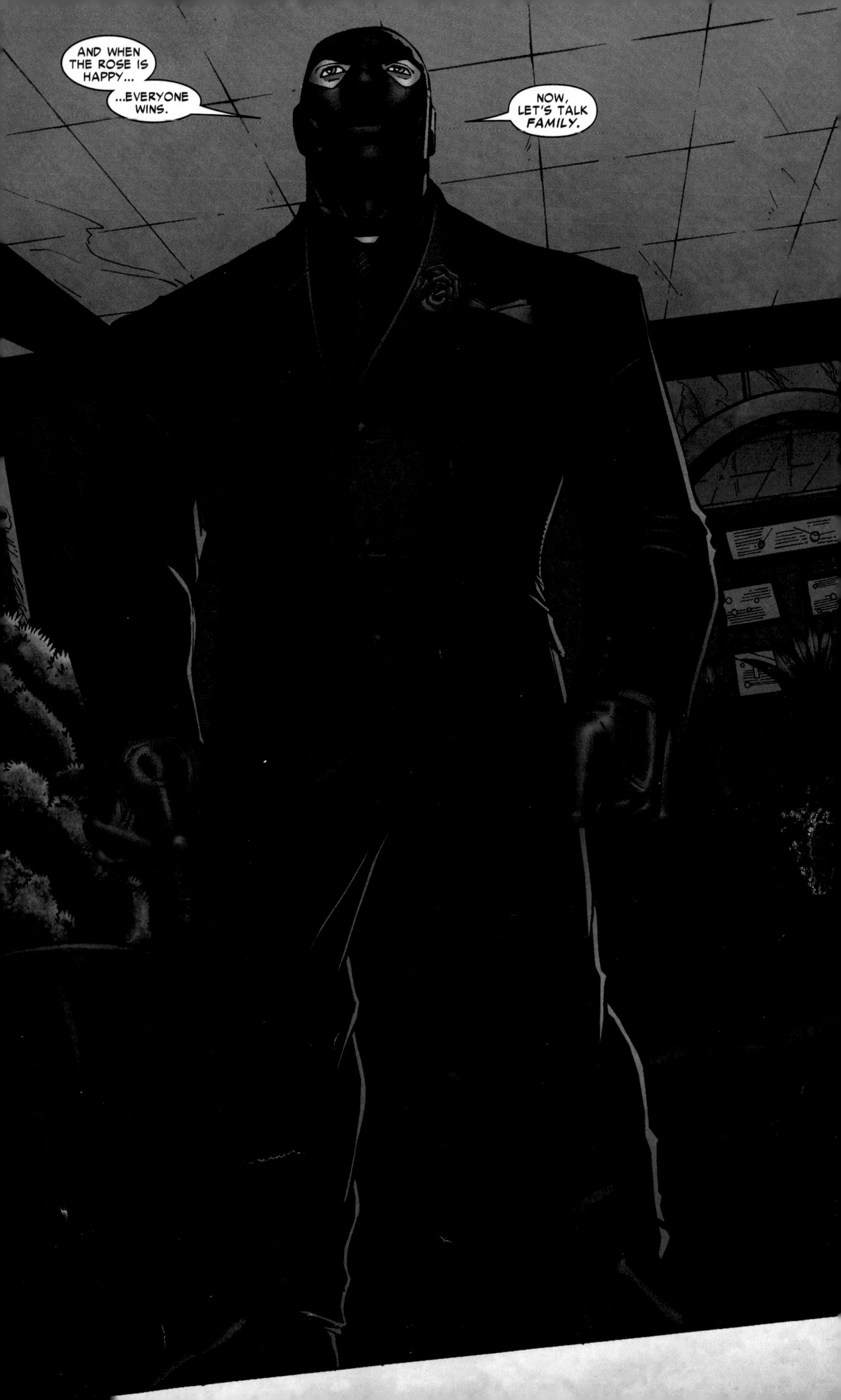
AND WHEN THE ROSE IS HAPPY...
...EVERYONE WINS.
NOW, LET'S TALK FAMILY.

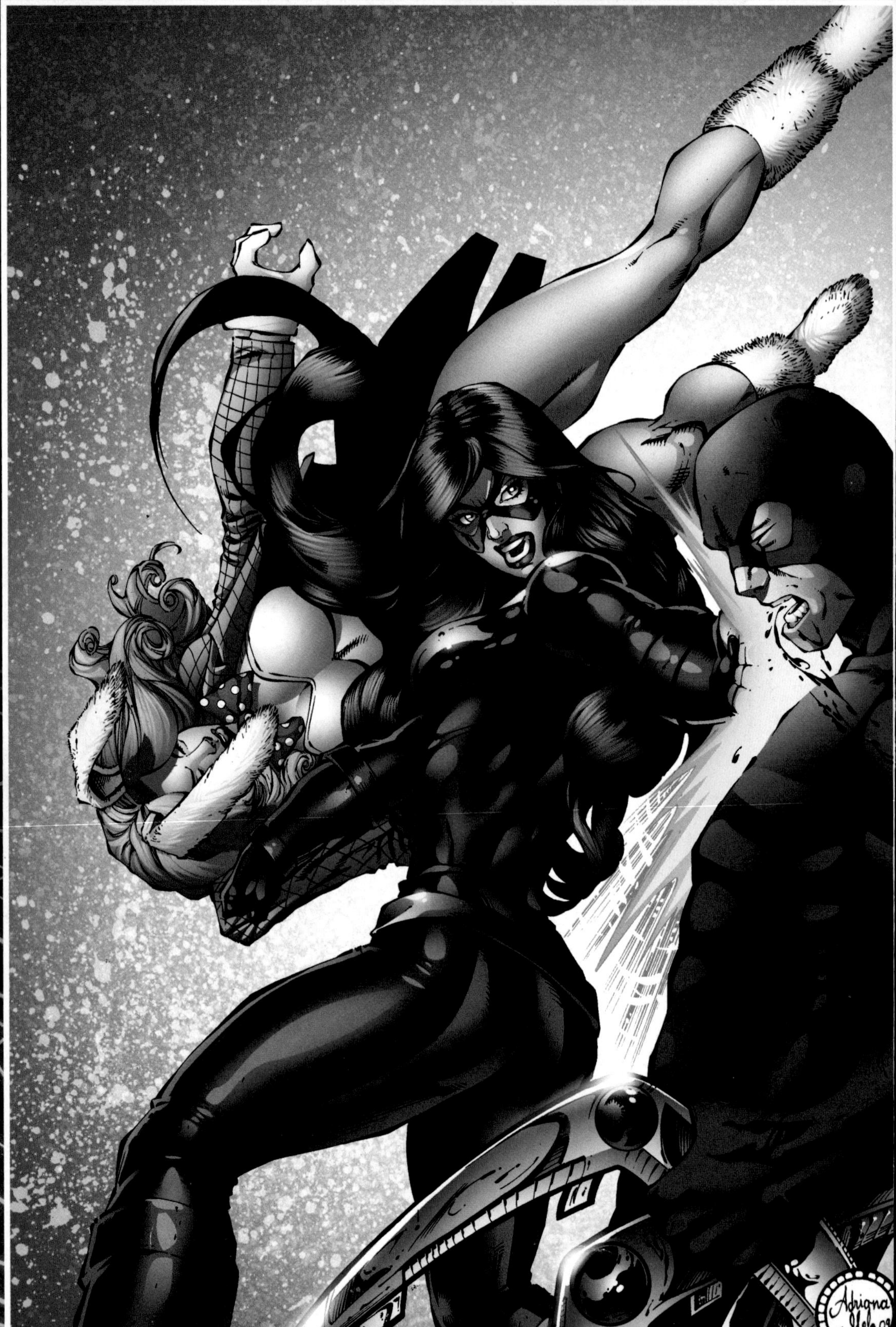

AMAZING SPIDER-MAN PRESENTS: JACKPOT #2

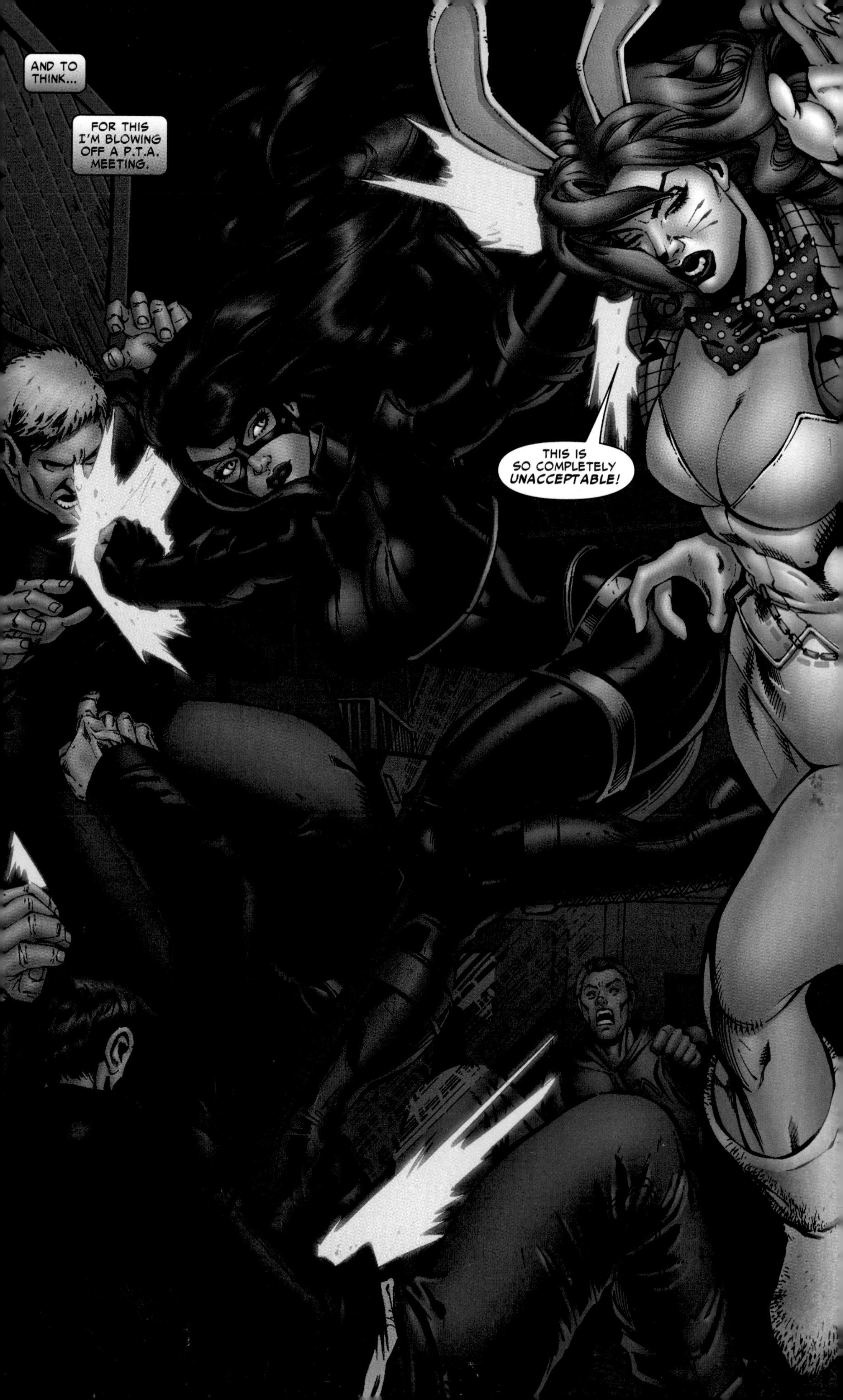
AND TO THINK...
FOR THIS I'M BLOWING OFF A P.T.A. MEETING.
THIS IS SO COMPLETELY *UNACCEPTABLE!*

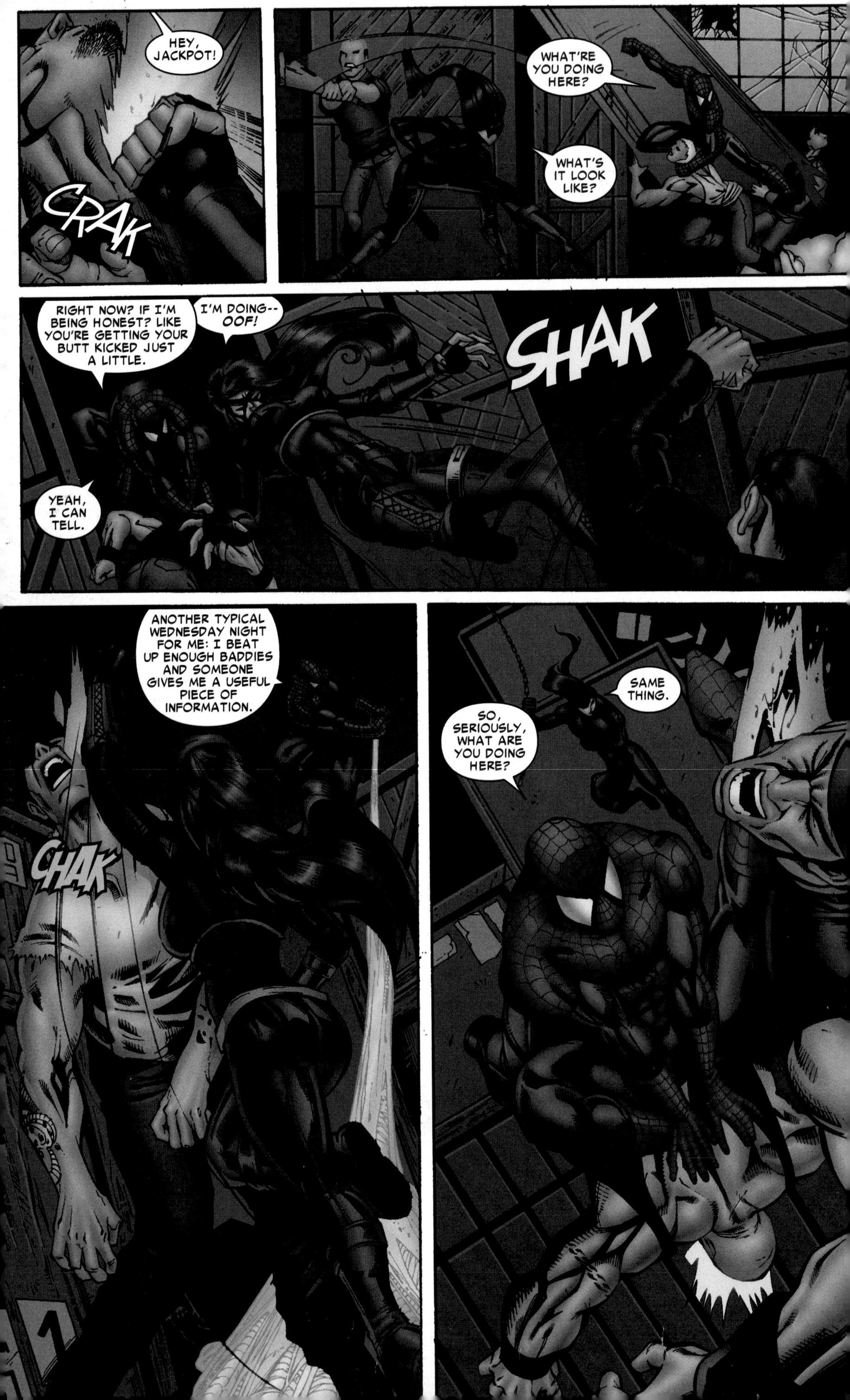
HEY, JACKPOT!
CRAK
WHAT'RE YOU DOING HERE?
WHAT'S IT LOOK LIKE?
RIGHT NOW? IF I'M BEING HONEST? LIKE YOU'RE GETTING YOUR BUTT KICKED JUST A LITTLE.
I'M DOING-- OOF!
SHAK
YEAH, I CAN TELL.
ANOTHER TYPICAL WEDNESDAY NIGHT FOR ME: I BEAT UP ENOUGH BADDIES AND SOMEONE GIVES ME A USEFUL PIECE OF INFORMATION.
CHAK
SAME THING.
SO, SERIOUSLY, WHAT ARE YOU DOING HERE?

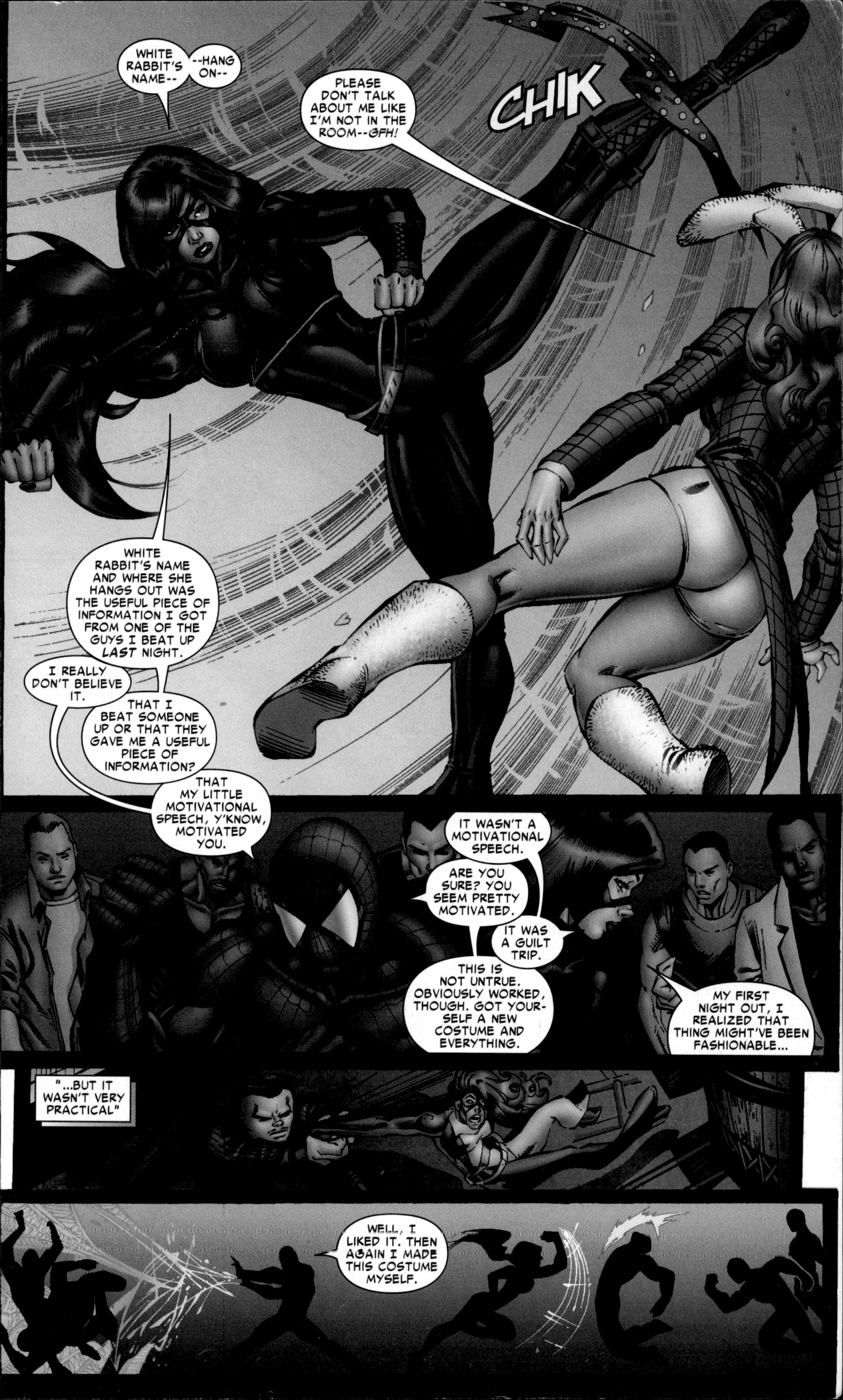
WHITE RABBIT'S NAME--
--HANG ON--
PLEASE DON'T TALK ABOUT ME LIKE I'M NOT IN THE ROOM--GFH!
CHIK
WHITE RABBIT'S NAME AND WHERE SHE HANGS OUT WAS THE USEFUL PIECE OF INFORMATION I GOT FROM ONE OF THE GUYS I BEAT UP LAST NIGHT.
I REALLY DON'T BELIEVE IT.
THAT I BEAT SOMEONE UP OR THAT THEY GAVE ME A USEFUL PIECE OF INFORMATION?
THAT MY LITTLE MOTIVATIONAL SPEECH, Y'KNOW, MOTIVATED YOU.
IT WASN'T A MOTIVATIONAL SPEECH.
ARE YOU SURE? YOU SEEM PRETTY MOTIVATED.
IT WAS A GUILT TRIP.
THIS IS NOT UNTRUE. OBVIOUSLY WORKED, THOUGH. GOT YOURSELF A NEW COSTUME AND EVERYTHING.
MY FIRST NIGHT OUT, I REALIZED THAT THING MIGHT'VE BEEN FASHIONABLE...
"...BUT IT WASN'T VERY PRACTICAL"
WELL, I LIKED IT. THEN AGAIN I MADE THIS COSTUME MYSELF.

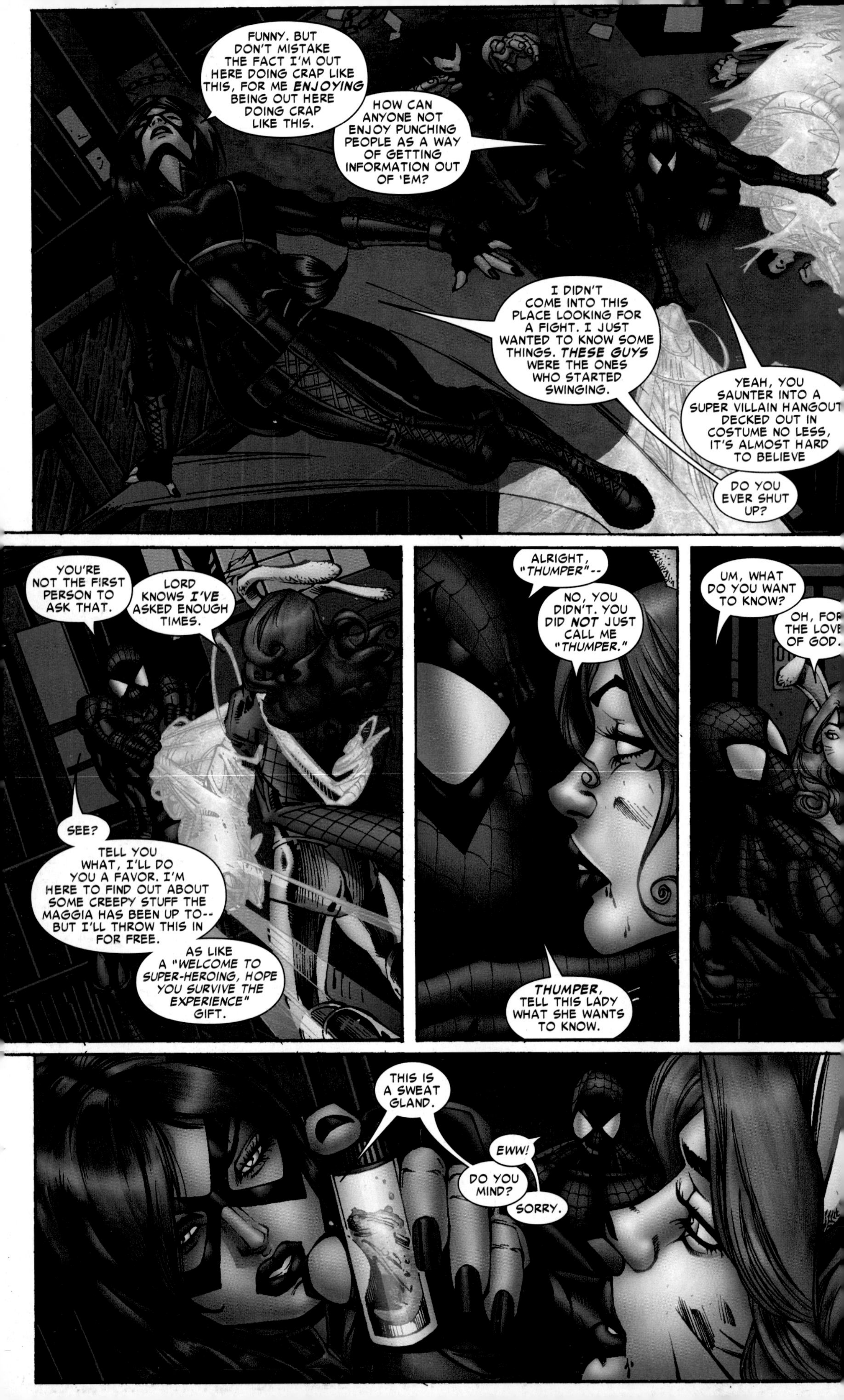
FUNNY. BUT DON'T MISTAKE THE FACT I'M OUT HERE DOING CRAP LIKE THIS, FOR ME *ENJOYING* BEING OUT HERE DOING CRAP LIKE THIS.
HOW CAN ANYONE NOT ENJOY PUNCHING PEOPLE AS A WAY OF GETTING INFORMATION OUT OF 'EM?
I DIDN'T COME INTO THIS PLACE LOOKING FOR A FIGHT. I JUST WANTED TO KNOW SOME THINGS. *THESE GUYS* WERE THE ONES WHO STARTED SWINGING.
YEAH, YOU SAUNTER INTO A SUPER VILLAIN HANGOUT DECKED OUT IN COSTUME NO LESS, IT'S ALMOST HARD TO BELIEVE
DO YOU EVER SHUT UP?
YOU'RE NOT THE FIRST PERSON TO ASK THAT.
LORD KNOWS *I'VE* ASKED ENOUGH TIMES.
SEE?
TELL YOU WHAT, I'LL DO YOU A FAVOR. I'M HERE TO FIND OUT ABOUT SOME CREEPY STUFF THE MAGGIA HAS BEEN UP TO-- BUT I'LL THROW THIS IN FOR FREE.
AS LIKE A "*WELCOME TO SUPER-HEROING, HOPE YOU SURVIVE THE EXPERIENCE*" GIFT.
ALRIGHT, "*THUMPER*"--
NO, YOU DIDN'T. YOU DID *NOT* JUST CALL ME "*THUMPER.*"
THUMPER, TELL THIS LADY WHAT SHE WANTS TO KNOW.
UM, WHAT DO YOU WANT TO KNOW?
OH, FOR THE LOVE OF GOD.
THIS IS A SWEAT GLAND.
EWW!
DO YOU MIND?
SORRY.

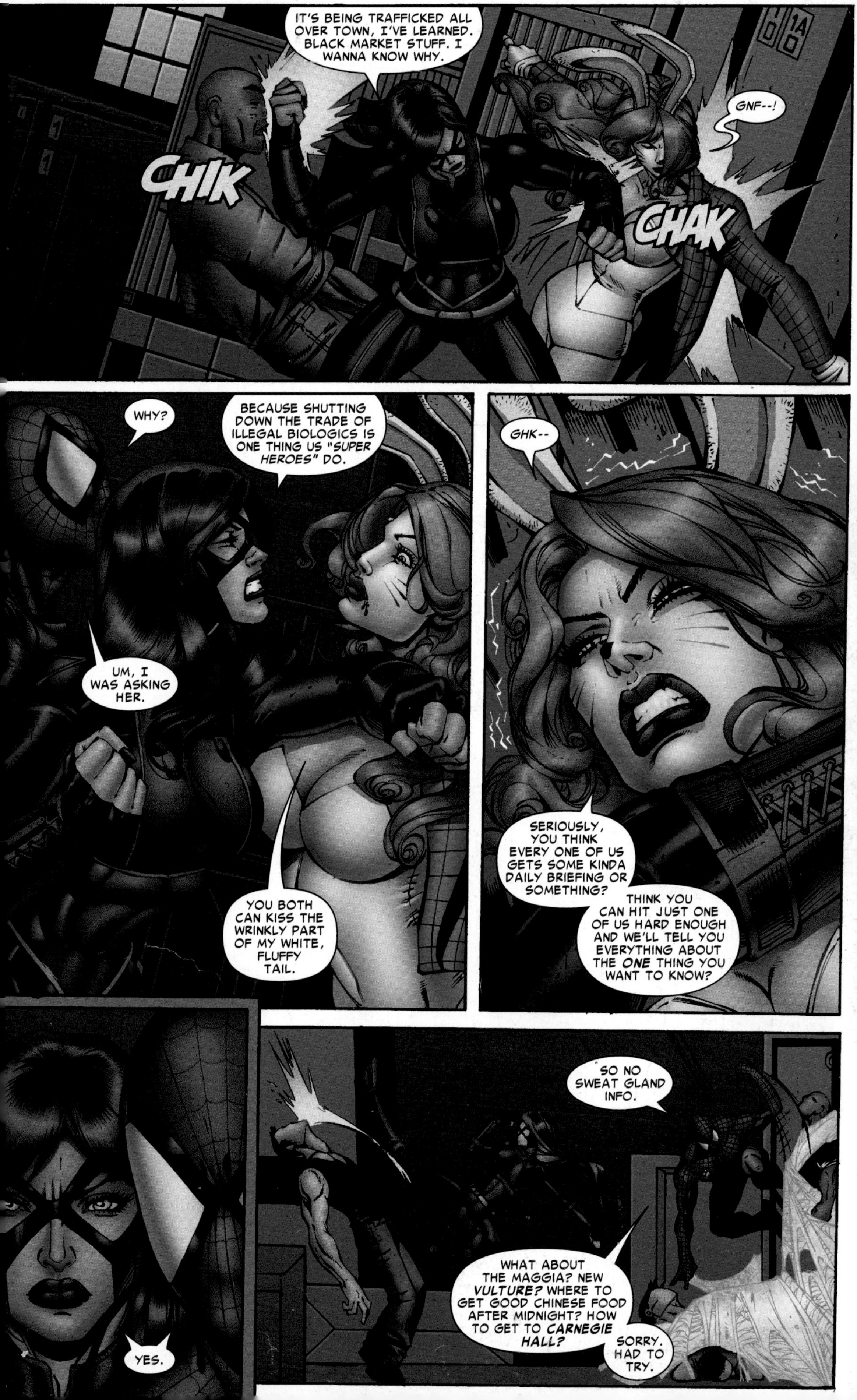
IT'S BEING TRAFFICKED ALL OVER TOWN, I'VE LEARNED. BLACK MARKET STUFF. I WANNA KNOW WHY.
CHIK
GNF--!
CHAK
WHY?
BECAUSE SHUTTING DOWN THE TRADE OF ILLEGAL BIOLOGICS IS ONE THING US "SUPER HEROES" DO.
UM, I WAS ASKING HER.
YOU BOTH CAN KISS THE WRINKLY PART OF MY WHITE, FLUFFY TAIL.
GHK--
SERIOUSLY, YOU THINK EVERY ONE OF US GETS SOME KINDA DAILY BRIEFING OR SOMETHING?
THINK YOU CAN HIT JUST ONE OF US HARD ENOUGH AND WE'LL TELL YOU EVERYTHING ABOUT THE ONE THING YOU WANT TO KNOW?
YES.
SO NO SWEAT GLAND INFO.
WHAT ABOUT THE MAGGIA? NEW VULTURE? WHERE TO GET GOOD CHINESE FOOD AFTER MIDNIGHT? HOW TO GET TO CARNEGIE HALL?
SORRY. HAD TO TRY.

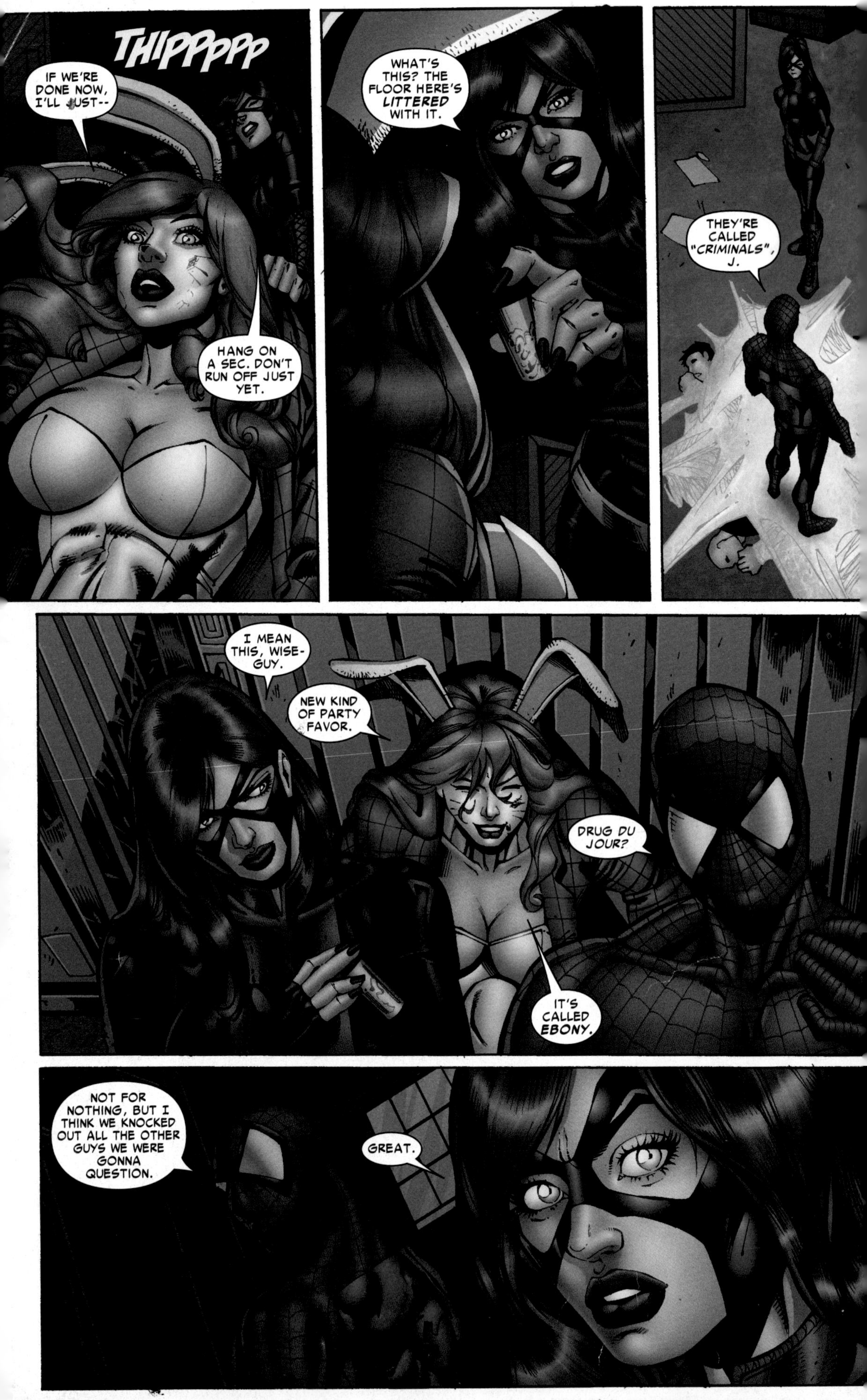
THIPPPPP
IF WE'RE DONE NOW, I'LL JUST--
HANG ON A SEC. DON'T RUN OFF JUST YET.
WHAT'S THIS? THE FLOOR HERE'S *LITTERED* WITH IT.
THEY'RE CALLED "*CRIMINALS*", J.
I MEAN THIS, WISE-GUY.
NEW KIND OF PARTY FAVOR.
DRUG DU JOUR?
IT'S CALLED *EBONY*.
NOT FOR NOTHING, BUT I THINK WE KNOCKED OUT ALL THE OTHER GUYS WE WERE GONNA QUESTION.
GREAT.

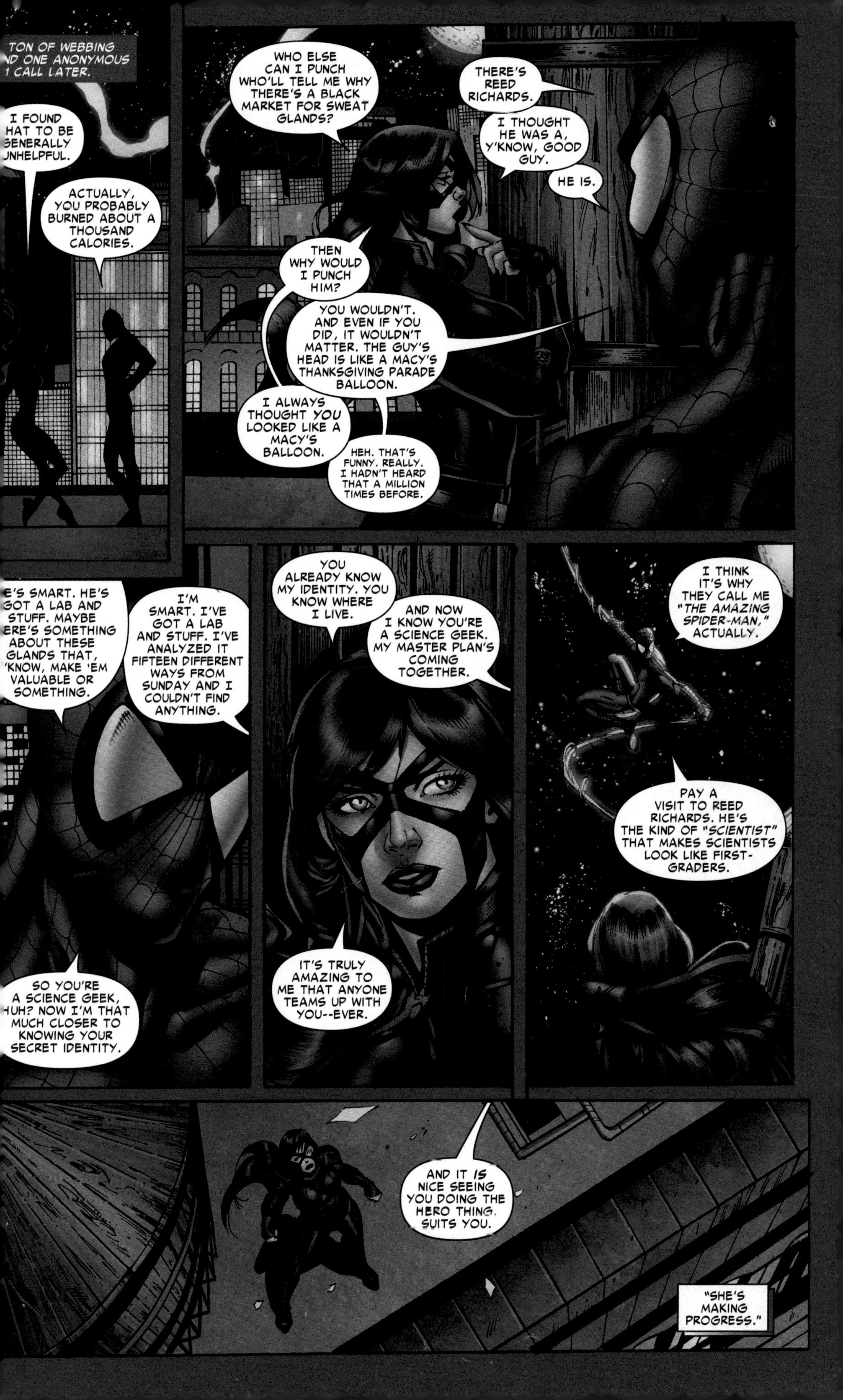
TON OF WEBBING
ND ONE ANONYMOUS
1 CALL LATER.
I FOUND HAT TO BE GENERALLY UNHELPFUL.
ACTUALLY, YOU PROBABLY BURNED ABOUT A THOUSAND CALORIES.
WHO ELSE CAN I PUNCH WHO'LL TELL ME WHY THERE'S A BLACK MARKET FOR SWEAT GLANDS?
THERE'S REED RICHARDS.
I THOUGHT HE WAS A, Y'KNOW, GOOD GUY.
HE IS.
THEN WHY WOULD I PUNCH HIM?
YOU WOULDN'T. AND EVEN IF YOU DID, IT WOULDN'T MATTER. THE GUY'S HEAD IS LIKE A MACY'S THANKSGIVING PARADE BALLOON.
I ALWAYS THOUGHT *YOU* LOOKED LIKE A MACY'S BALLOON.
HEH. THAT'S FUNNY. REALLY. I HADN'T HEARD THAT A MILLION TIMES BEFORE.
E'S SMART. HE'S GOT A LAB AND STUFF. MAYBE ERE'S SOMETHING ABOUT THESE GLANDS THAT, 'KNOW, MAKE 'EM VALUABLE OR SOMETHING.
I'M SMART. I'VE GOT A LAB AND STUFF. I'VE ANALYZED IT FIFTEEN DIFFERENT WAYS FROM SUNDAY AND I COULDN'T FIND ANYTHING.
SO YOU'RE A SCIENCE GEEK, HUH? NOW I'M THAT MUCH CLOSER TO KNOWING YOUR SECRET IDENTITY.
YOU ALREADY KNOW MY IDENTITY. YOU KNOW WHERE I LIVE.
AND NOW I KNOW YOU'RE A SCIENCE GEEK. MY MASTER PLAN'S COMING TOGETHER.
IT'S TRULY AMAZING TO ME THAT ANYONE TEAMS UP WITH YOU--EVER.
I THINK IT'S WHY THEY CALL ME "*THE AMAZING SPIDER-MAN*," ACTUALLY.
PAY A VISIT TO REED RICHARDS. HE'S THE KIND OF "*SCIENTIST*" THAT MAKES SCIENTISTS LOOK LIKE FIRST-GRADERS.
AND IT *IS* NICE SEEING YOU DOING THE HERO THING. SUITS YOU.
"SHE'S MAKING PROGRESS."

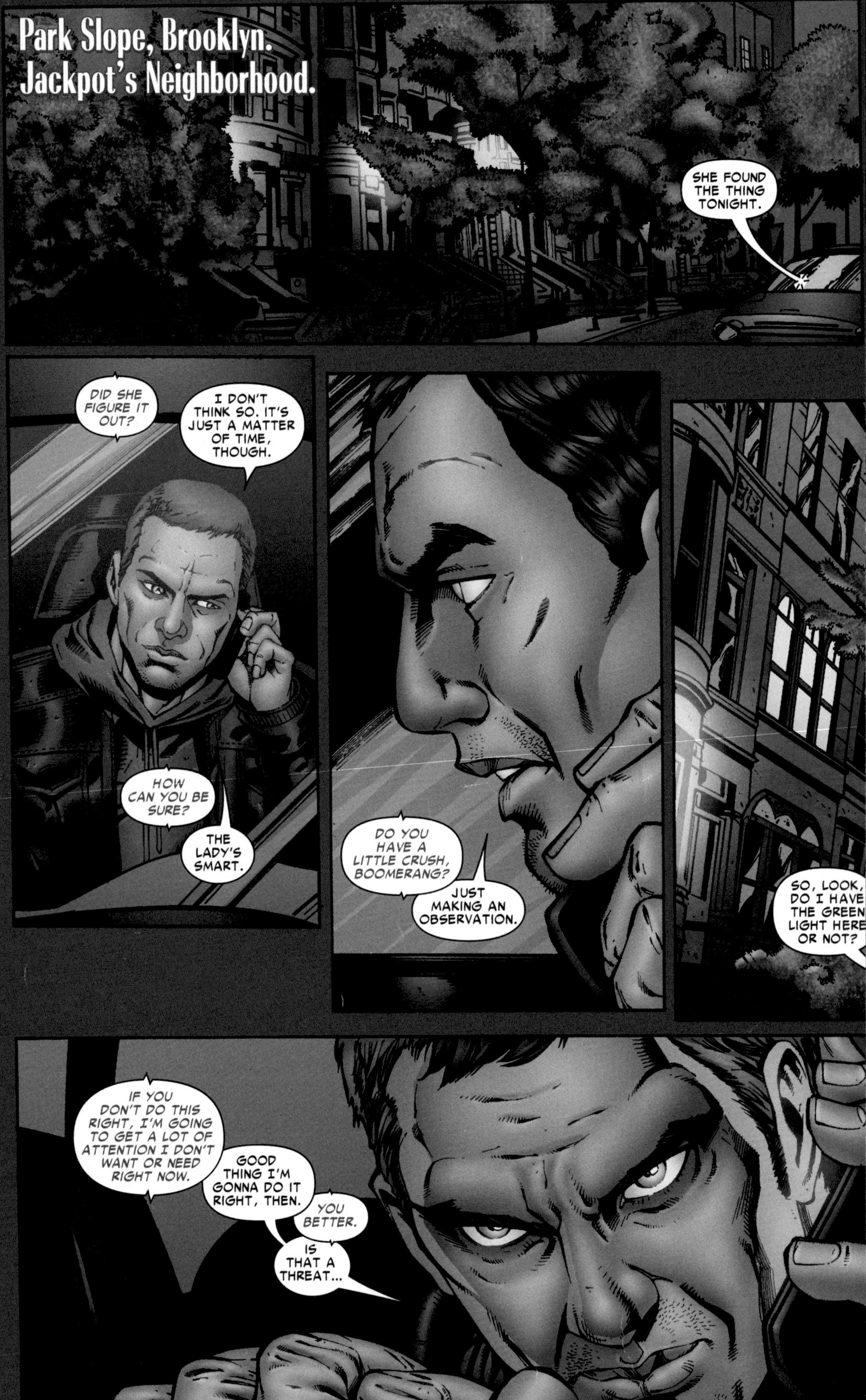
Park Slope, Brooklyn.
Jackpot's Neighborhood.
SHE FOUND THE THING TONIGHT.
DID SHE FIGURE IT OUT?
I DON'T THINK SO. IT'S JUST A MATTER OF TIME, THOUGH.
HOW CAN YOU BE SURE?
THE LADY'S SMART.
DO YOU HAVE A LITTLE CRUSH, BOOMERANG?
JUST MAKING AN OBSERVATION.
SO, LOOK, DO I HAVE THE GREEN LIGHT HERE OR NOT?
IF YOU DON'T DO THIS RIGHT, I'M GOING TO GET A LOT OF ATTENTION I DON'T WANT OR NEED RIGHT NOW.
GOOD THING I'M GONNA DO IT RIGHT, THEN.
YOU BETTER.
IS THAT A THREAT...

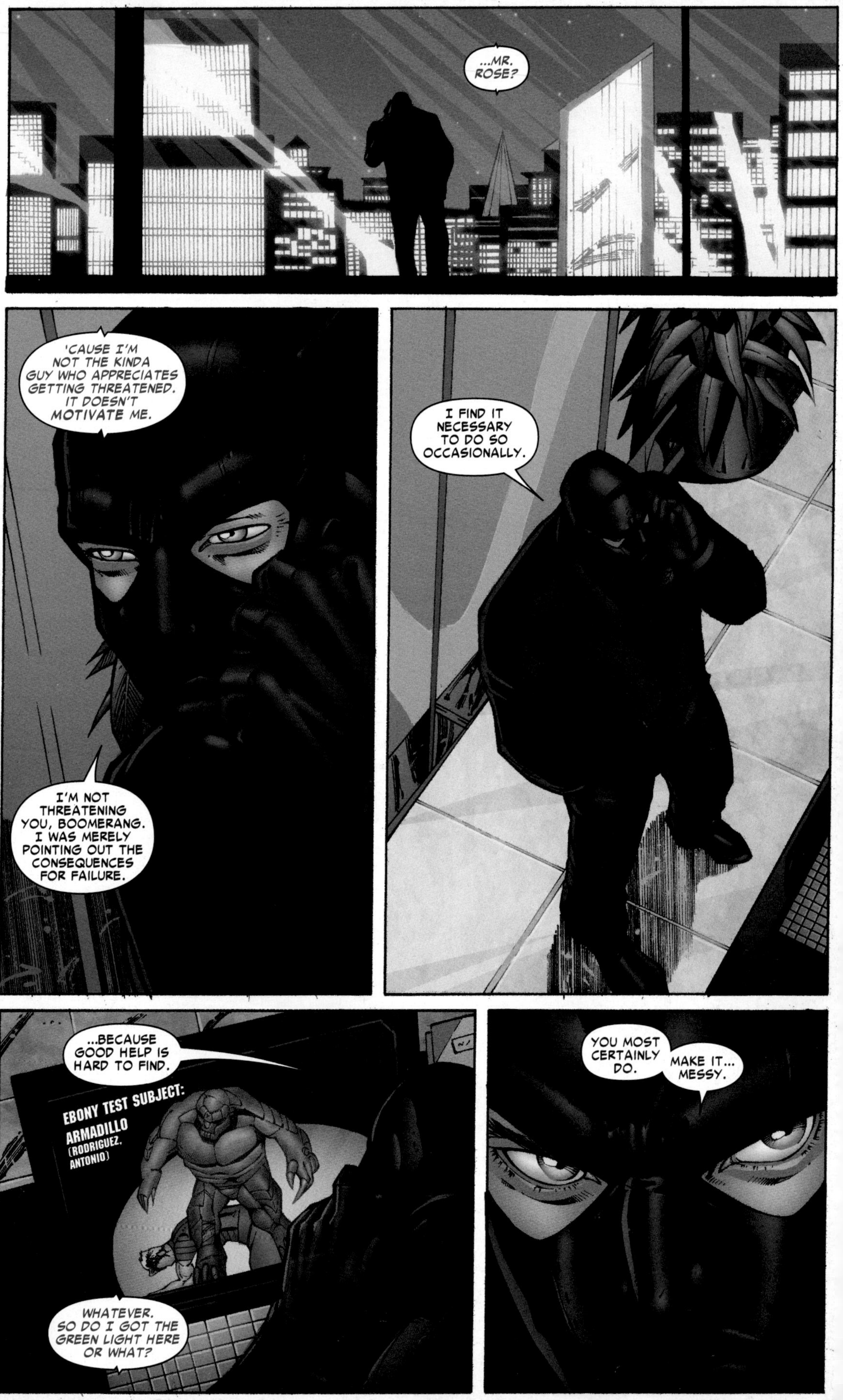
...MR. ROSE?
'CAUSE I'M NOT THE KINDA GUY WHO APPRECIATES GETTING THREATENED. IT DOESN'T MOTIVATE ME.
I FIND IT NECESSARY TO DO SO OCCASIONALLY.
I'M NOT THREATENING YOU, BOOMERANG. I WAS MERELY POINTING OUT THE CONSEQUENCES FOR FAILURE.
...BECAUSE GOOD HELP IS HARD TO FIND.
EBONY TEST SUBJECT:
ARMADILLO
(RODRIGUEZ, ANTONIO)
WHATEVER. SO DO I GOT THE GREEN LIGHT HERE OR WHAT?
YOU MOST CERTAINLY DO.
MAKE IT... MESSY.

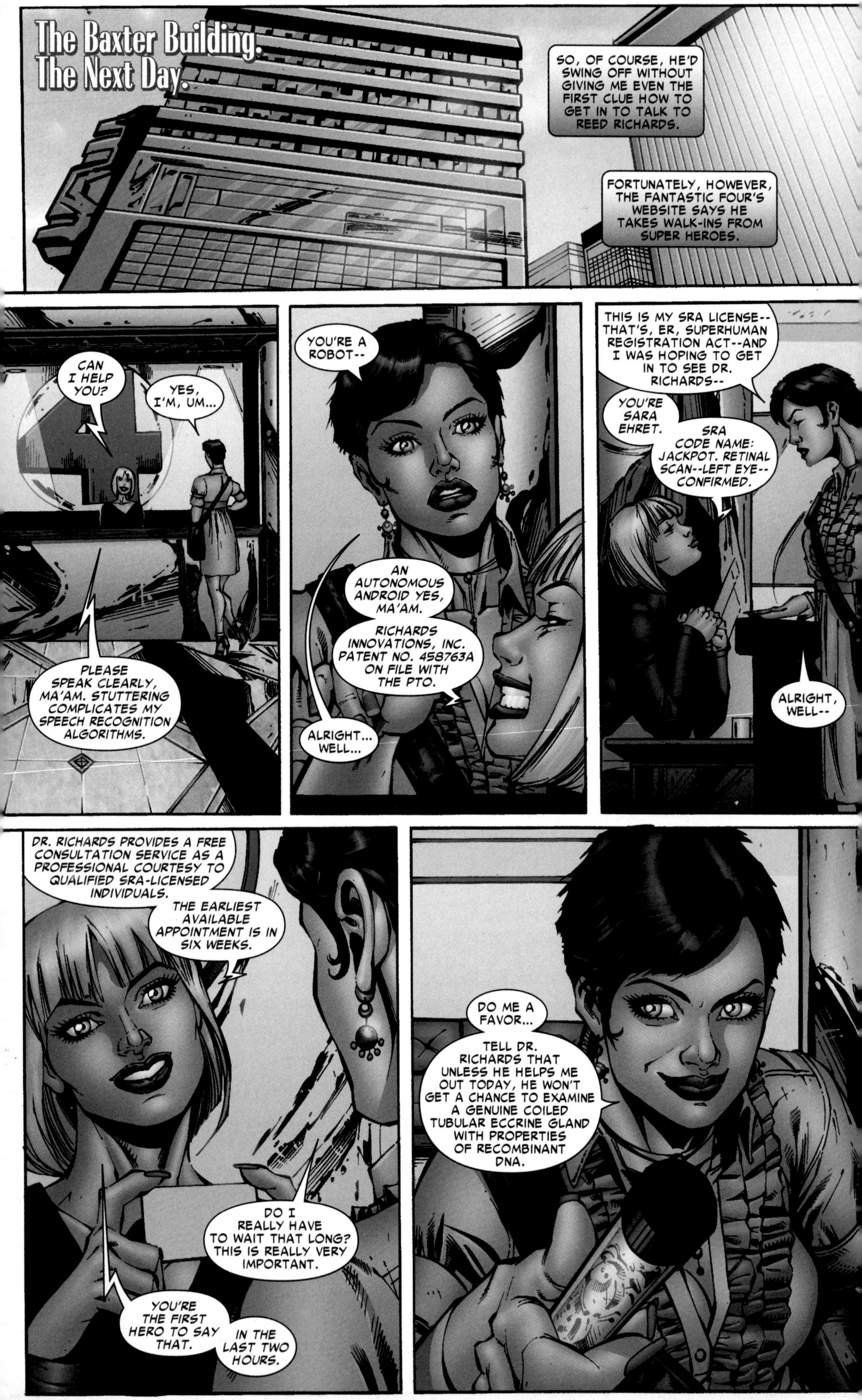
The Baxter Building.
The Next Day.
SO, OF COURSE, HE'D SWING OFF WITHOUT GIVING ME EVEN THE FIRST CLUE HOW TO GET IN TO TALK TO REED RICHARDS.
FORTUNATELY, HOWEVER, THE FANTASTIC FOUR'S WEBSITE SAYS HE TAKES WALK-INS FROM SUPER HEROES.
CAN I HELP YOU?
YES, I'M, UM...
PLEASE SPEAK CLEARLY, MA'AM. STUTTERING COMPLICATES MY SPEECH RECOGNITION ALGORITHMS.
YOU'RE A ROBOT--
AN AUTONOMOUS ANDROID YES, MA'AM.
RICHARDS INNOVATIONS, INC. PATENT NO. 458763A ON FILE WITH THE PTO.
ALRIGHT... WELL...
THIS IS MY SRA LICENSE--THAT'S, ER, SUPERHUMAN REGISTRATION ACT--AND I WAS HOPING TO GET IN TO SEE DR. RICHARDS--
YOU'RE SARA EHRET.
SRA CODE NAME: JACKPOT. RETINAL SCAN--LEFT EYE--CONFIRMED.
ALRIGHT, WELL--
DR. RICHARDS PROVIDES A FREE CONSULTATION SERVICE AS A PROFESSIONAL COURTESY TO QUALIFIED SRA-LICENSED INDIVIDUALS.
THE EARLIEST AVAILABLE APPOINTMENT IS IN SIX WEEKS.
DO I REALLY HAVE TO WAIT THAT LONG? THIS IS REALLY VERY IMPORTANT.
YOU'RE THE FIRST HERO TO SAY THAT.
IN THE LAST TWO HOURS.
DO ME A FAVOR...
TELL DR. RICHARDS THAT UNLESS HE HELPS ME OUT TODAY, HE WON'T GET A CHANCE TO EXAMINE A GENUINE COILED TUBULAR ECCRINE GLAND WITH PROPERTIES OF RECOMBINANT DNA.

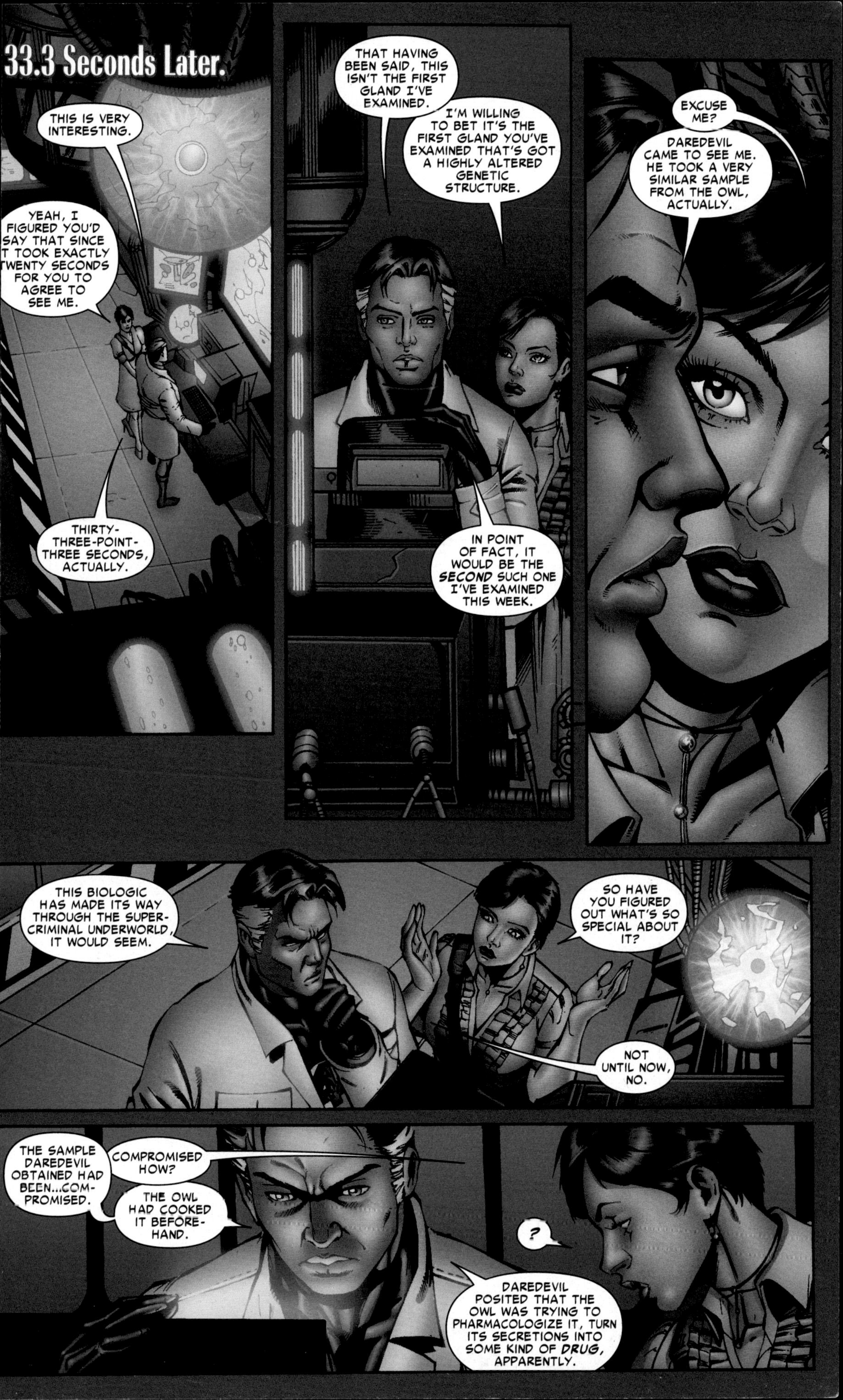
33.3 Seconds Later.
THIS IS VERY INTERESTING.
YEAH, I FIGURED YOU'D SAY THAT SINCE IT TOOK EXACTLY TWENTY SECONDS FOR YOU TO AGREE TO SEE ME.
THIRTY-THREE-POINT-THREE SECONDS, ACTUALLY.
THAT HAVING BEEN SAID, THIS ISN'T THE FIRST GLAND I'VE EXAMINED.
I'M WILLING TO BET IT'S THE FIRST GLAND YOU'VE EXAMINED THAT'S GOT A HIGHLY ALTERED GENETIC STRUCTURE.
IN POINT OF FACT, IT WOULD BE THE SECOND SUCH ONE I'VE EXAMINED THIS WEEK.
EXCUSE ME?
DAREDEVIL CAME TO SEE ME. HE TOOK A VERY SIMILAR SAMPLE FROM THE OWL, ACTUALLY.
THIS BIOLOGIC HAS MADE ITS WAY THROUGH THE SUPER-CRIMINAL UNDERWORLD, IT WOULD SEEM.
SO HAVE YOU FIGURED OUT WHAT'S SO SPECIAL ABOUT IT?
NOT UNTIL NOW, NO.
THE SAMPLE DAREDEVIL OBTAINED HAD BEEN...COMPROMISED.
COMPROMISED HOW?
THE OWL HAD COOKED IT BEFOREHAND.
?
DAREDEVIL POSITED THAT THE OWL WAS TRYING TO PHARMACOLOGIZE IT, TURN ITS SECRETIONS INTO SOME KIND OF DRUG, APPARENTLY.

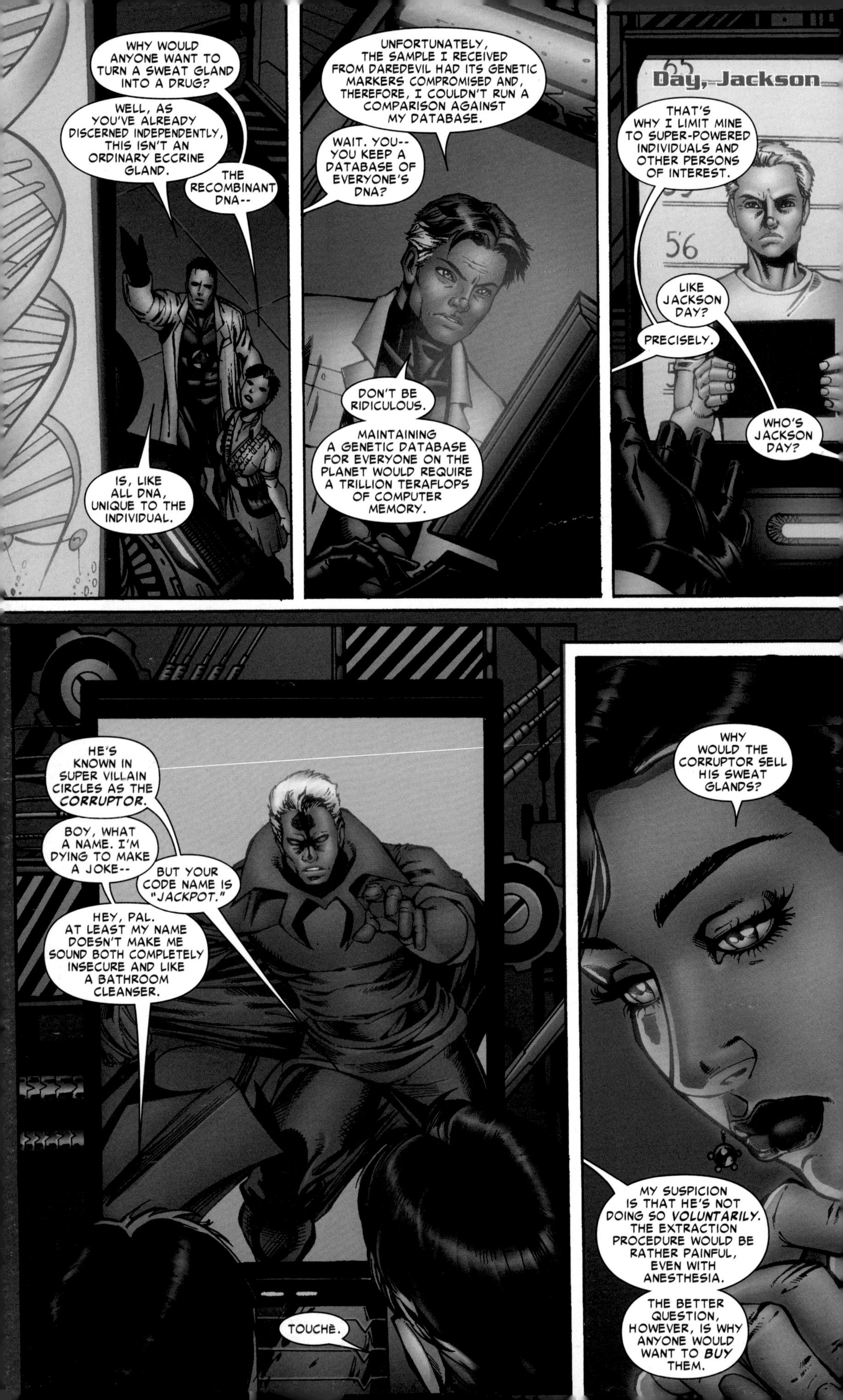

WHY WOULD ANYONE WANT TO TURN A SWEAT GLAND INTO A DRUG?
WELL, AS YOU'VE ALREADY DISCERNED INDEPENDENTLY, THIS ISN'T AN ORDINARY ECCRINE GLAND.
THE RECOMBINANT DNA--
IS, LIKE ALL DNA, UNIQUE TO THE INDIVIDUAL.
UNFORTUNATELY, THE SAMPLE I RECEIVED FROM DAREDEVIL HAD ITS GENETIC MARKERS COMPROMISED AND, THEREFORE, I COULDN'T RUN A COMPARISON AGAINST MY DATABASE.
WAIT. YOU-- YOU KEEP A DATABASE OF EVERYONE'S DNA?
DON'T BE RIDICULOUS.
MAINTAINING A GENETIC DATABASE FOR EVERYONE ON THE PLANET WOULD REQUIRE A TRILLION TERAFLOPS OF COMPUTER MEMORY.
Day, Jackson
56
THAT'S WHY I LIMIT MINE TO SUPER-POWERED INDIVIDUALS AND OTHER PERSONS OF INTEREST.
LIKE JACKSON DAY?
PRECISELY.
WHO'S JACKSON DAY?
HE'S KNOWN IN SUPER VILLAIN CIRCLES AS THE *CORRUPTOR*.
BOY, WHAT A NAME. I'M DYING TO MAKE A JOKE--
BUT YOUR CODE NAME IS "*JACKPOT*."
HEY, PAL. AT LEAST MY NAME DOESN'T MAKE ME SOUND BOTH COMPLETELY INSECURE AND LIKE A BATHROOM CLEANSER.
TOUCHÈ.
WHY WOULD THE CORRUPTOR SELL HIS SWEAT GLANDS?
MY SUSPICION IS THAT HE'S NOT DOING SO *VOLUNTARILY*. THE EXTRACTION PROCEDURE WOULD BE RATHER PAINFUL, EVEN WITH ANESTHESIA.
THE BETTER QUESTION, HOWEVER, IS WHY ANYONE WOULD WANT TO *BUY* THEM.

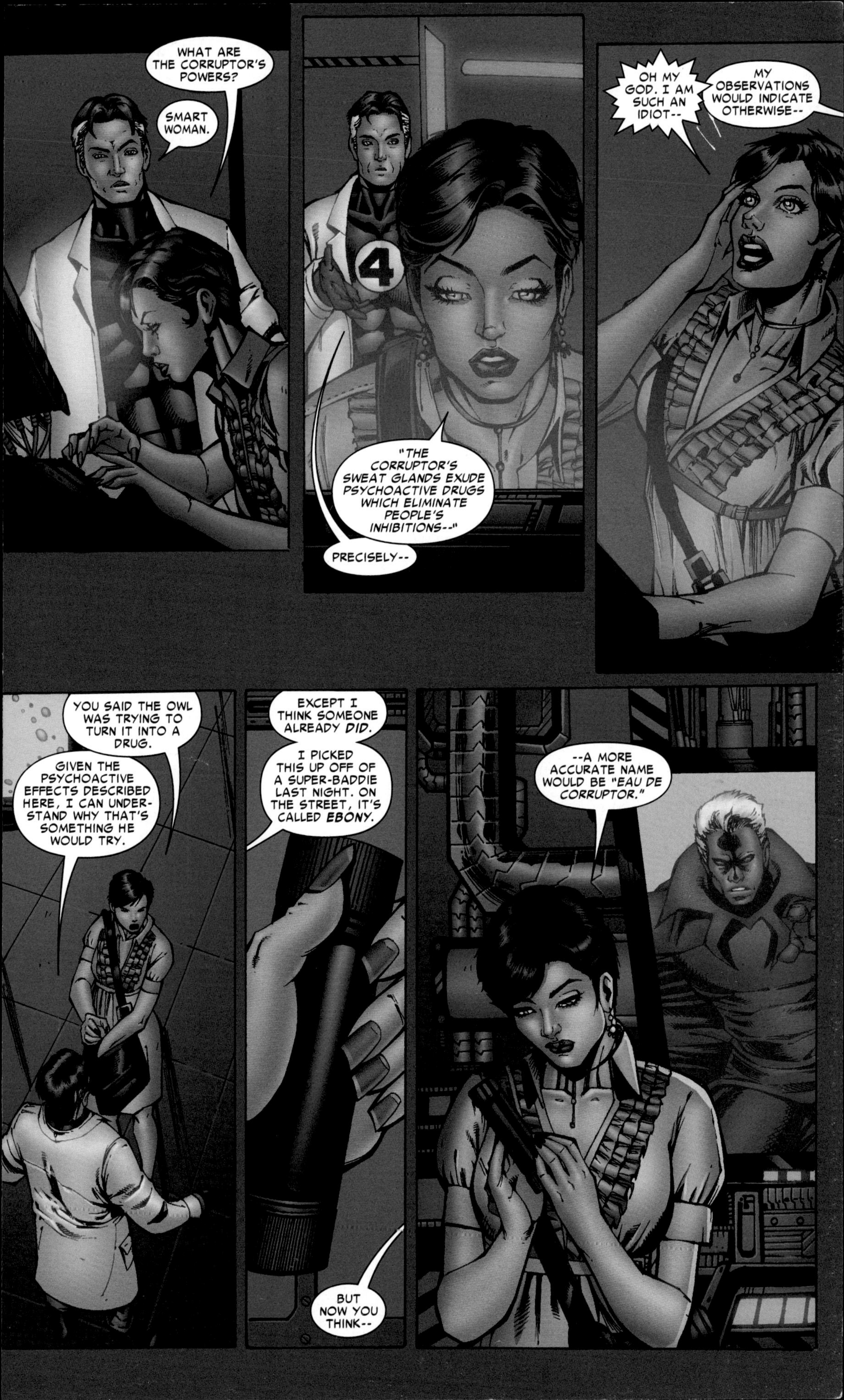
WHAT ARE THE CORRUPTOR'S POWERS?
SMART WOMAN.
"THE CORRUPTOR'S SWEAT GLANDS EXUDE PSYCHOACTIVE DRUGS WHICH ELIMINATE PEOPLE'S INHIBITIONS--"
PRECISELY--
OH MY GOD. I AM SUCH AN IDIOT--
MY OBSERVATIONS WOULD INDICATE OTHERWISE--
YOU SAID THE OWL WAS TRYING TO TURN IT INTO A DRUG.
GIVEN THE PSYCHOACTIVE EFFECTS DESCRIBED HERE, I CAN UNDERSTAND WHY THAT'S SOMETHING HE WOULD TRY.
EXCEPT I THINK SOMEONE ALREADY *DID*.
I PICKED THIS UP OFF OF A SUPER-BADDIE LAST NIGHT. ON THE STREET, IT'S CALLED *EBONY*.
BUT NOW YOU THINK--
--A MORE ACCURATE NAME WOULD BE "*EAU DE CORRUPTOR.*"

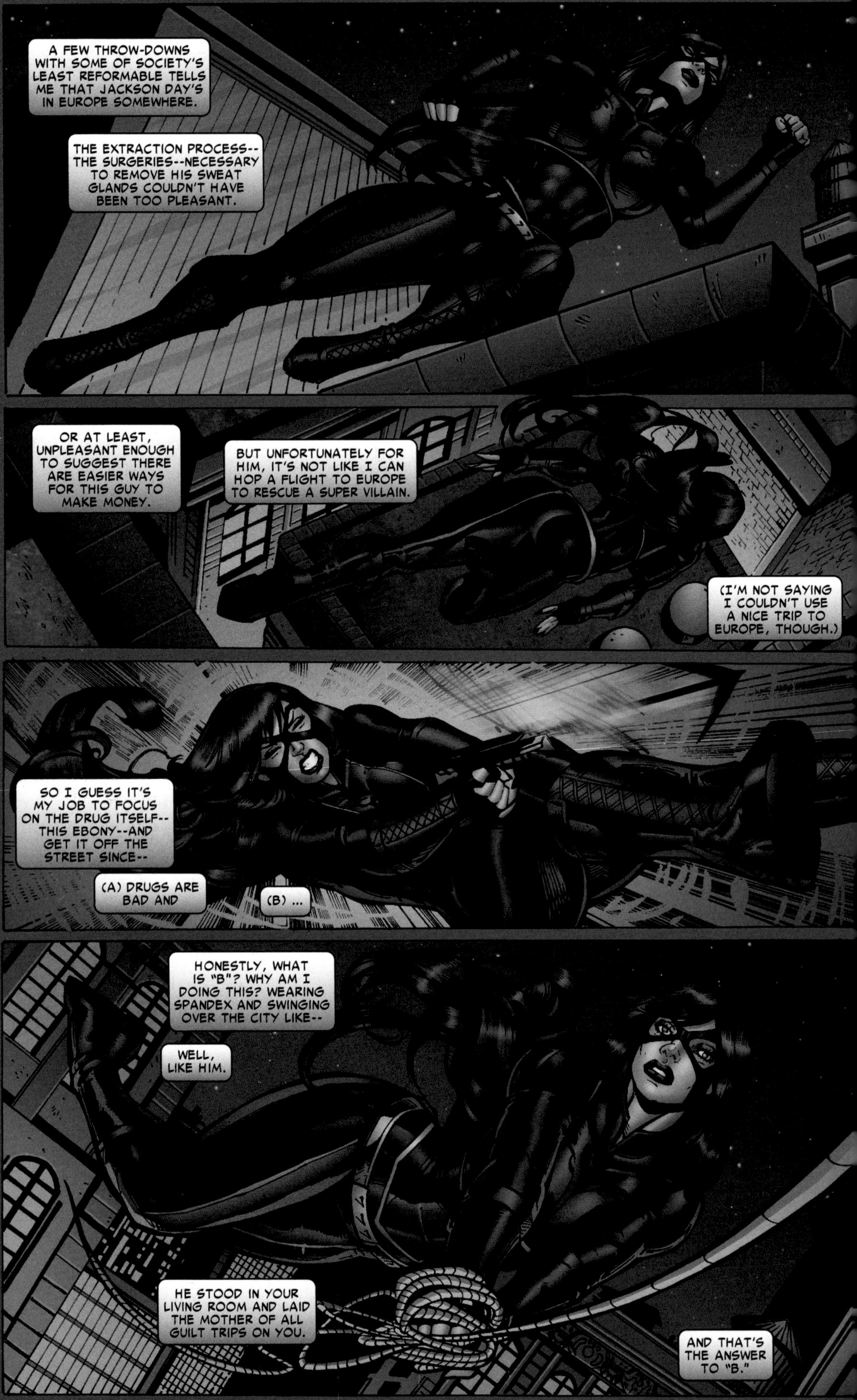
A FEW THROW-DOWNS WITH SOME OF SOCIETY'S LEAST REFORMABLE TELLS ME THAT JACKSON DAY'S IN EUROPE SOMEWHERE.
THE EXTRACTION PROCESS--THE SURGERIES--NECESSARY TO REMOVE HIS SWEAT GLANDS COULDN'T HAVE BEEN TOO PLEASANT.
OR AT LEAST, UNPLEASANT ENOUGH TO SUGGEST THERE ARE EASIER WAYS FOR THIS GUY TO MAKE MONEY.
BUT UNFORTUNATELY FOR HIM, IT'S NOT LIKE I CAN HOP A FLIGHT TO EUROPE TO RESCUE A SUPER VILLAIN.
(I'M NOT SAYING I COULDN'T USE A NICE TRIP TO EUROPE, THOUGH.)
SO I GUESS IT'S MY JOB TO FOCUS ON THE DRUG ITSELF--THIS EBONY--AND GET IT OFF THE STREET SINCE--
(A) DRUGS ARE BAD AND
(B) ...
HONESTLY, WHAT IS "B"? WHY AM I DOING THIS? WEARING SPANDEX AND SWINGING OVER THE CITY LIKE--
WELL, LIKE HIM.
HE STOOD IN YOUR LIVING ROOM AND LAID THE MOTHER OF ALL GUILT TRIPS ON YOU.
AND THAT'S THE ANSWER TO "B."

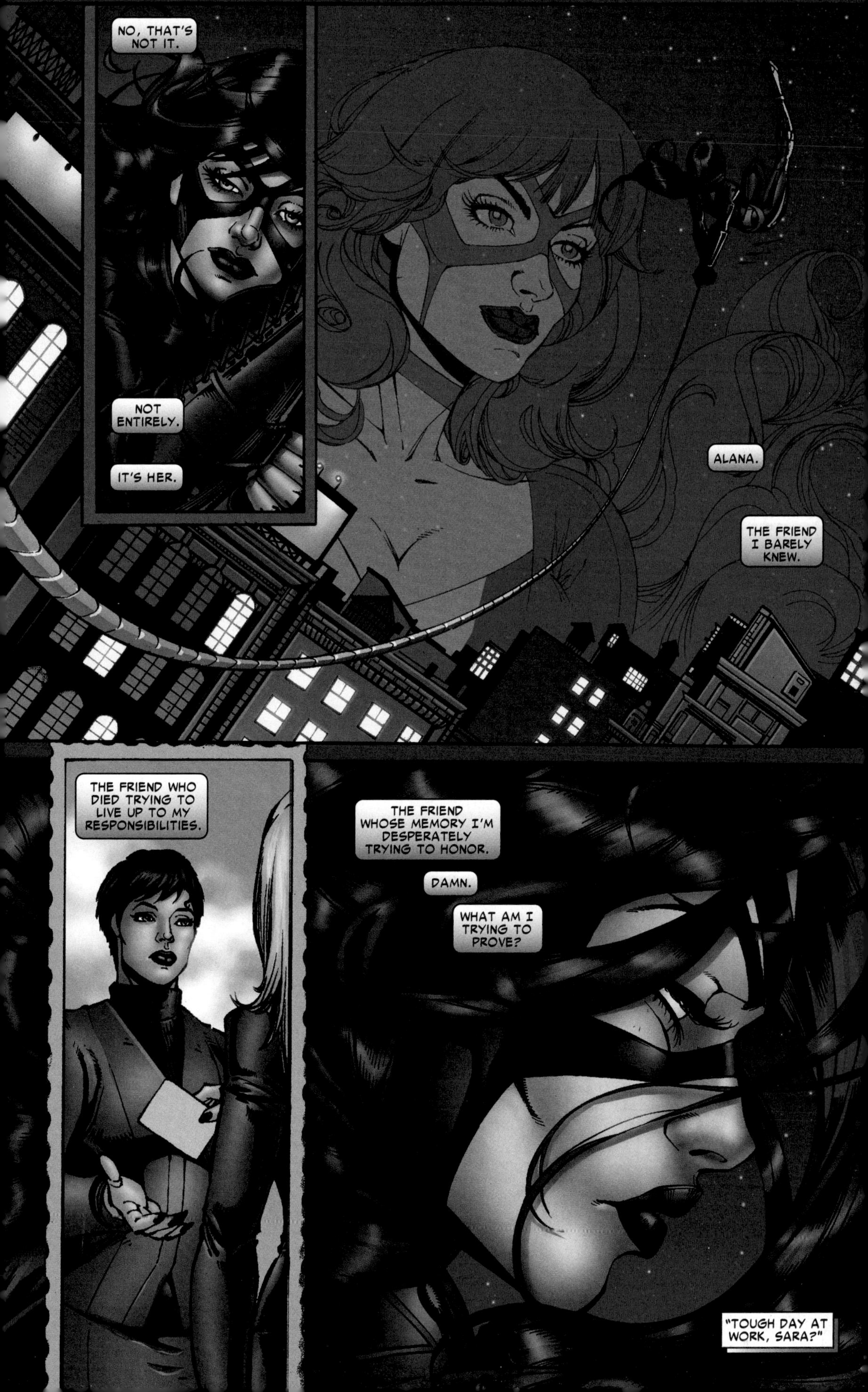
NO, THAT'S NOT IT.
NOT ENTIRELY.
IT'S HER.
ALANA.
THE FRIEND I BARELY KNEW.
THE FRIEND WHO DIED TRYING TO LIVE UP TO MY RESPONSIBILITIES.
THE FRIEND WHOSE MEMORY I'M DESPERATELY TRYING TO HONOR.
DAMN.
WHAT AM I TRYING TO PROVE?
"TOUGH DAY AT WORK, SARA?"

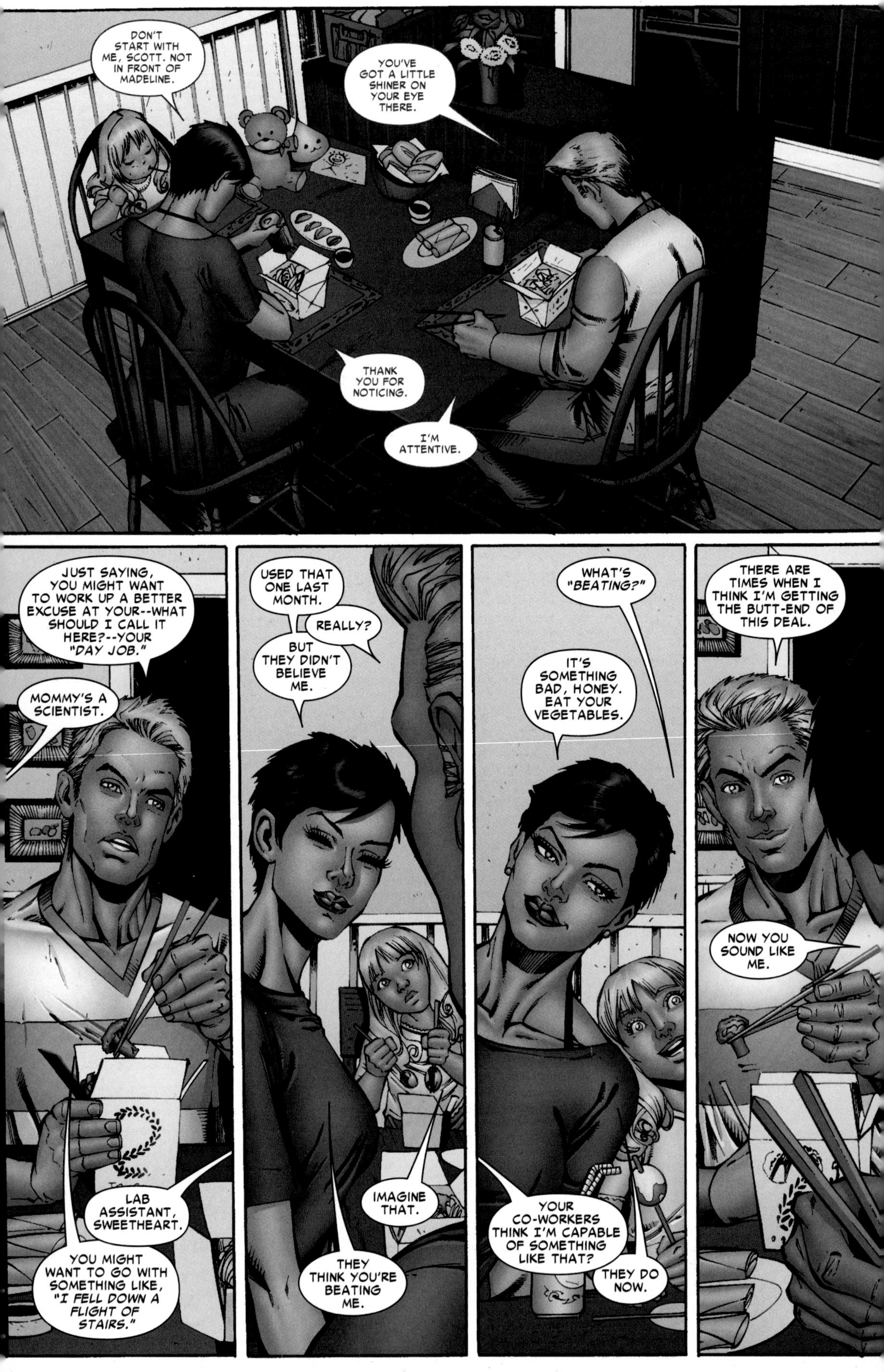
DON'T START WITH ME, SCOTT. NOT IN FRONT OF MADELINE.
YOU'VE GOT A LITTLE SHINER ON YOUR EYE THERE.
THANK YOU FOR NOTICING.
I'M ATTENTIVE.
JUST SAYING, YOU MIGHT WANT TO WORK UP A BETTER EXCUSE AT YOUR--WHAT SHOULD I CALL IT HERE?--YOUR *"DAY JOB."*
MOMMY'S A SCIENTIST.
LAB ASSISTANT, SWEETHEART.
YOU MIGHT WANT TO GO WITH SOMETHING LIKE, *"I FELL DOWN A FLIGHT OF STAIRS."*
USED THAT ONE LAST MONTH.
REALLY?
BUT THEY DIDN'T BELIEVE ME.
IMAGINE THAT.
THEY THINK YOU'RE BEATING ME.
WHAT'S *"BEATING?"*
IT'S SOMETHING BAD, HONEY. EAT YOUR VEGETABLES.
YOUR CO-WORKERS THINK I'M CAPABLE OF SOMETHING LIKE THAT?
THEY DO NOW.
THERE ARE TIMES WHEN I THINK I'M GETTING THE BUTT-END OF THIS DEAL.
NOW YOU SOUND LIKE ME.

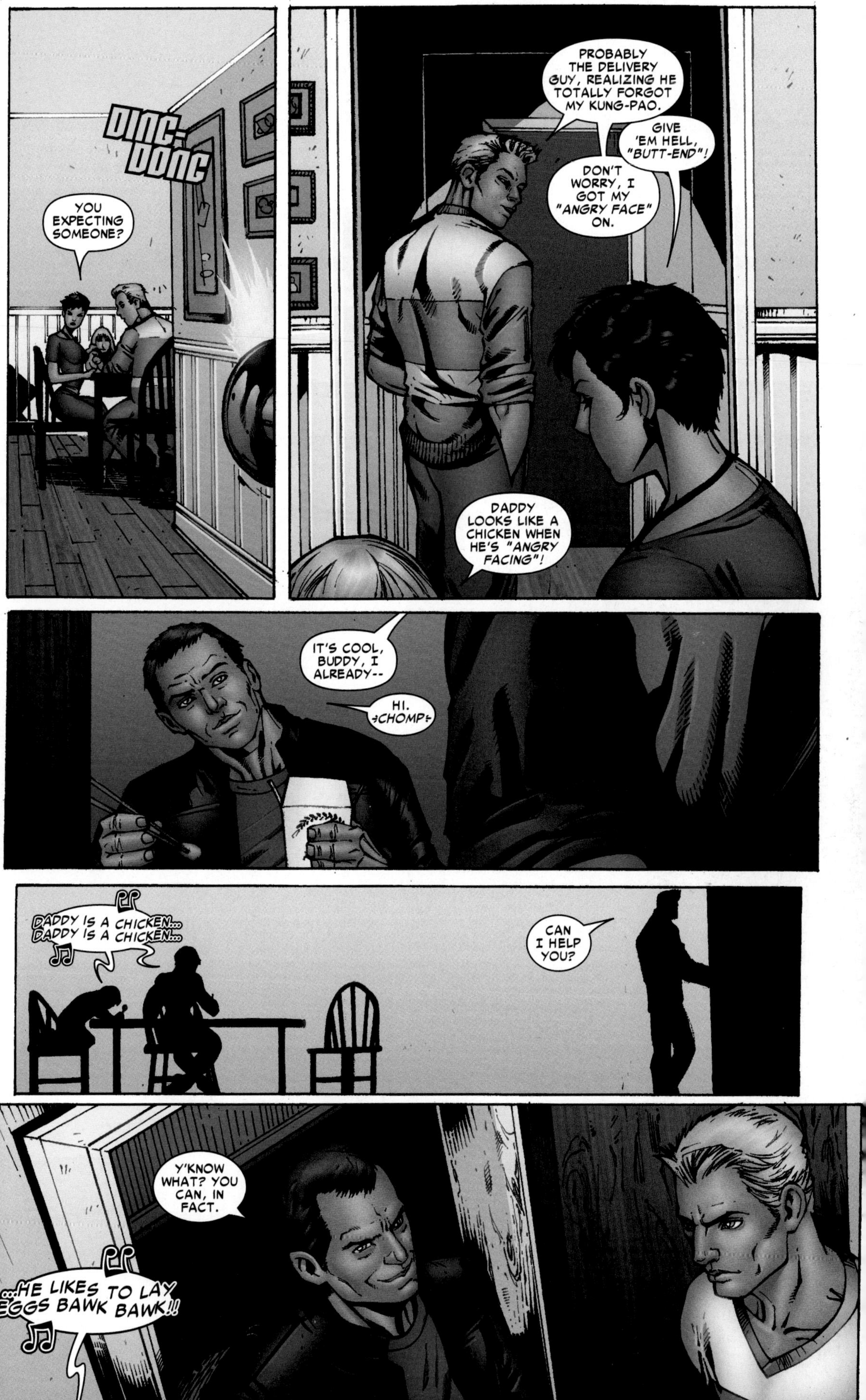
DING-DONG
YOU EXPECTING SOMEONE?
PROBABLY THE DELIVERY GUY, REALIZING HE TOTALLY FORGOT MY KUNG-PAO.
DON'T WORRY, I GOT MY "ANGRY FACE" ON.
GIVE 'EM HELL, "BUTT-END"!
DADDY LOOKS LIKE A CHICKEN WHEN HE'S "ANGRY FACING"!
IT'S COOL, BUDDY, I ALREADY--
HI. *CHOMP*
DADDY IS A CHICKEN... DADDY IS A CHICKEN...
CAN I HELP YOU?
Y'KNOW WHAT? YOU CAN, IN FACT.
...HE LIKES TO LAY EGGS BAWK BAWK!!

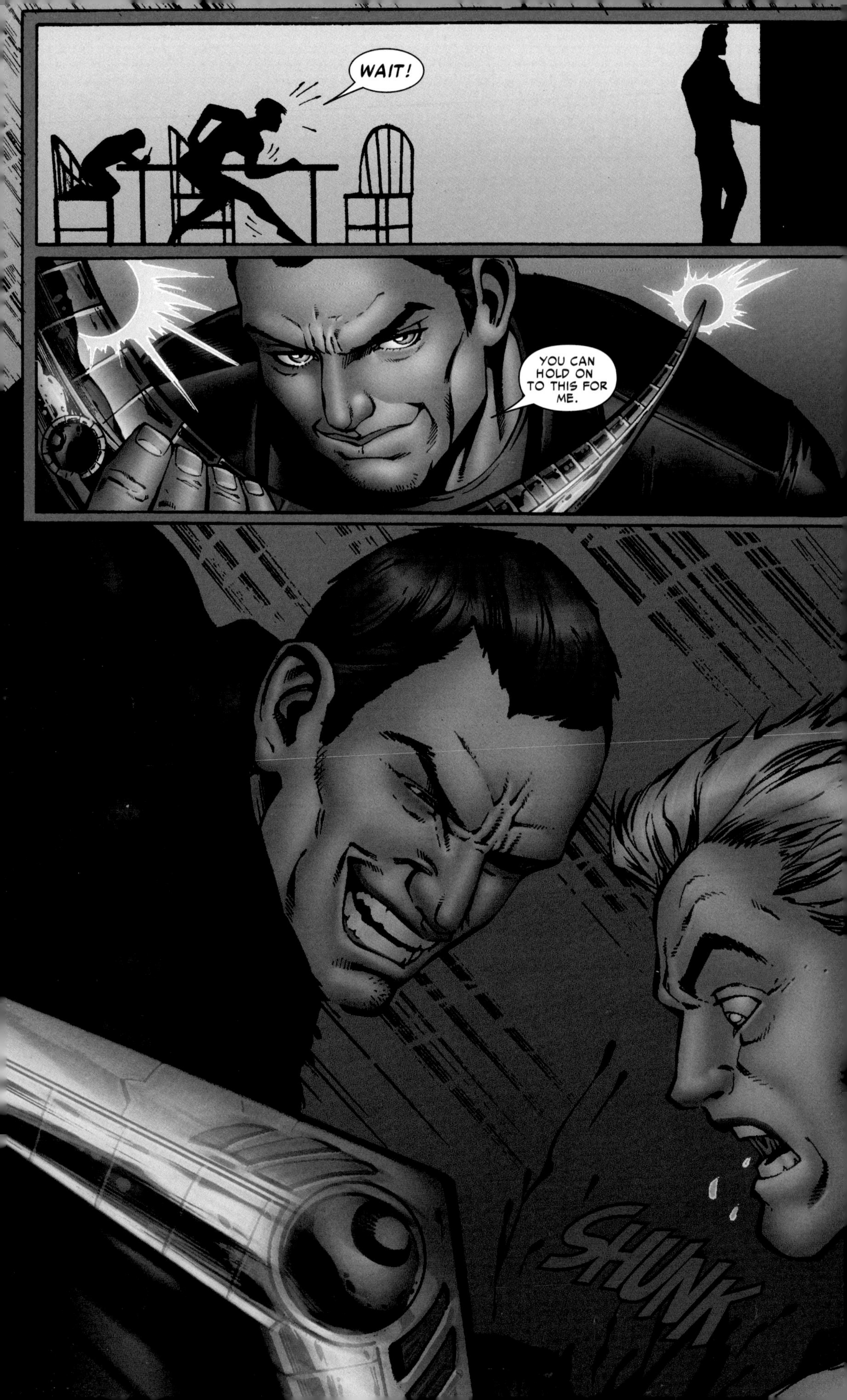
WAIT!
YOU CAN HOLD ON TO THIS FOR ME.
SHUNK

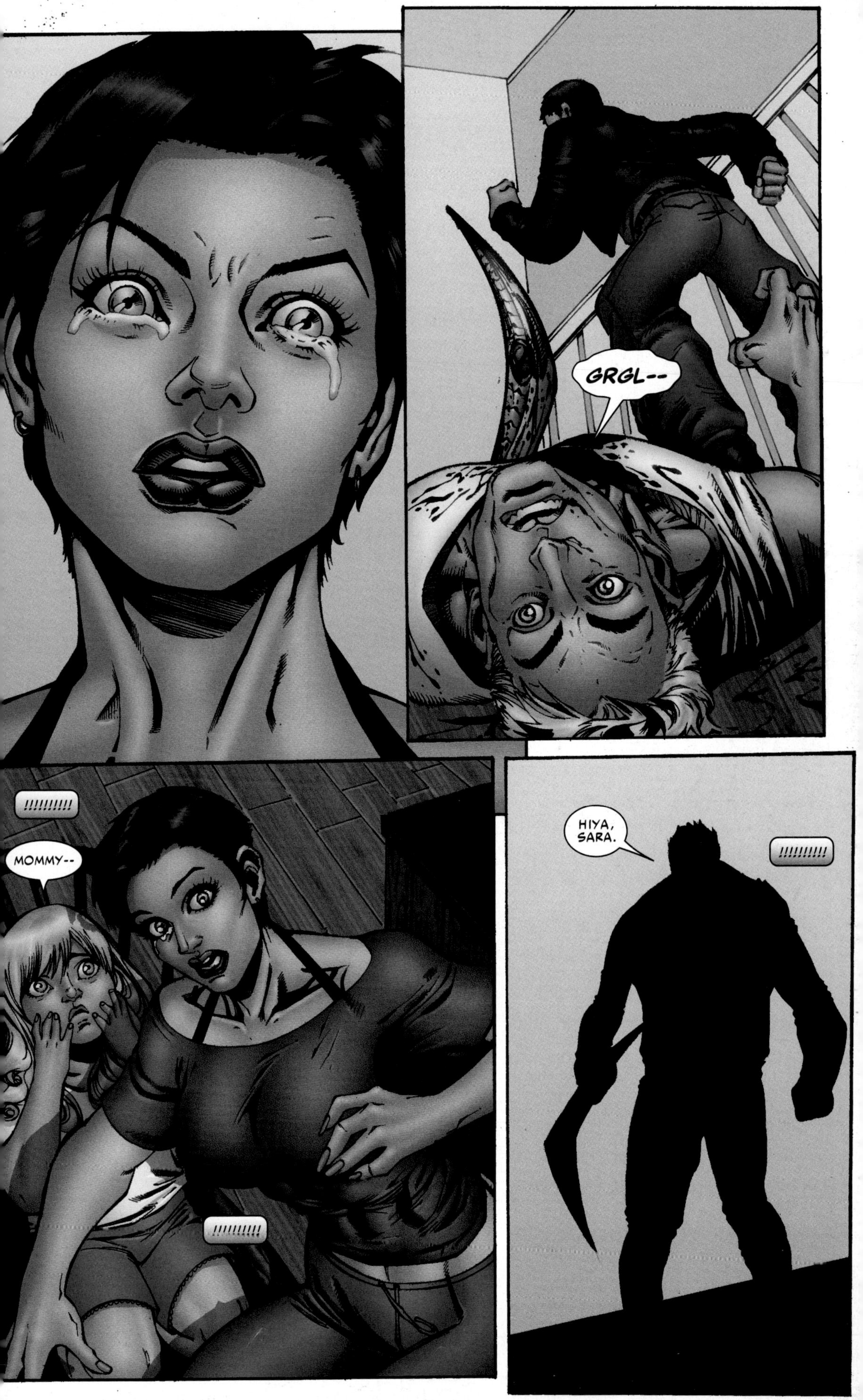
GRGL--
!!!!!!!!!!
MOMMY--
!!!!!!!!!!
HIYA, SARA.
!!!!!!!!!!

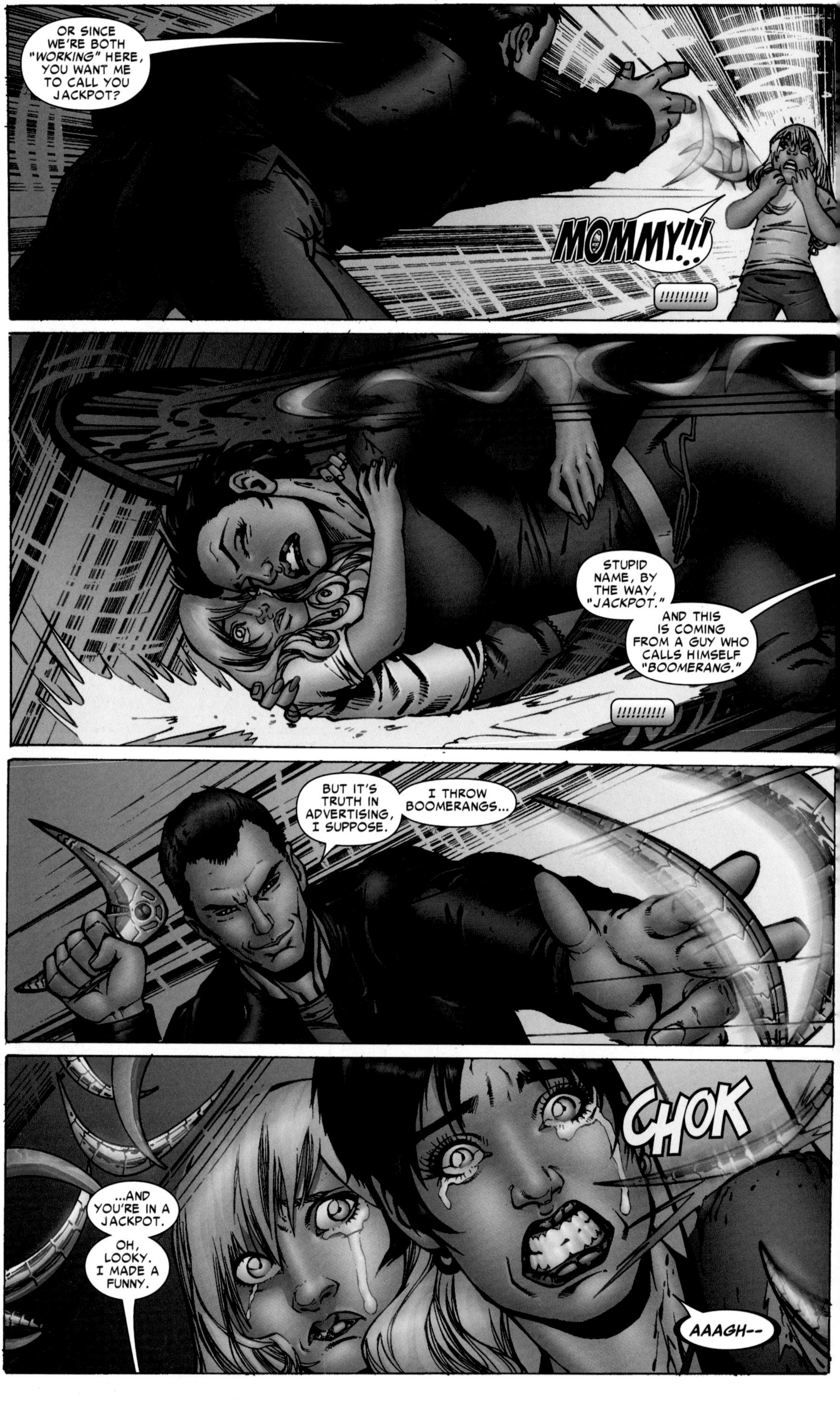
OR SINCE WE'RE BOTH "WORKING" HERE, YOU WANT ME TO CALL YOU JACKPOT?
MOMMY!!!...
!!!!!!!!!!
STUPID NAME, BY THE WAY, "JACKPOT."
AND THIS IS COMING FROM A GUY WHO CALLS HIMSELF "BOOMERANG."
!!!!!!!!!!
BUT IT'S TRUTH IN ADVERTISING, I SUPPOSE.
I THROW BOOMERANGS...
CHOK
...AND YOU'RE IN A JACKPOT.
OH, LOOKY. I MADE A FUNNY.
AAAGH--

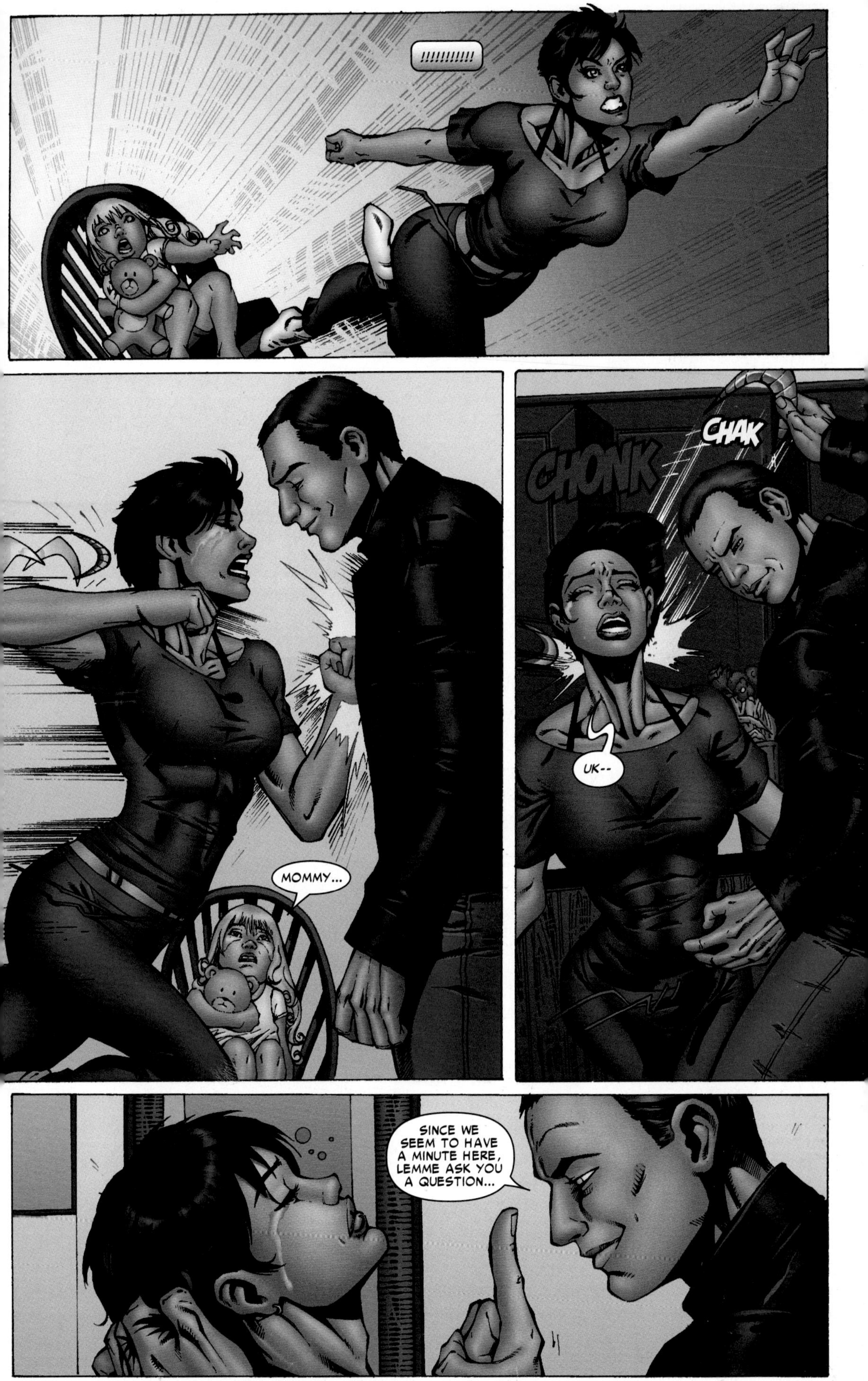
!!!!!!!!!!
MOMMY...
CHONK
CHAK
UK--
SINCE WE SEEM TO HAVE A MINUTE HERE, LEMME ASK YOU A QUESTION...

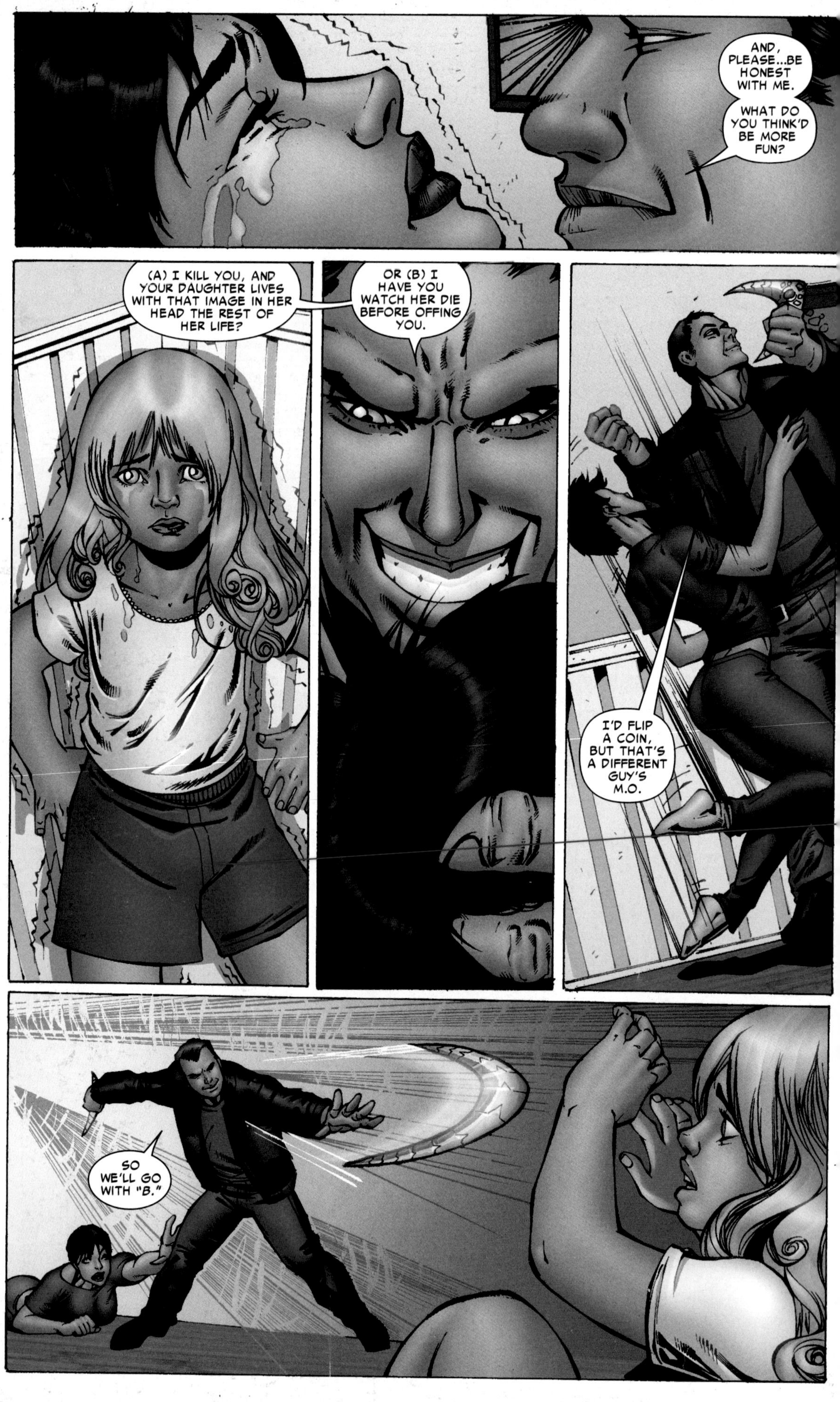
AND, PLEASE...BE HONEST WITH ME.
WHAT DO YOU THINK'D BE MORE FUN?
(A) I KILL YOU, AND YOUR DAUGHTER LIVES WITH THAT IMAGE IN HER HEAD THE REST OF HER LIFE?
OR (B) I HAVE YOU WATCH HER DIE BEFORE OFFING YOU.
I'D FLIP A COIN, BUT THAT'S A DIFFERENT GUY'S M.O.
SO WE'LL GO WITH "B."

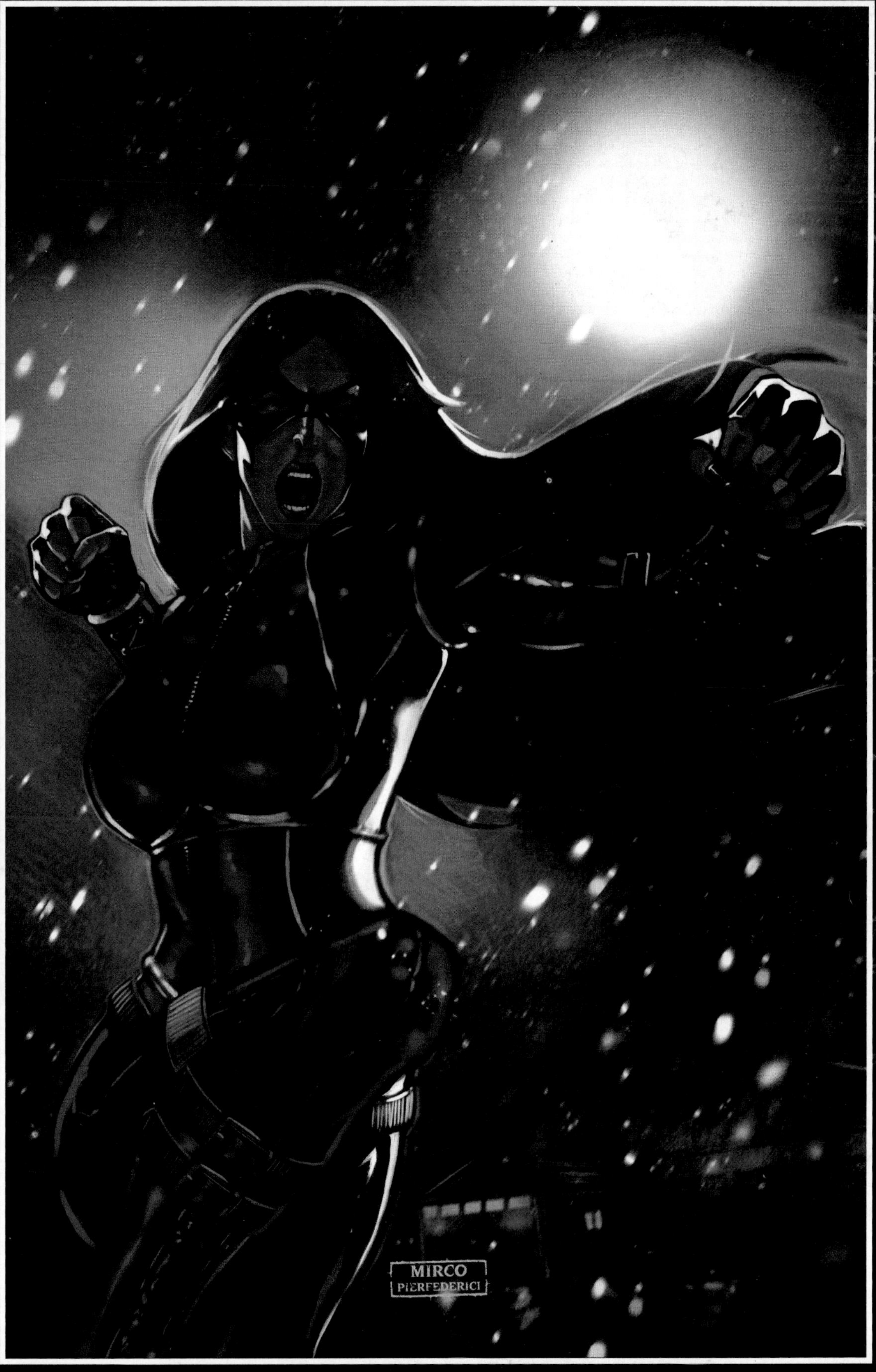
MIRCO
PIERFEDERICI

AMAZING SPIDER-MAN PRESENTS: JACKPOT #3

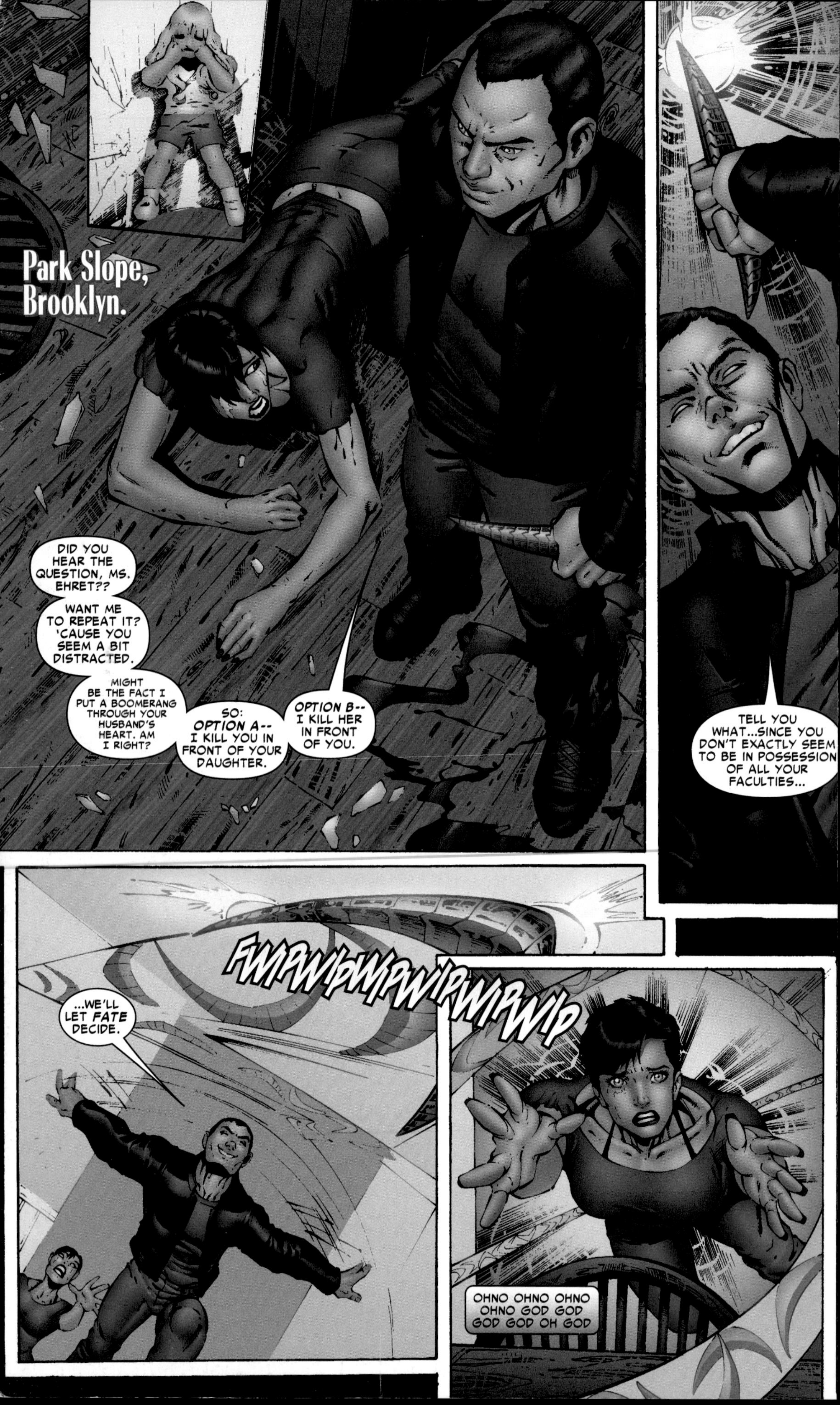
Park Slope, Brooklyn.
DID YOU HEAR THE QUESTION, MS. EHRET??
WANT ME TO REPEAT IT? 'CAUSE YOU SEEM A BIT DISTRACTED.
MIGHT BE THE FACT I PUT A BOOMERANG THROUGH YOUR HUSBAND'S HEART. AM I RIGHT?
SO: OPTION A-- I KILL YOU IN FRONT OF YOUR DAUGHTER.
OPTION B-- I KILL HER IN FRONT OF YOU.
TELL YOU WHAT...SINCE YOU DON'T EXACTLY SEEM TO BE IN POSSESSION OF ALL YOUR FACULTIES...
FWIPWIPWIPWIPWIPWIP
...WE'LL LET FATE DECIDE.
OHNO OHNO OHNO OHNO GOD GOD GOD GOD OH GOD

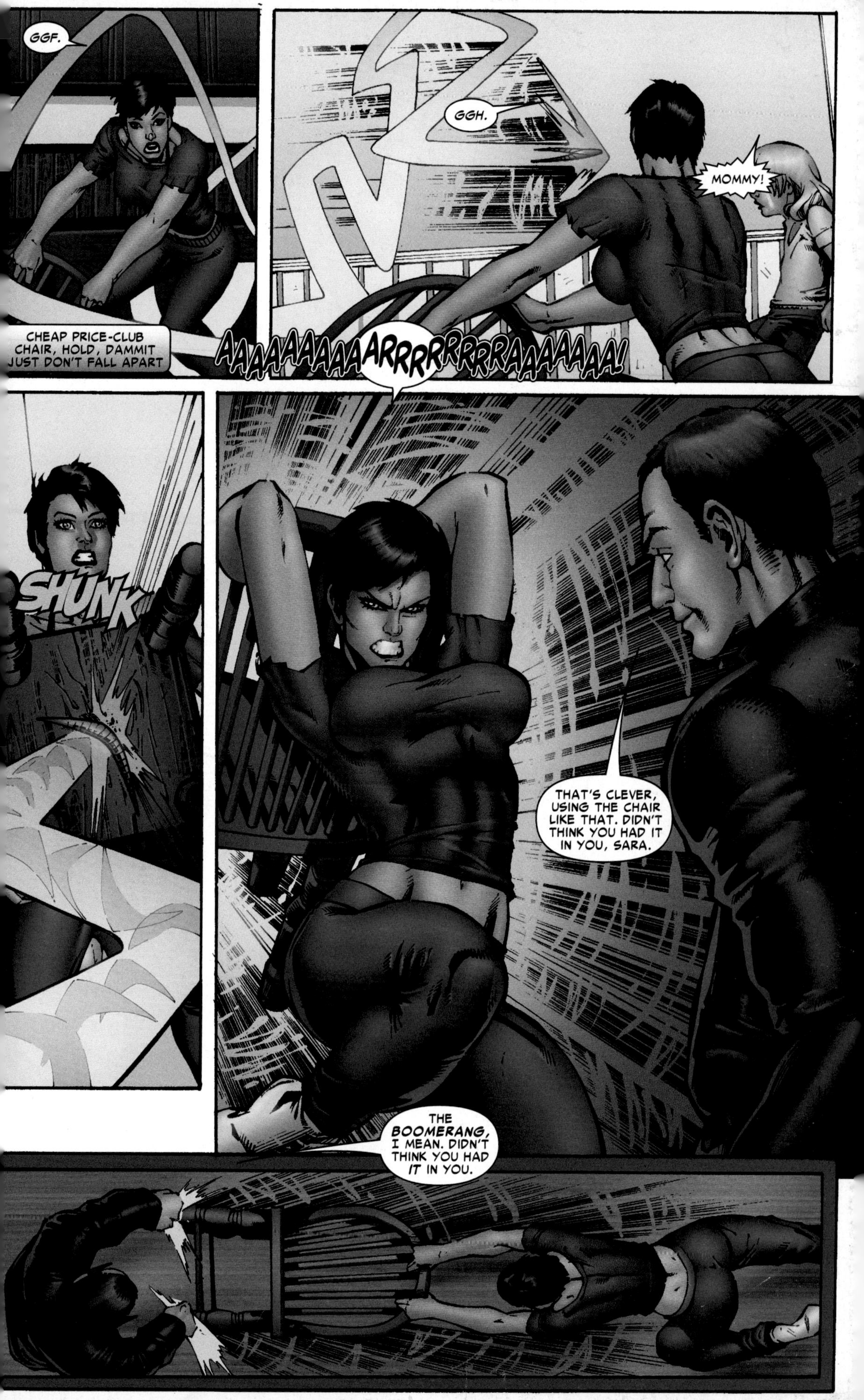
GGF.
CHEAP PRICE-CLUB CHAIR, HOLD, DAMMIT JUST DON'T FALL APART
GGH.
MOMMY!
AAAAAAAAAARRRRRRRAAAAAAA!
SHUNK
THAT'S CLEVER, USING THE CHAIR LIKE THAT. DIDN'T THINK YOU HAD IT IN YOU, SARA.
THE BOOMERANG, I MEAN. DIDN'T THINK YOU HAD IT IN YOU.

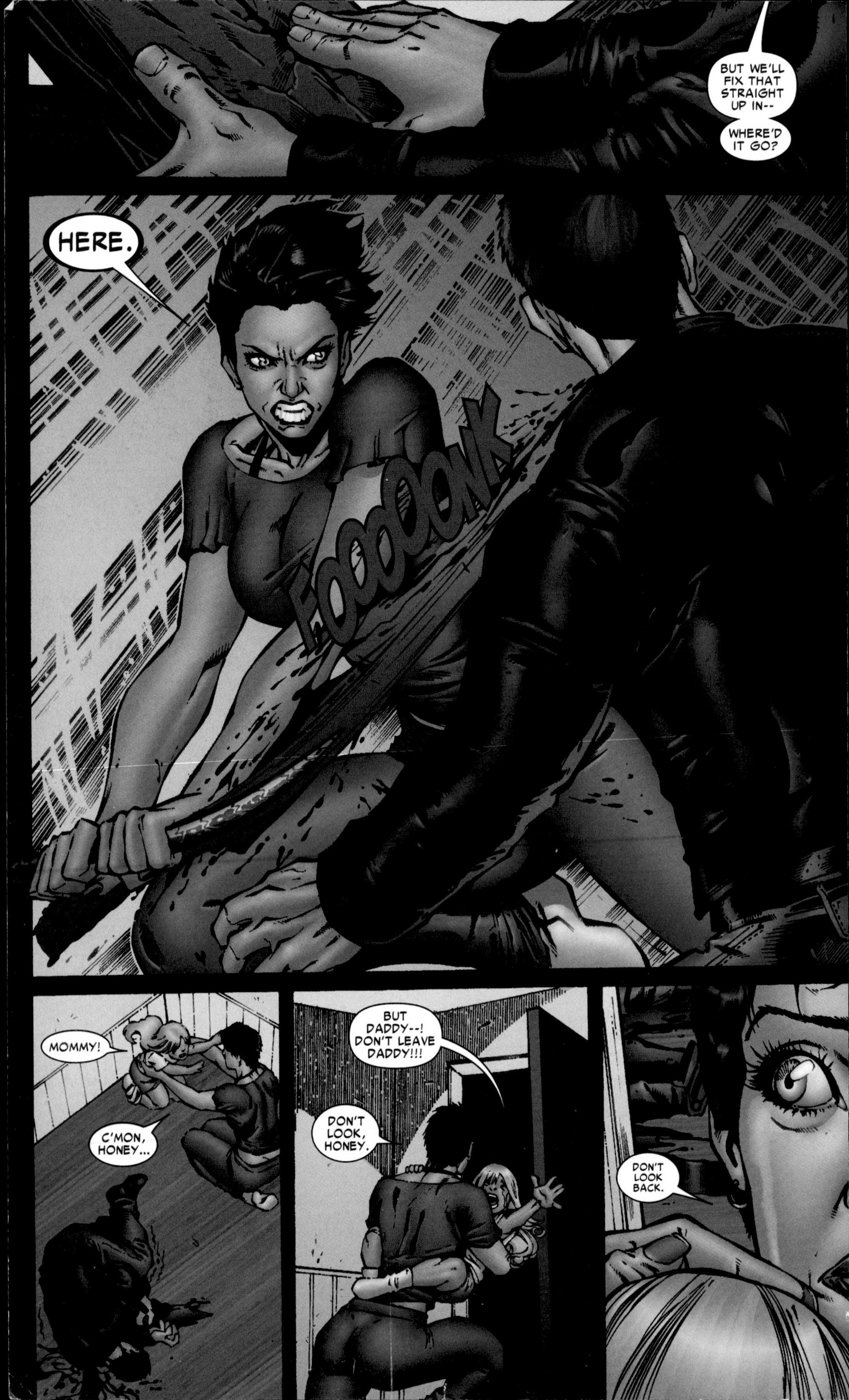
BUT WE'LL FIX THAT STRAIGHT UP IN--
WHERE'D IT GO?
HERE.
FOOOOONK
MOMMY!
C'MON, HONEY...
BUT DADDY--! DON'T LEAVE DADDY!!!
DON'T LOOK, HONEY.
DON'T LOOK BACK.

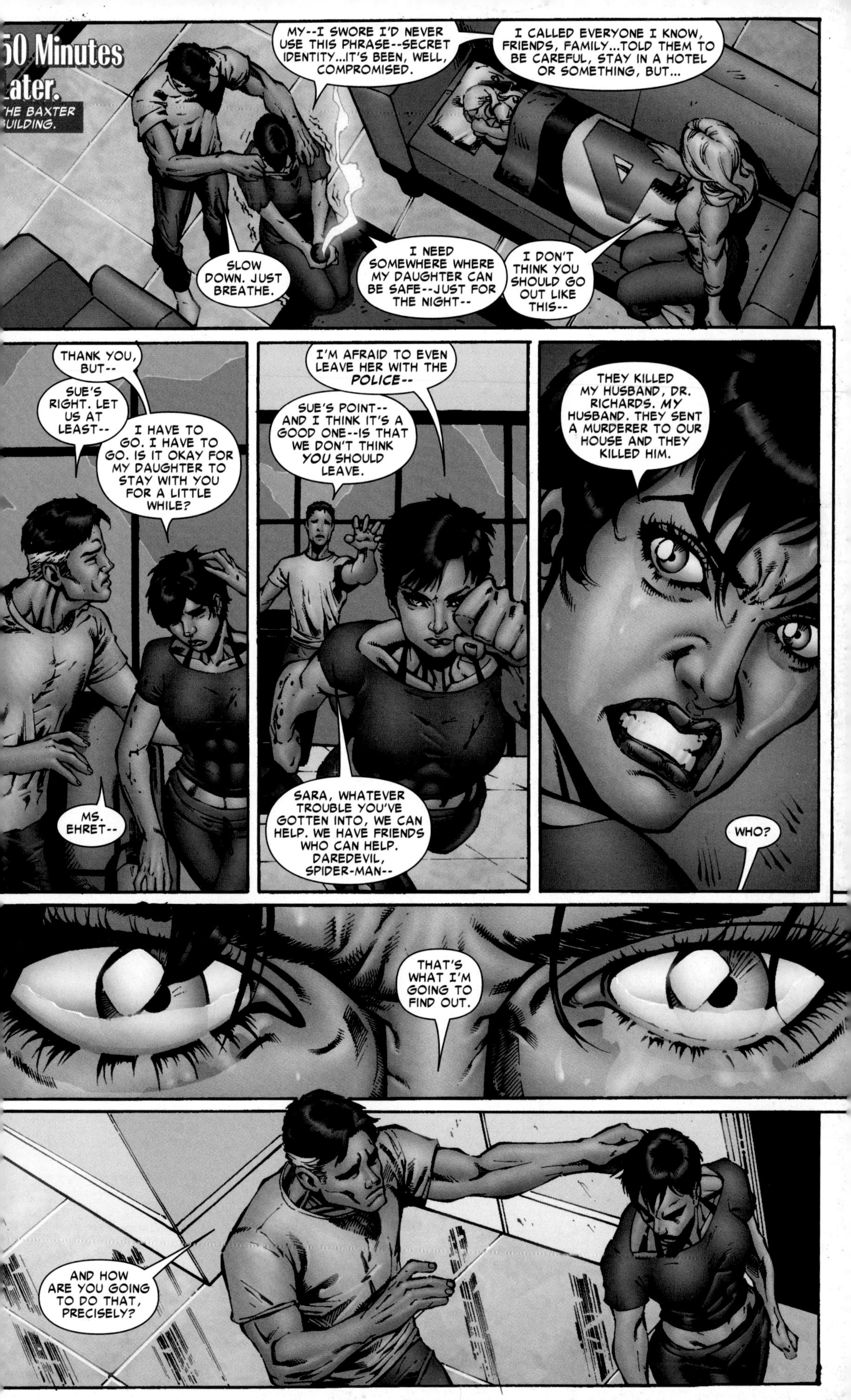
50 Minutes Later.
THE BAXTER BUILDING.
MY--I SWORE I'D NEVER USE THIS PHRASE--SECRET IDENTITY...IT'S BEEN, WELL, COMPROMISED.
I CALLED EVERYONE I KNOW, FRIENDS, FAMILY...TOLD THEM TO BE CAREFUL, STAY IN A HOTEL OR SOMETHING, BUT...
SLOW DOWN. JUST BREATHE.
I NEED SOMEWHERE WHERE MY DAUGHTER CAN BE SAFE--JUST FOR THE NIGHT--
I DON'T THINK YOU SHOULD GO OUT LIKE THIS--
THANK YOU, BUT--
SUE'S RIGHT. LET US AT LEAST--
I HAVE TO GO. I HAVE TO GO. IS IT OKAY FOR MY DAUGHTER TO STAY WITH YOU FOR A LITTLE WHILE?
MS. EHRET--
I'M AFRAID TO EVEN LEAVE HER WITH THE POLICE--
SUE'S POINT--AND I THINK IT'S A GOOD ONE--IS THAT WE DON'T THINK YOU SHOULD LEAVE.
SARA, WHATEVER TROUBLE YOU'VE GOTTEN INTO, WE CAN HELP. WE HAVE FRIENDS WHO CAN HELP. DAREDEVIL, SPIDER-MAN--
THEY KILLED MY HUSBAND, DR. RICHARDS. MY HUSBAND. THEY SENT A MURDERER TO OUR HOUSE AND THEY KILLED HIM.
WHO?
THAT'S WHAT I'M GOING TO FIND OUT.
AND HOW ARE YOU GOING TO DO THAT, PRECISELY?

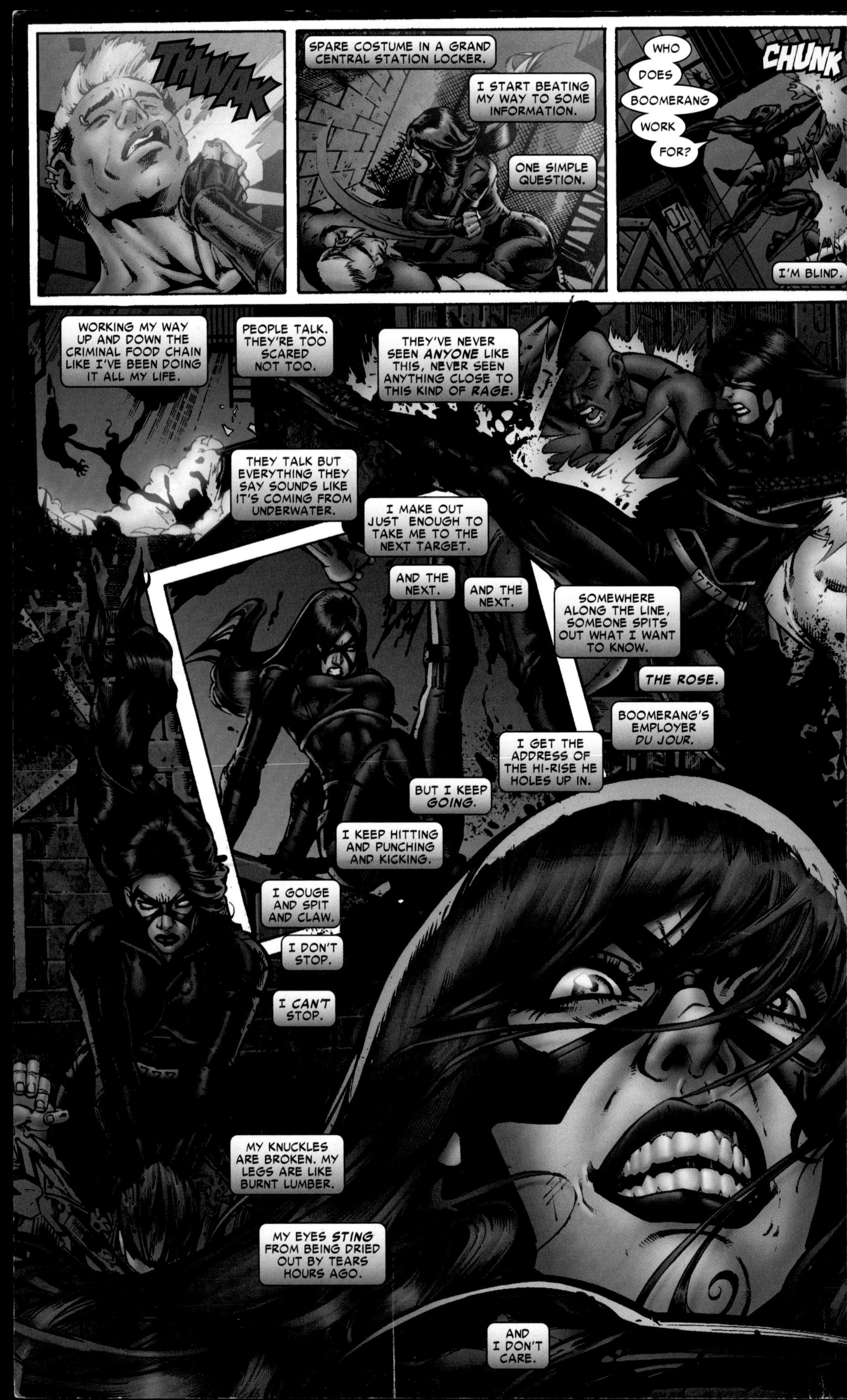
THWAK
SPARE COSTUME IN A GRAND CENTRAL STATION LOCKER.
I START BEATING MY WAY TO SOME INFORMATION.
ONE SIMPLE QUESTION.
WHO DOES BOOMERANG WORK FOR?
CHUNK
I'M BLIND.
WORKING MY WAY UP AND DOWN THE CRIMINAL FOOD CHAIN LIKE I'VE BEEN DOING IT ALL MY LIFE.
PEOPLE TALK. THEY'RE TOO SCARED NOT TOO.
THEY'VE NEVER SEEN ANYONE LIKE THIS, NEVER SEEN ANYTHING CLOSE TO THIS KIND OF RAGE.
THEY TALK BUT EVERYTHING THEY SAY SOUNDS LIKE IT'S COMING FROM UNDERWATER.
I MAKE OUT JUST ENOUGH TO TAKE ME TO THE NEXT TARGET.
AND THE NEXT.
AND THE NEXT.
SOMEWHERE ALONG THE LINE, SOMEONE SPITS OUT WHAT I WANT TO KNOW.
THE ROSE.
BOOMERANG'S EMPLOYER DU JOUR.
I GET THE ADDRESS OF THE HI-RISE HE HOLES UP IN.
BUT I KEEP GOING.
I KEEP HITTING AND PUNCHING AND KICKING.
I GOUGE AND SPIT AND CLAW.
I DON'T STOP.
I CAN'T STOP.
MY KNUCKLES ARE BROKEN. MY LEGS ARE LIKE BURNT LUMBER.
MY EYES STING FROM BEING DRIED OUT BY TEARS HOURS AGO.
AND I DON'T CARE.

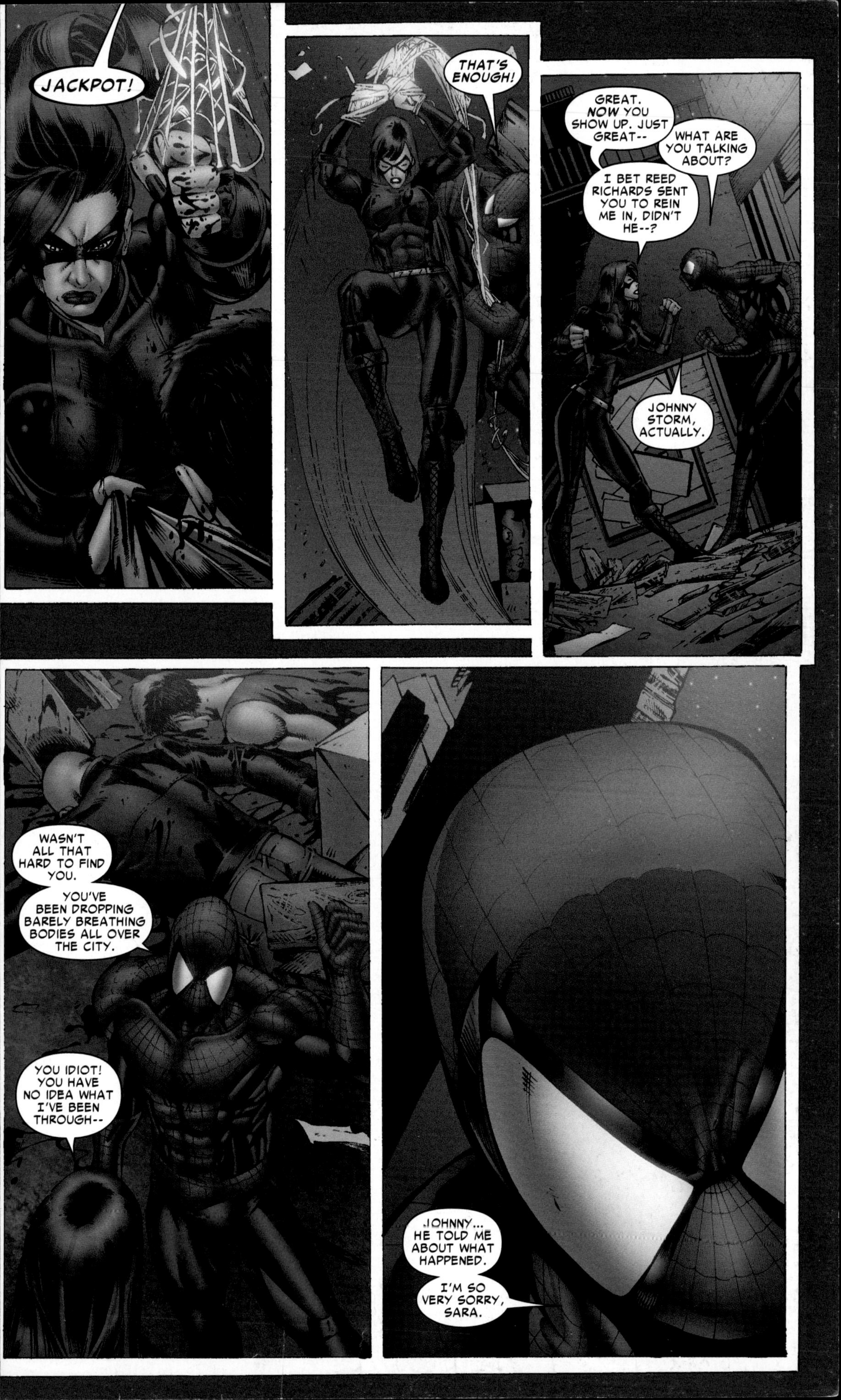
JACKPOT!
THAT'S ENOUGH!
GREAT. NOW YOU SHOW UP. JUST GREAT--
WHAT ARE YOU TALKING ABOUT?
I BET REED RICHARDS SENT YOU TO REIN ME IN, DIDN'T HE--?
JOHNNY STORM, ACTUALLY.
WASN'T ALL THAT HARD TO FIND YOU.
YOU'VE BEEN DROPPING BARELY BREATHING BODIES ALL OVER THE CITY.
YOU IDIOT! YOU HAVE NO IDEA WHAT I'VE BEEN THROUGH--
JOHNNY... HE TOLD ME ABOUT WHAT HAPPENED.
I'M SO VERY SORRY, SARA.

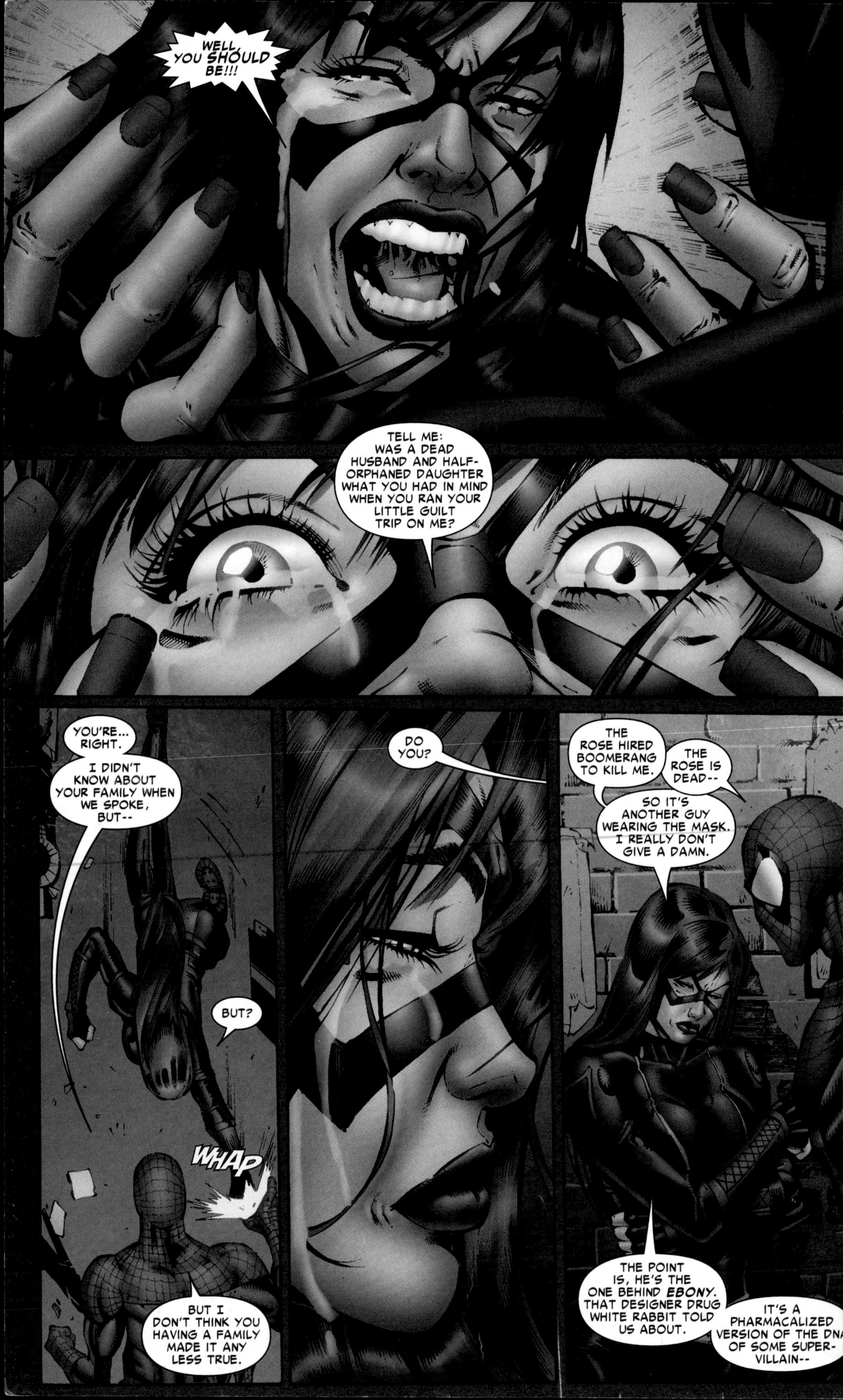
WELL, YOU SHOULD BE!!!
TELL ME: WAS A DEAD HUSBAND AND HALF-ORPHANED DAUGHTER WHAT YOU HAD IN MIND WHEN YOU RAN YOUR LITTLE GUILT TRIP ON ME?
YOU'RE... RIGHT.
I DIDN'T KNOW ABOUT YOUR FAMILY WHEN WE SPOKE, BUT--
BUT?
WHAP
BUT I DON'T THINK YOU HAVING A FAMILY MADE IT ANY LESS TRUE.
DO YOU?
THE ROSE HIRED BOOMERANG TO KILL ME.
THE ROSE IS DEAD--
SO IT'S ANOTHER GUY WEARING THE MASK. I REALLY DON'T GIVE A DAMN.
THE POINT IS, HE'S THE ONE BEHIND EBONY. THAT DESIGNER DRUG WHITE RABBIT TOLD US ABOUT.
IT'S A PHARMACALIZED VERSION OF THE DNA OF SOME SUPER-VILLAIN--

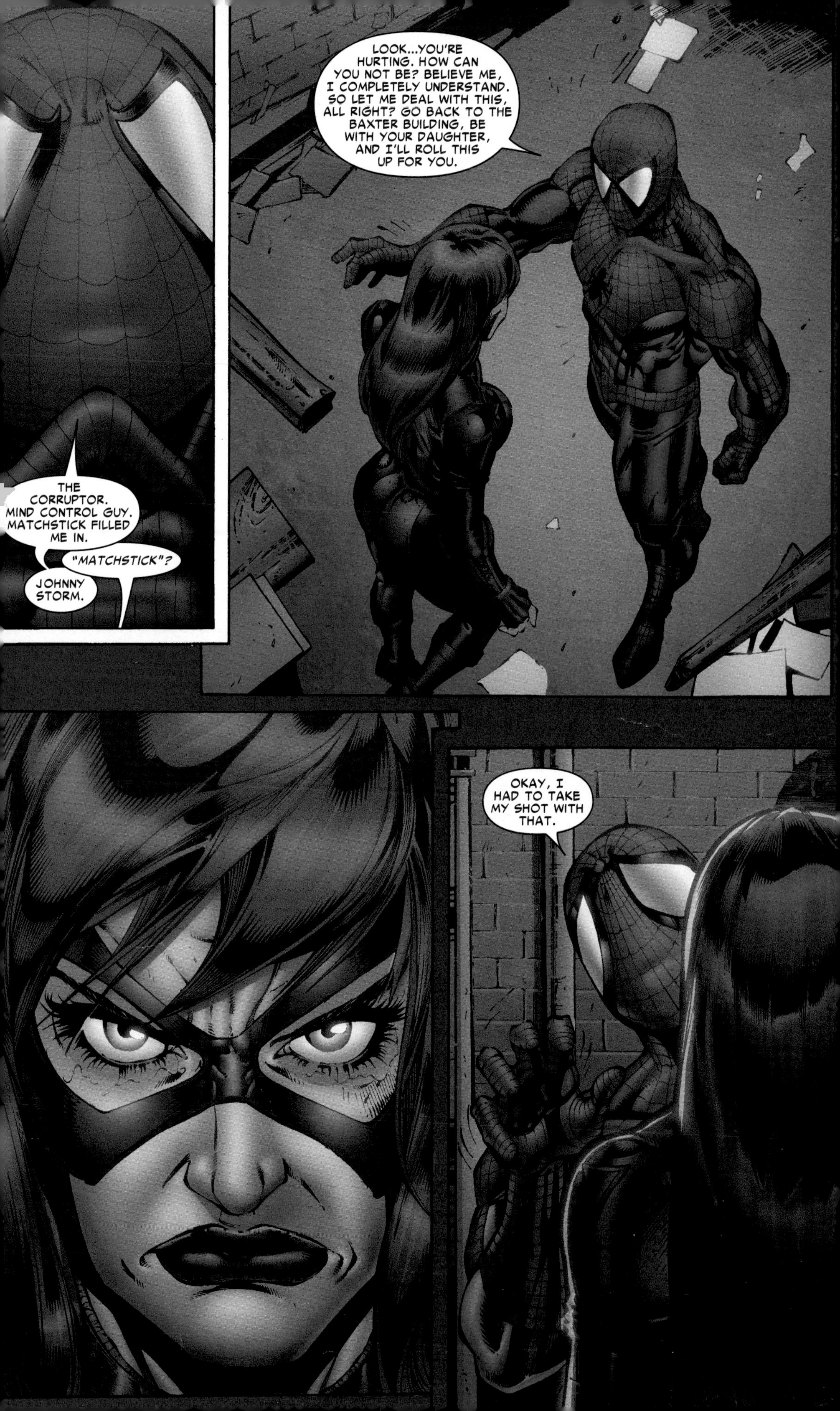
THE CORRUPTOR. MIND CONTROL GUY. MATCHSTICK FILLED ME IN.
"MATCHSTICK"?
JOHNNY STORM.
LOOK...YOU'RE HURTING. HOW CAN YOU NOT BE? BELIEVE ME, I COMPLETELY UNDERSTAND. SO LET ME DEAL WITH THIS, ALL RIGHT? GO BACK TO THE BAXTER BUILDING, BE WITH YOUR DAUGHTER, AND I'LL ROLL THIS UP FOR YOU.
OKAY, I HAD TO TAKE MY SHOT WITH THAT.

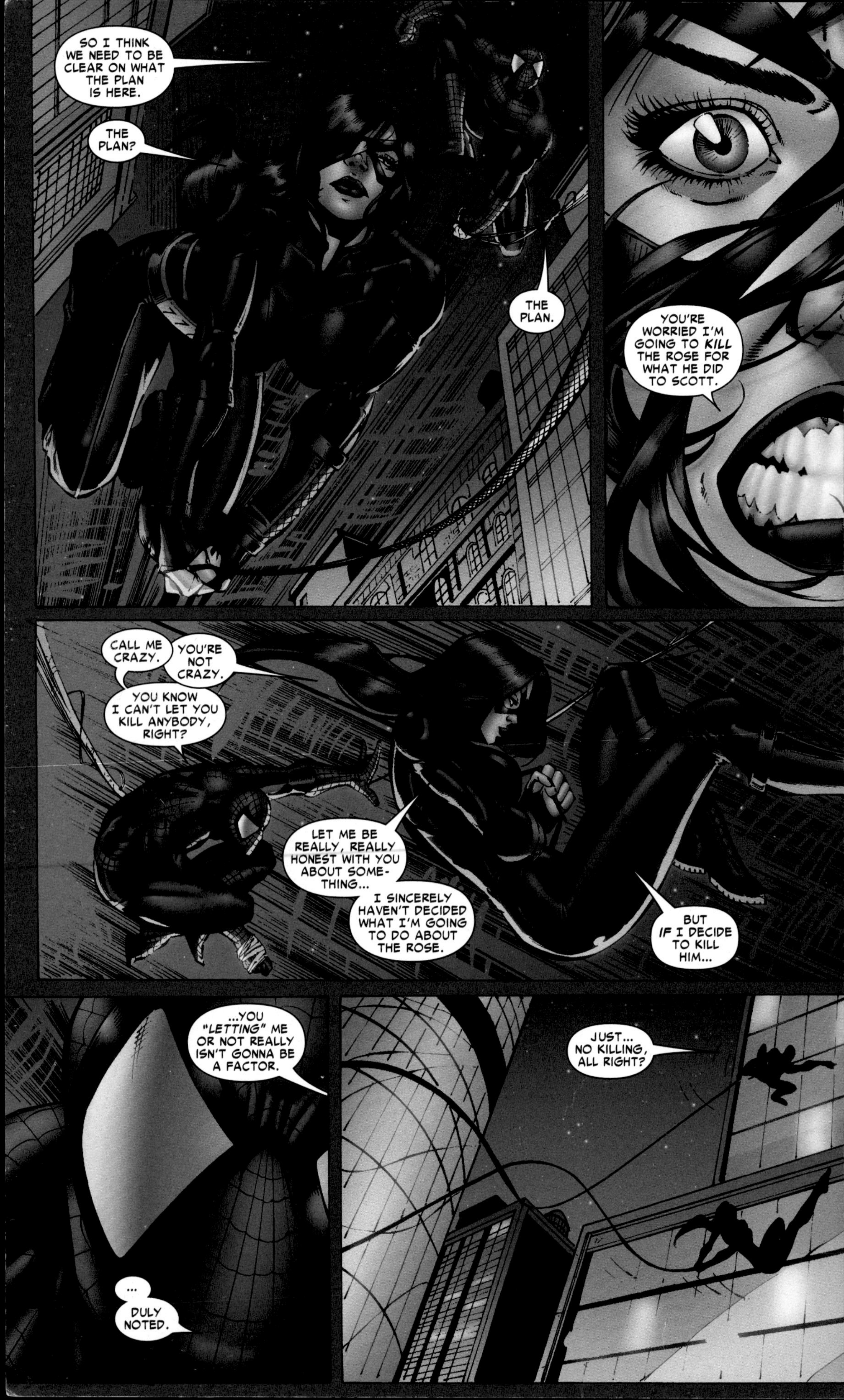
SO I THINK WE NEED TO BE CLEAR ON WHAT THE PLAN IS HERE.
THE PLAN?
THE PLAN.
YOU'RE WORRIED I'M GOING TO KILL THE ROSE FOR WHAT HE DID TO SCOTT.
CALL ME CRAZY.
YOU'RE NOT CRAZY.
YOU KNOW I CAN'T LET YOU KILL ANYBODY, RIGHT?
LET ME BE REALLY, REALLY HONEST WITH YOU ABOUT SOME-THING...
I SINCERELY HAVEN'T DECIDED WHAT I'M GOING TO DO ABOUT THE ROSE.
BUT IF I DECIDE TO KILL HIM...
...YOU "LETTING" ME OR NOT REALLY ISN'T GONNA BE A FACTOR.
...
DULY NOTED.
JUST... NO KILLING, ALL RIGHT?

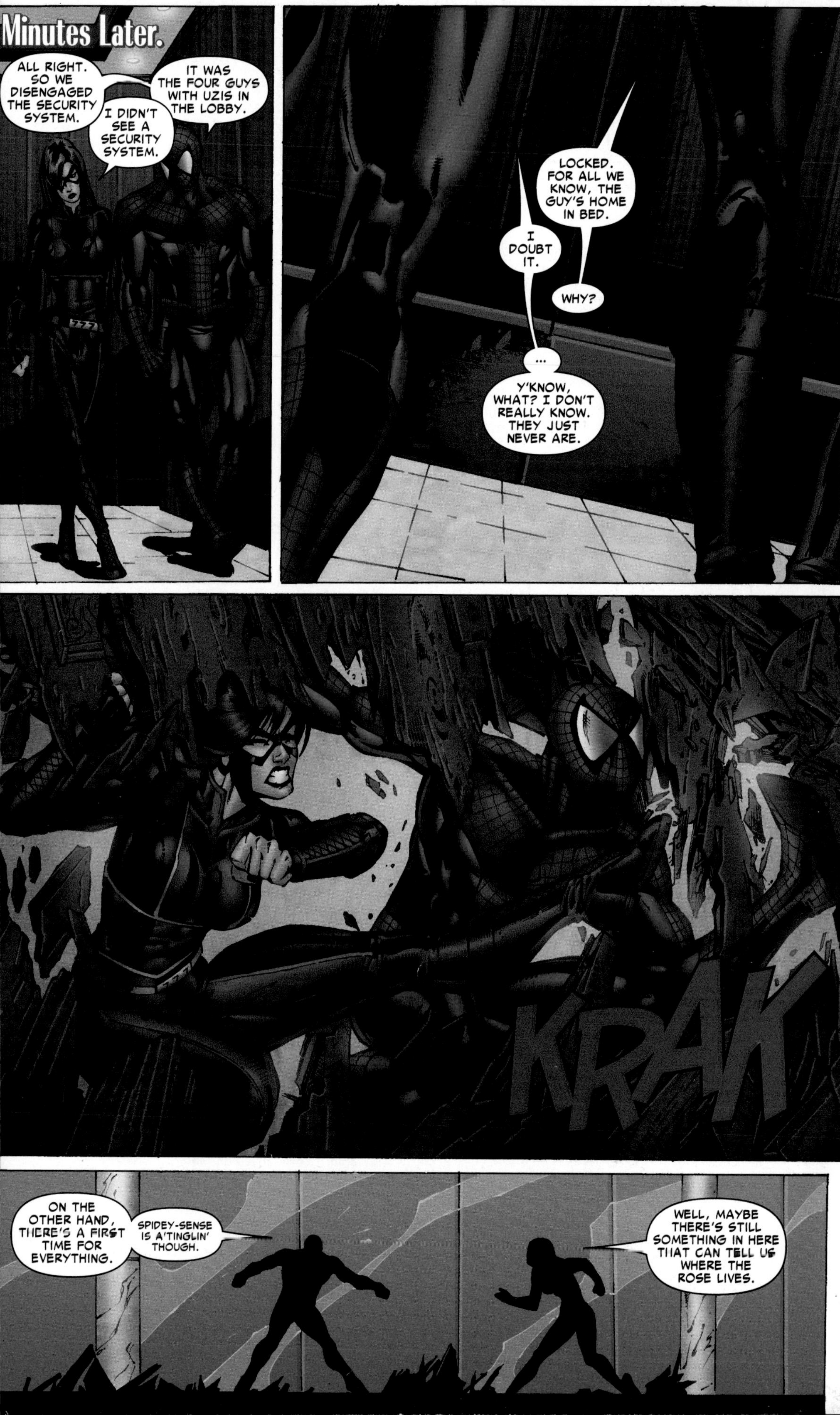
Minutes Later.
ALL RIGHT. SO WE DISENGAGED THE SECURITY SYSTEM.
IT WAS THE FOUR GUYS WITH UZIS IN THE LOBBY.
I DIDN'T SEE A SECURITY SYSTEM.
LOCKED. FOR ALL WE KNOW, THE GUY'S HOME IN BED.
I DOUBT IT.
WHY?
...
Y'KNOW, WHAT? I DON'T REALLY KNOW. THEY JUST NEVER ARE.
KRAK
ON THE OTHER HAND, THERE'S A FIRST TIME FOR EVERYTHING.
SPIDEY-SENSE IS A'TINGLIN' THOUGH.
WELL, MAYBE THERE'S STILL SOMETHING IN HERE THAT CAN TELL US WHERE THE ROSE LIVES.

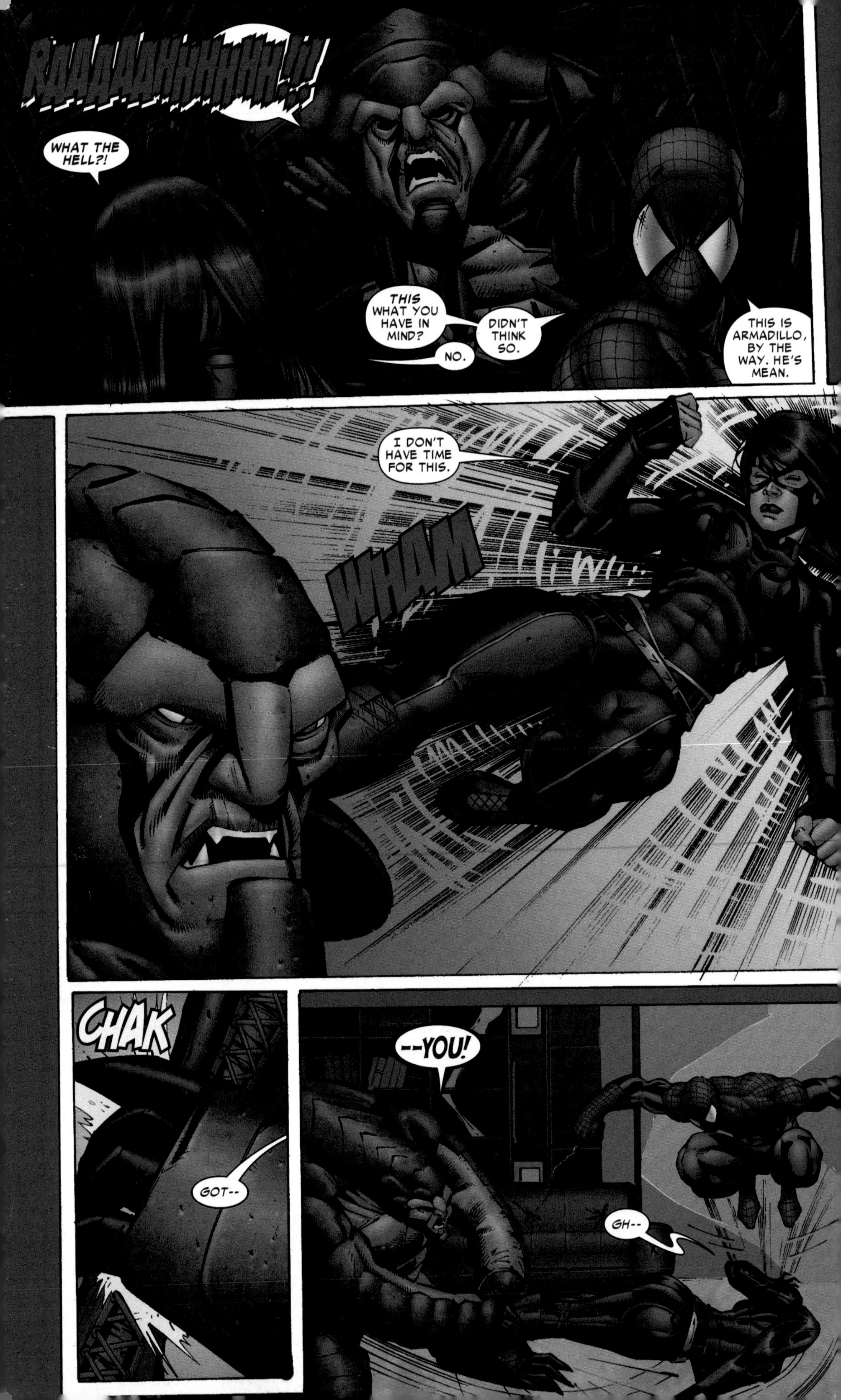
RAAAAAHHHHHH!!!
WHAT THE HELL?!
THIS WHAT YOU HAVE IN MIND?
NO.
DIDN'T THINK SO.
THIS IS ARMADILLO, BY THE WAY. HE'S MEAN.
I DON'T HAVE TIME FOR THIS.
WHAM
CHAK
GOT--
--YOU!
GH--

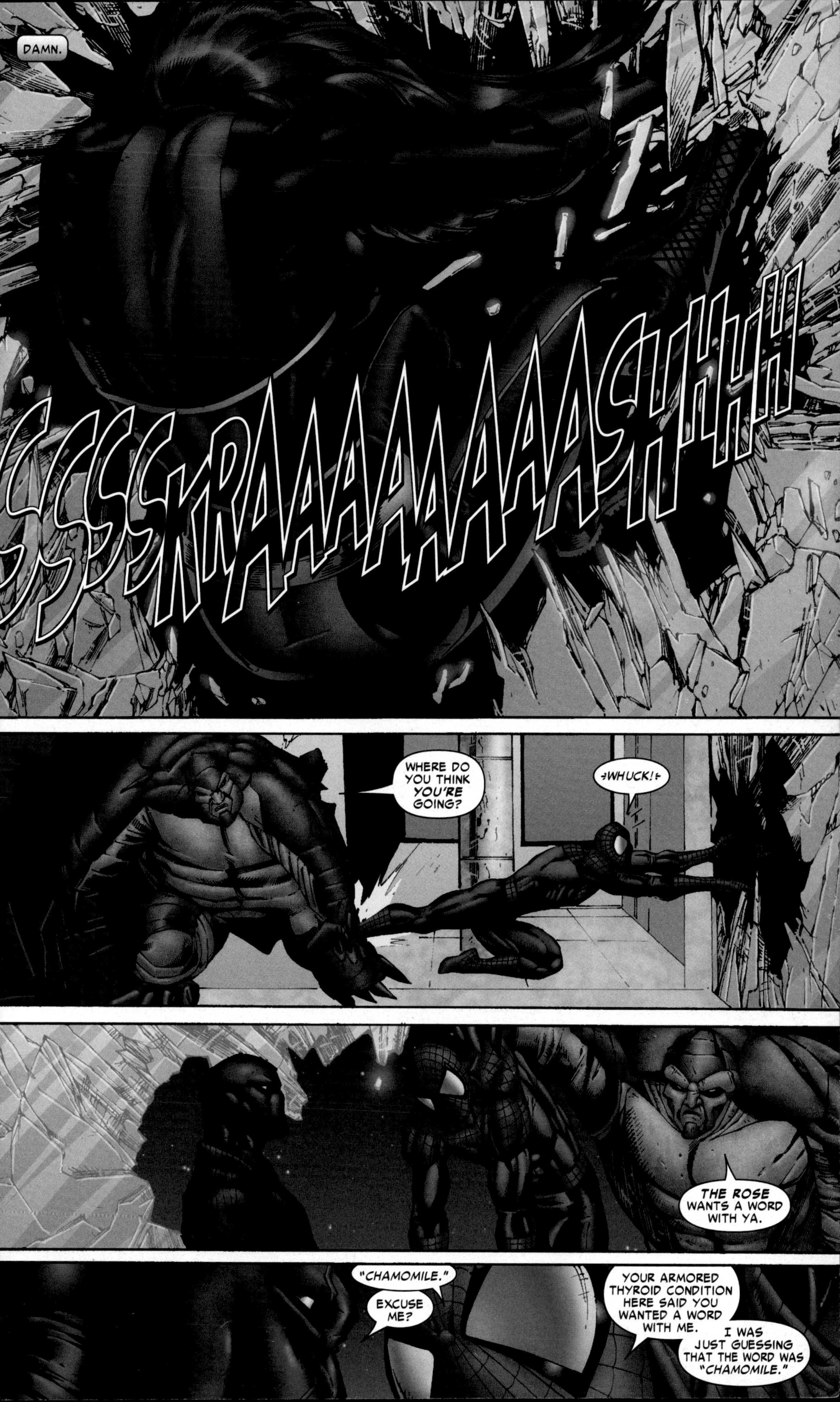
DAMN.
SSSSKRAAAAAAASHHH
WHERE DO YOU THINK YOU'RE GOING?
WHUCK!
THE ROSE WANTS A WORD WITH YA.
"CHAMOMILE."
EXCUSE ME?
YOUR ARMORED THYROID CONDITION HERE SAID YOU WANTED A WORD WITH ME.
I WAS JUST GUESSING THAT THE WORD WAS "CHAMOMILE."

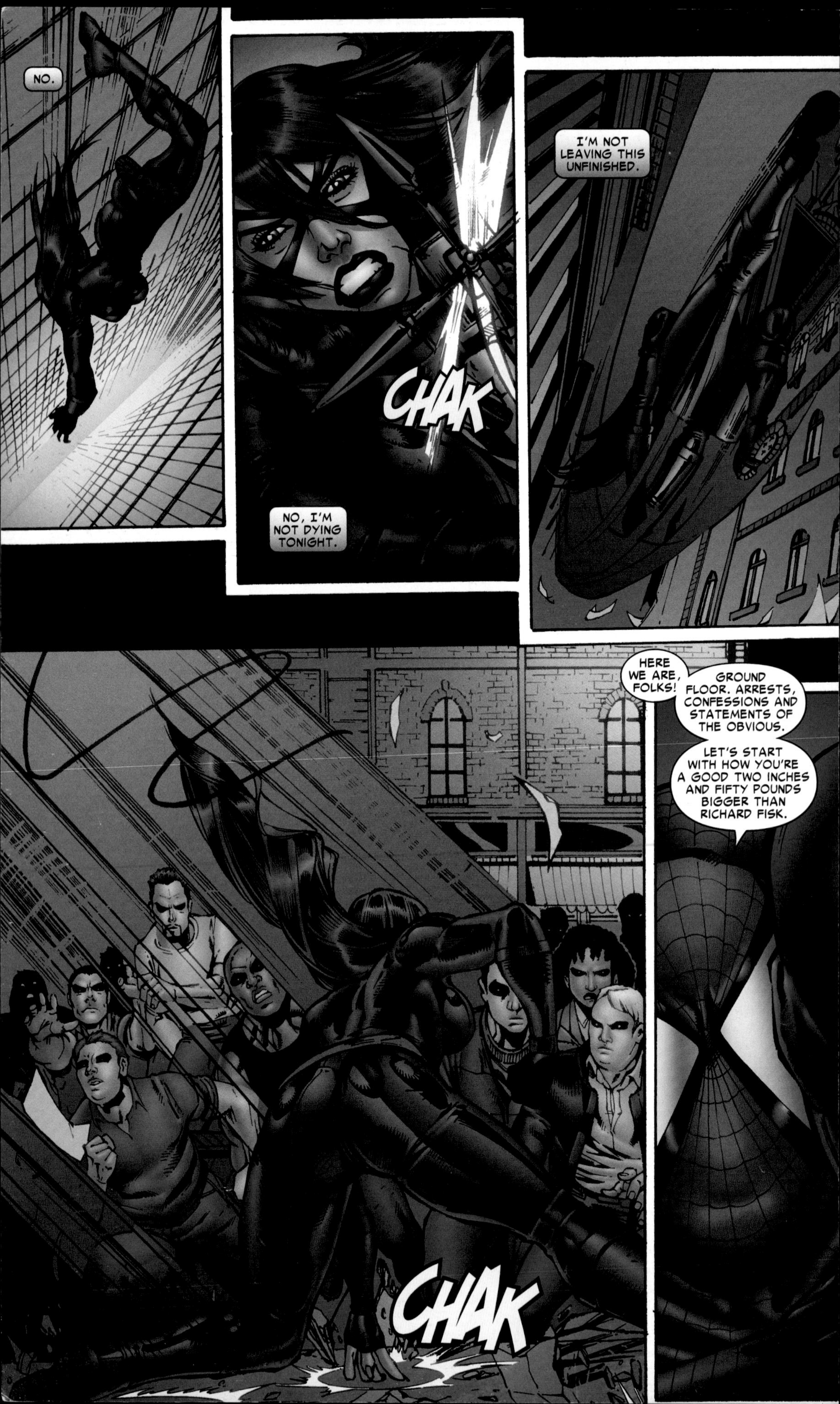

NO.
NO, I'M NOT DYING TONIGHT.
CHAK
I'M NOT LEAVING THIS UNFINISHED.
HERE WE ARE, FOLKS!
GROUND FLOOR. ARRESTS, CONFESSIONS AND STATEMENTS OF THE OBVIOUS.
LET'S START WITH HOW YOU'RE A GOOD TWO INCHES AND FIFTY POUNDS BIGGER THAN RICHARD FISK.
CHAK

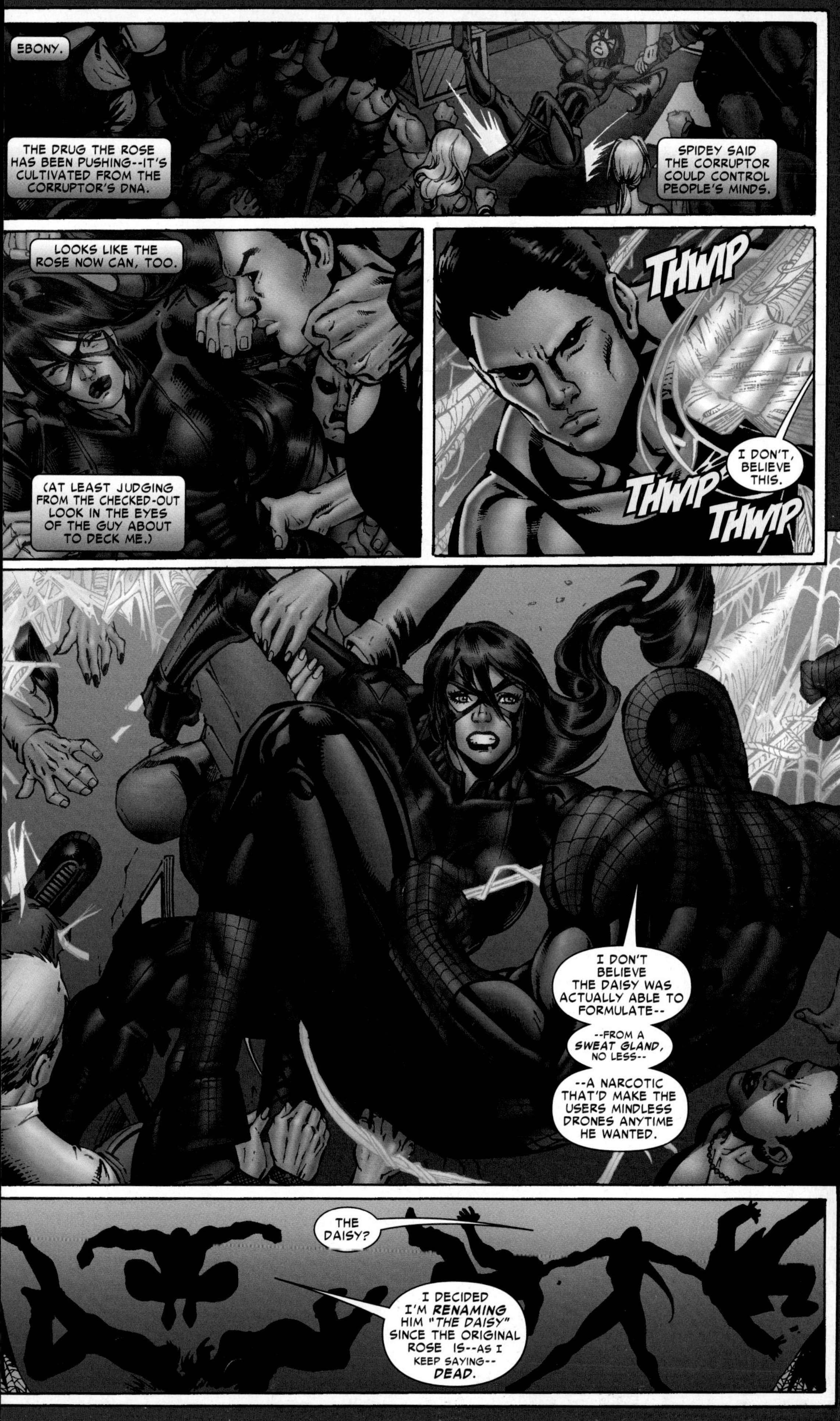
EBONY.
THE DRUG THE ROSE HAS BEEN PUSHING--IT'S CULTIVATED FROM THE CORRUPTOR'S DNA.
SPIDEY SAID THE CORRUPTOR COULD CONTROL PEOPLE'S MINDS.
LOOKS LIKE THE ROSE NOW CAN, TOO.
(AT LEAST JUDGING FROM THE CHECKED-OUT LOOK IN THE EYES OF THE GUY ABOUT TO DECK ME.)
THWIP
I DON'T, BELIEVE THIS.
THWIP
THWIP
I DON'T BELIEVE THE DAISY WAS ACTUALLY ABLE TO FORMULATE--
--FROM A *SWEAT GLAND*, NO LESS--
--A NARCOTIC THAT'D MAKE THE USERS MINDLESS DRONES ANYTIME HE WANTED.
THE DAISY?
I DECIDED I'M ***RENAMING*** HIM *"THE DAISY"* SINCE THE ORIGINAL ROSE IS--AS I KEEP SAYING-- ***DEAD.***

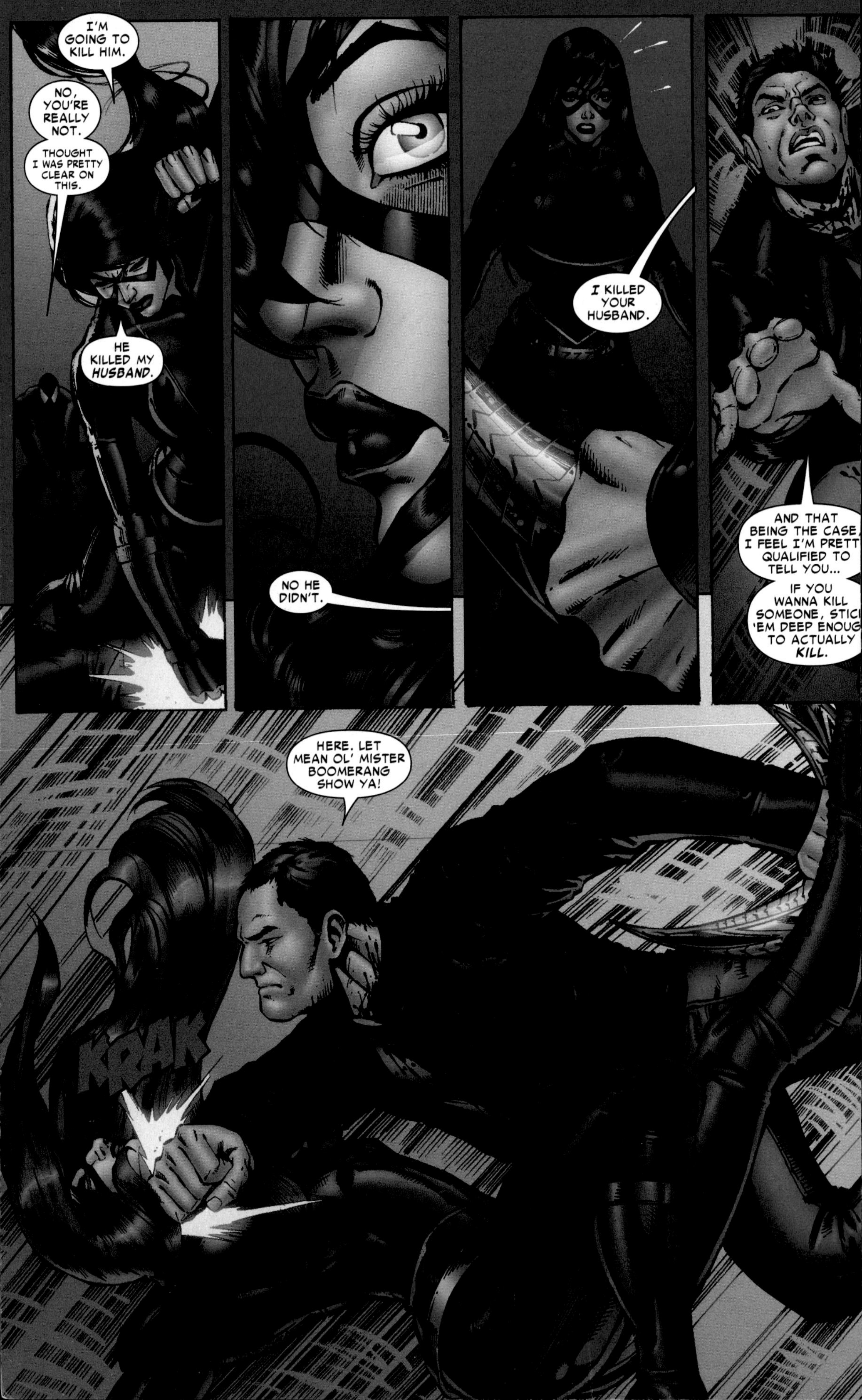
I'M GOING TO KILL HIM.
NO, YOU'RE REALLY NOT.
THOUGHT I WAS PRETTY CLEAR ON THIS.
HE KILLED MY HUSBAND.
NO HE DIDN'T.
I KILLED YOUR HUSBAND.
AND THAT BEING THE CASE, I FEEL I'M PRETT QUALIFIED TO TELL YOU...
IF YOU WANNA KILL SOMEONE, STIC 'EM DEEP ENOUG TO ACTUALLY KILL.
HERE. LET MEAN OL' MISTER BOOMERANG SHOW YA!
KRAK

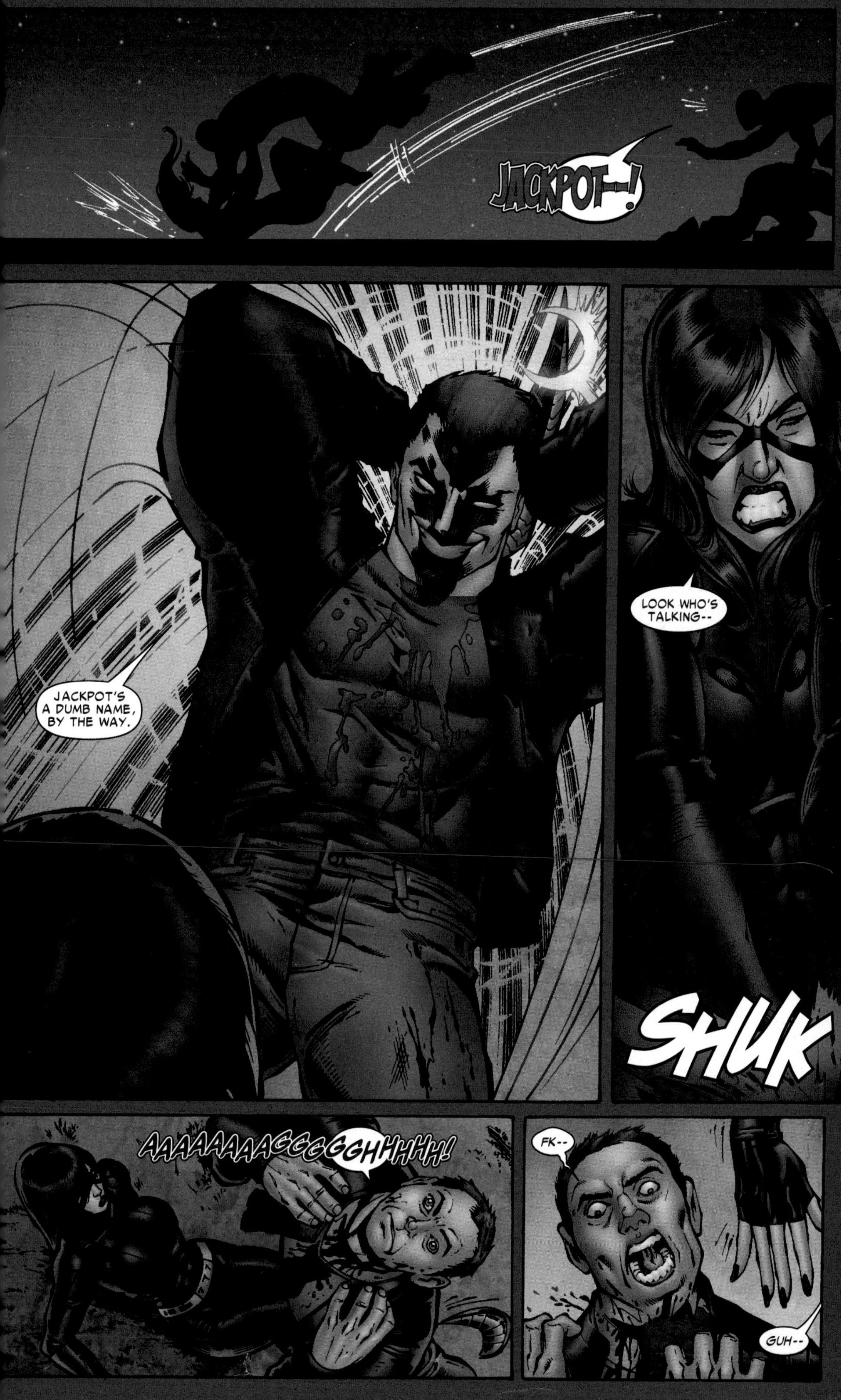
JACKPOT--!
JACKPOT'S A DUMB NAME, BY THE WAY.
LOOK WHO'S TALKING--
SHUK
AAAAAAAAGGGGGHHHHHH!
FK--
GUH--

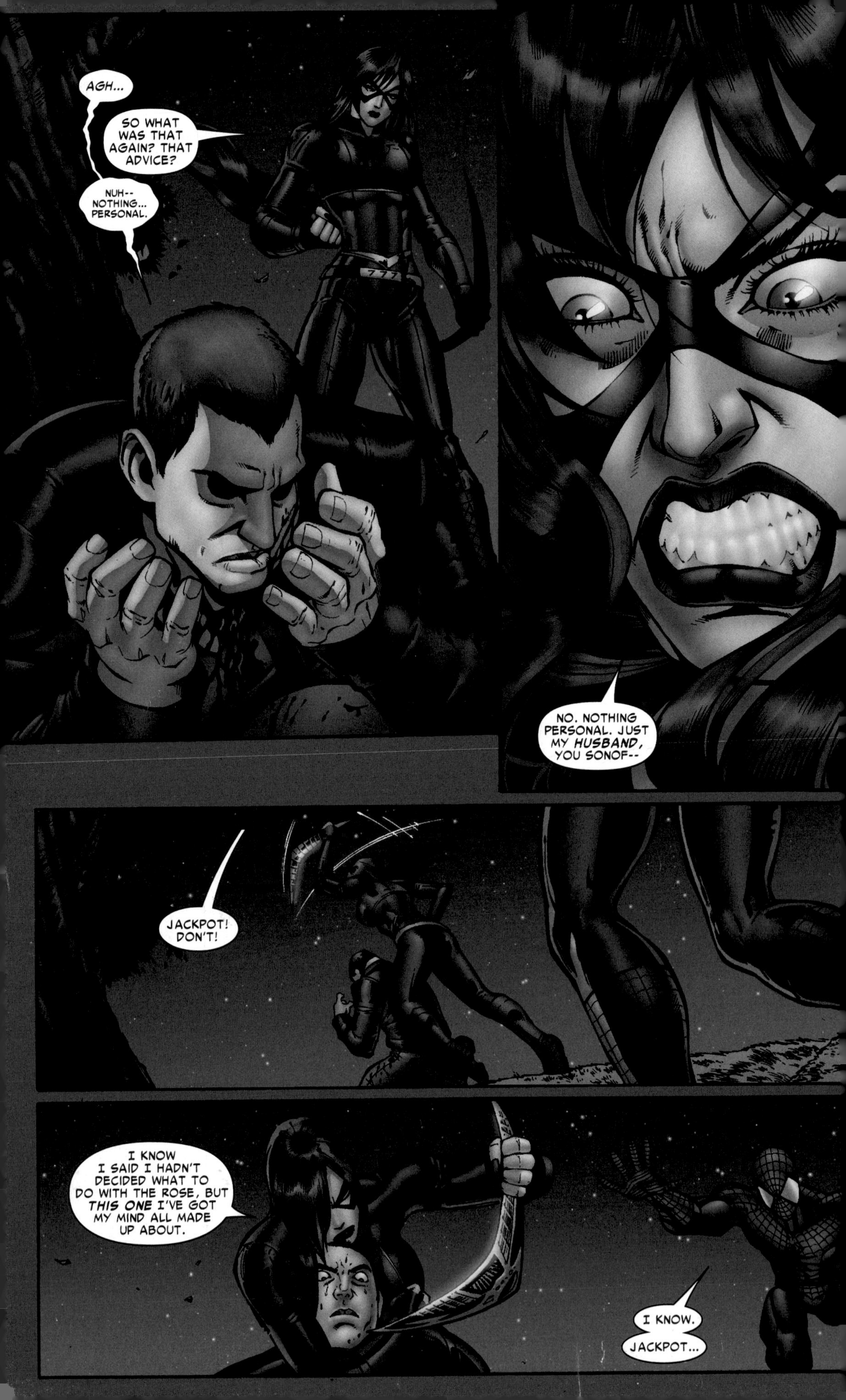

AGH...
SO WHAT WAS THAT AGAIN? THAT ADVICE?
NUH-- NOTHING... PERSONAL.
NO. NOTHING PERSONAL. JUST MY *HUSBAND*, YOU SONOF--
JACKPOT! DON'T!
I KNOW I SAID I HADN'T DECIDED WHAT TO DO WITH THE ROSE, BUT *THIS ONE* I'VE GOT MY MIND ALL MADE UP ABOUT.
I KNOW.
JACKPOT...

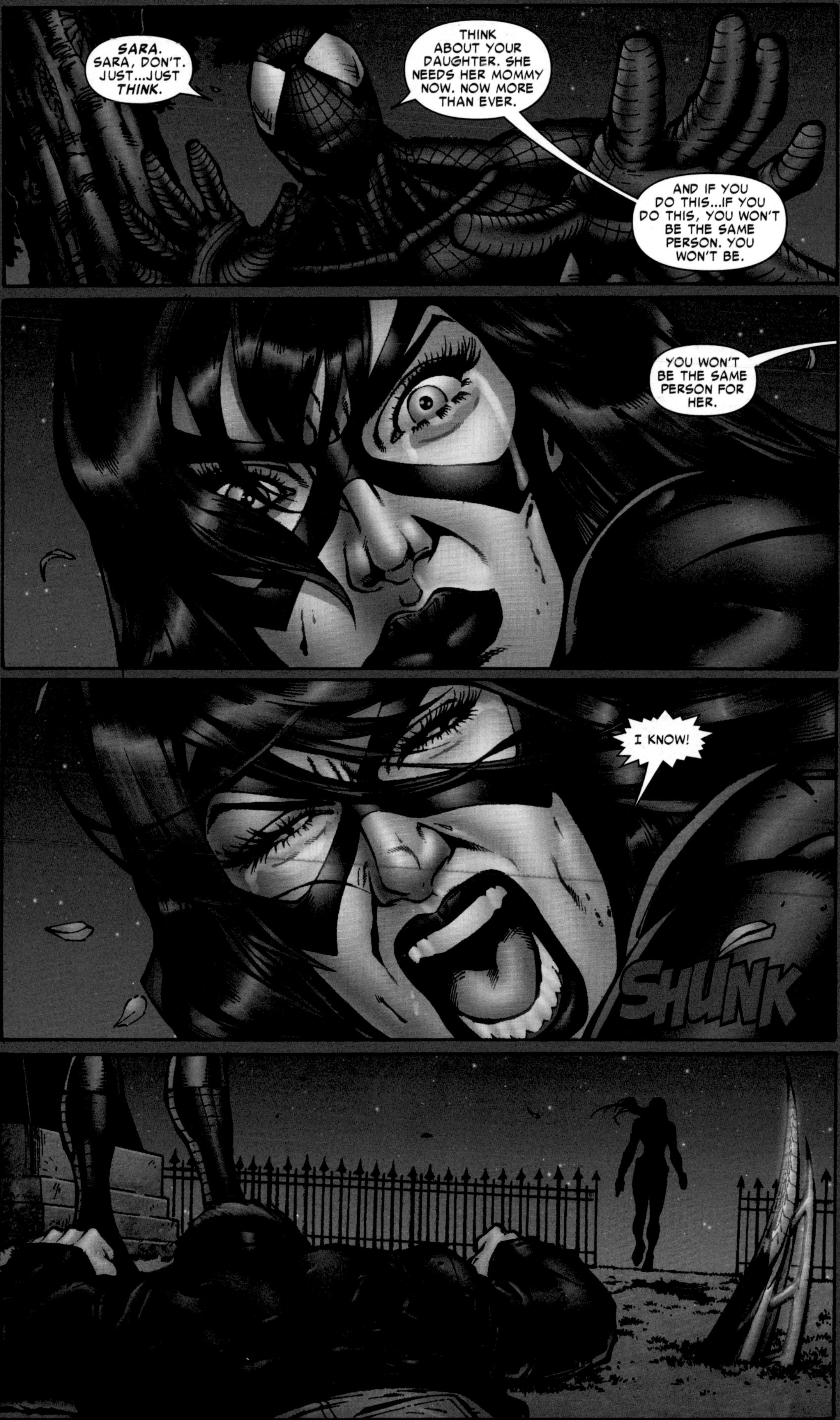
SARA. SARA, DON'T. JUST...JUST THINK.
THINK ABOUT YOUR DAUGHTER. SHE NEEDS HER MOMMY NOW. NOW MORE THAN EVER.
AND IF YOU DO THIS...IF YOU DO THIS, YOU WON'T BE THE SAME PERSON. YOU WON'T BE.
YOU WON'T BE THE SAME PERSON FOR HER.
I KNOW!
SHUNK

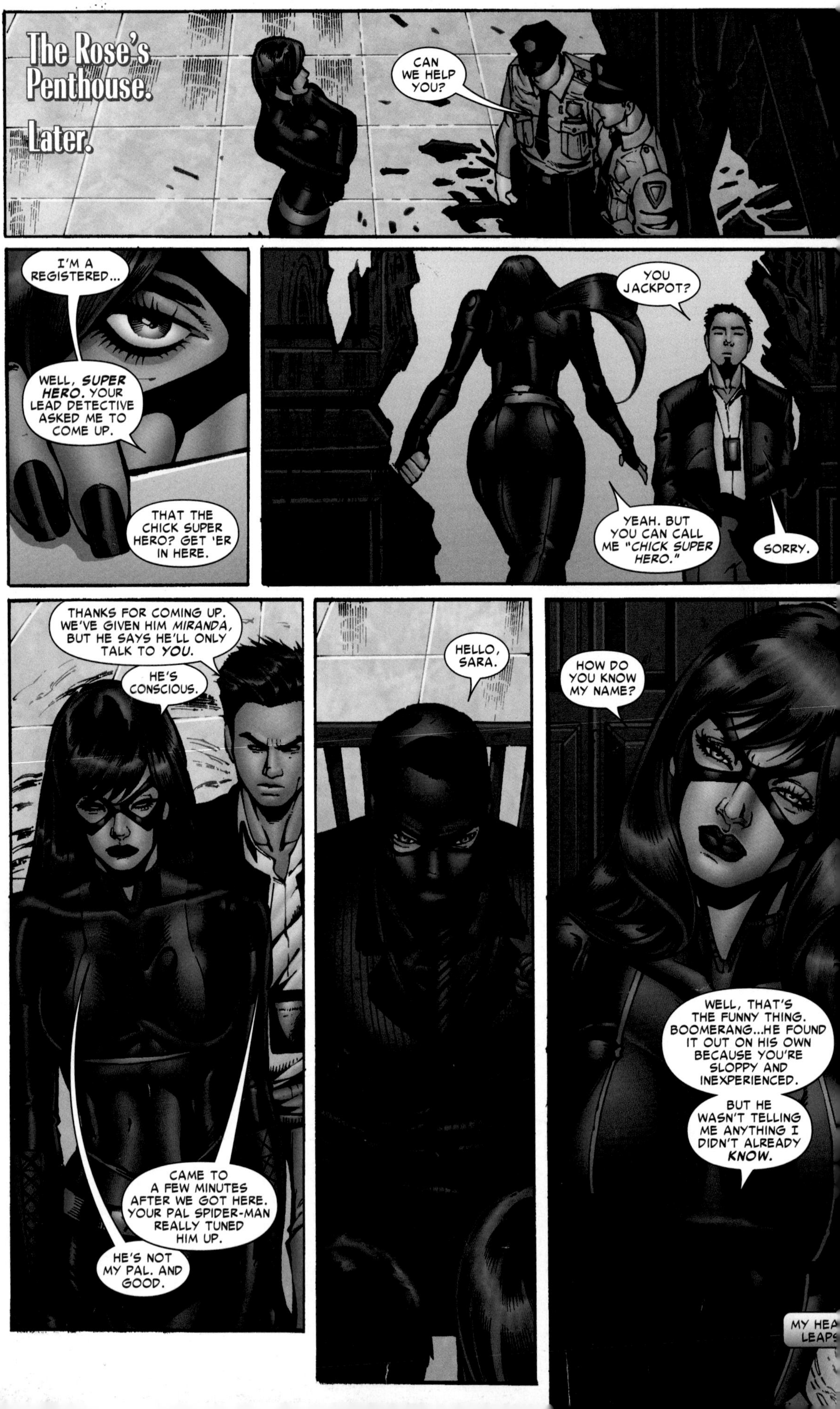

The Rose's Penthouse.
Later.
CAN WE HELP YOU?
I'M A REGISTERED...
WELL, SUPER HERO. YOUR LEAD DETECTIVE ASKED ME TO COME UP.
THAT THE CHICK SUPER HERO? GET 'ER IN HERE.
YOU JACKPOT?
YEAH. BUT YOU CAN CALL ME "CHICK SUPER HERO."
SORRY.
THANKS FOR COMING UP. WE'VE GIVEN HIM MIRANDA, BUT HE SAYS HE'LL ONLY TALK TO YOU.
HE'S CONSCIOUS.
CAME TO A FEW MINUTES AFTER WE GOT HERE. YOUR PAL SPIDER-MAN REALLY TUNED HIM UP.
HE'S NOT MY PAL. AND GOOD.
HELLO, SARA.
HOW DO YOU KNOW MY NAME?
WELL, THAT'S THE FUNNY THING. BOOMERANG...HE FOUND IT OUT ON HIS OWN BECAUSE YOU'RE SLOPPY AND INEXPERIENCED.
BUT HE WASN'T TELLING ME ANYTHING I DIDN'T ALREADY KNOW.

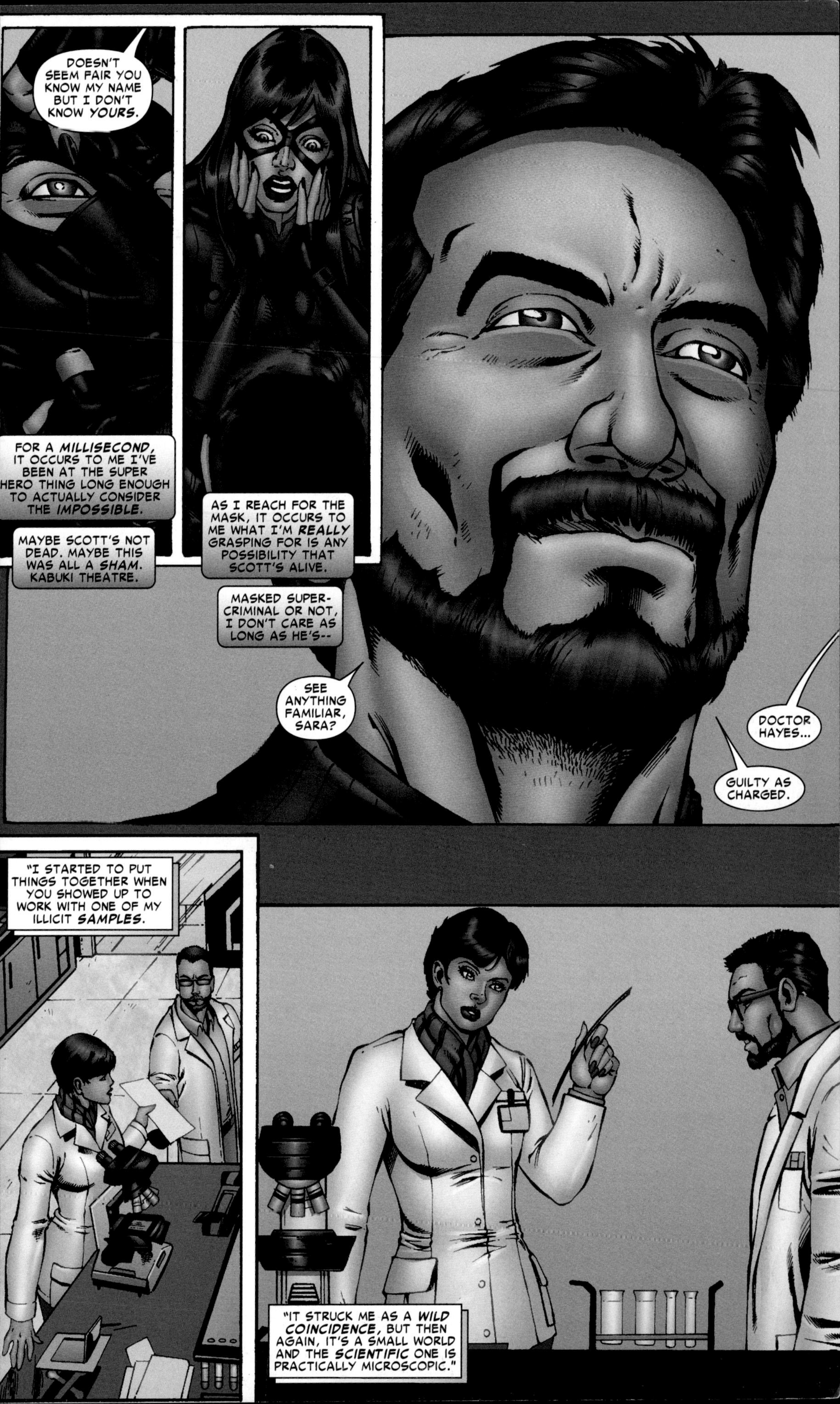
DOESN'T SEEM FAIR YOU KNOW MY NAME BUT I DON'T KNOW *YOURS*.
FOR A *MILLISECOND*, IT OCCURS TO ME I'VE BEEN AT THE SUPER HERO THING LONG ENOUGH TO ACTUALLY CONSIDER THE *IMPOSSIBLE*.
MAYBE SCOTT'S NOT DEAD. MAYBE THIS WAS ALL A *SHAM*. KABUKI THEATRE.
AS I REACH FOR THE MASK, IT OCCURS TO ME WHAT I'M *REALLY* GRASPING FOR IS ANY POSSIBILITY THAT SCOTT'S ALIVE.
MASKED SUPER-CRIMINAL OR NOT, I DON'T CARE AS LONG AS HE'S--
SEE ANYTHING FAMILIAR, SARA?
DOCTOR HAYES...
GUILTY AS CHARGED.
"I STARTED TO PUT THINGS TOGETHER WHEN YOU SHOWED UP TO WORK WITH ONE OF MY ILLICIT *SAMPLES*.
"IT STRUCK ME AS A *WILD COINCIDENCE*, BUT THEN AGAIN, IT'S A SMALL WORLD AND THE *SCIENTIFIC* ONE IS PRACTICALLY MICROSCOPIC."

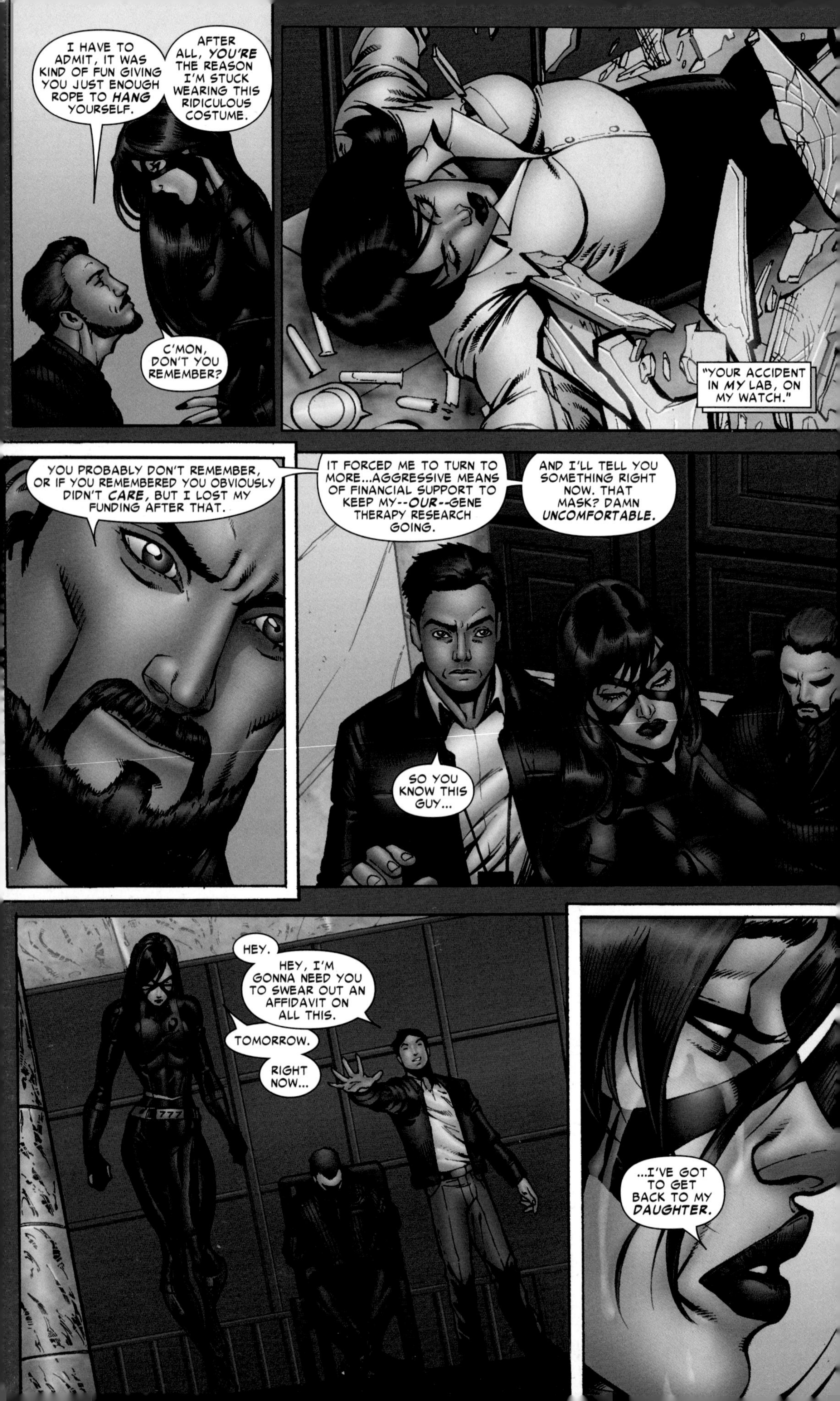
I HAVE TO ADMIT, IT WAS KIND OF FUN GIVING YOU JUST ENOUGH ROPE TO HANG YOURSELF.
AFTER ALL, YOU'RE THE REASON I'M STUCK WEARING THIS RIDICULOUS COSTUME.
C'MON, DON'T YOU REMEMBER?
"YOUR ACCIDENT IN MY LAB, ON MY WATCH."
YOU PROBABLY DON'T REMEMBER, OR IF YOU REMEMBERED YOU OBVIOUSLY DIDN'T CARE, BUT I LOST MY FUNDING AFTER THAT.
IT FORCED ME TO TURN TO MORE...AGGRESSIVE MEANS OF FINANCIAL SUPPORT TO KEEP MY--OUR--GENE THERAPY RESEARCH GOING.
AND I'LL TELL YOU SOMETHING RIGHT NOW. THAT MASK? DAMN UNCOMFORTABLE.
SO YOU KNOW THIS GUY...
HEY.
HEY, I'M GONNA NEED YOU TO SWEAR OUT AN AFFIDAVIT ON ALL THIS.
TOMORROW.
RIGHT NOW...
...I'VE GOT TO GET BACK TO MY DAUGHTER.

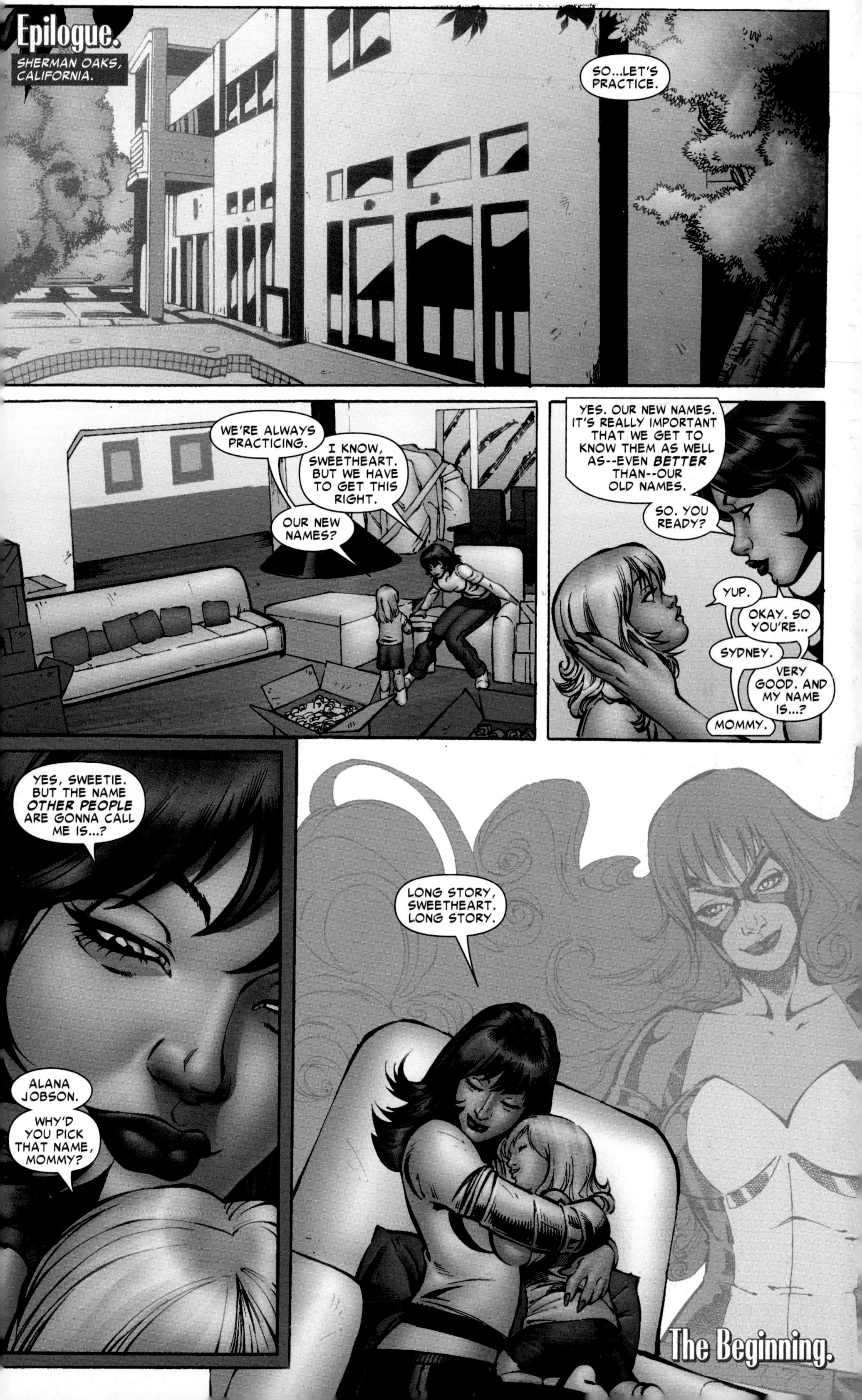

Epilogue.
SHERMAN OAKS, CALIFORNIA.
SO...LET'S PRACTICE.
WE'RE ALWAYS PRACTICING.
I KNOW, SWEETHEART. BUT WE HAVE TO GET THIS RIGHT.
OUR NEW NAMES?
YES. OUR NEW NAMES. IT'S REALLY IMPORTANT THAT WE GET TO KNOW THEM AS WELL AS--EVEN *BETTER* THAN--OUR OLD NAMES.
SO. YOU READY?
YUP.
OKAY. SO YOU'RE...
SYDNEY.
VERY GOOD. AND MY NAME IS...?
MOMMY.
YES, SWEETIE. BUT THE NAME *OTHER PEOPLE* ARE GONNA CALL ME IS...?
ALANA JOBSON.
WHY'D YOU PICK THAT NAME, MOMMY?
LONG STORY, SWEETHEART. LONG STORY.
The Beginning.

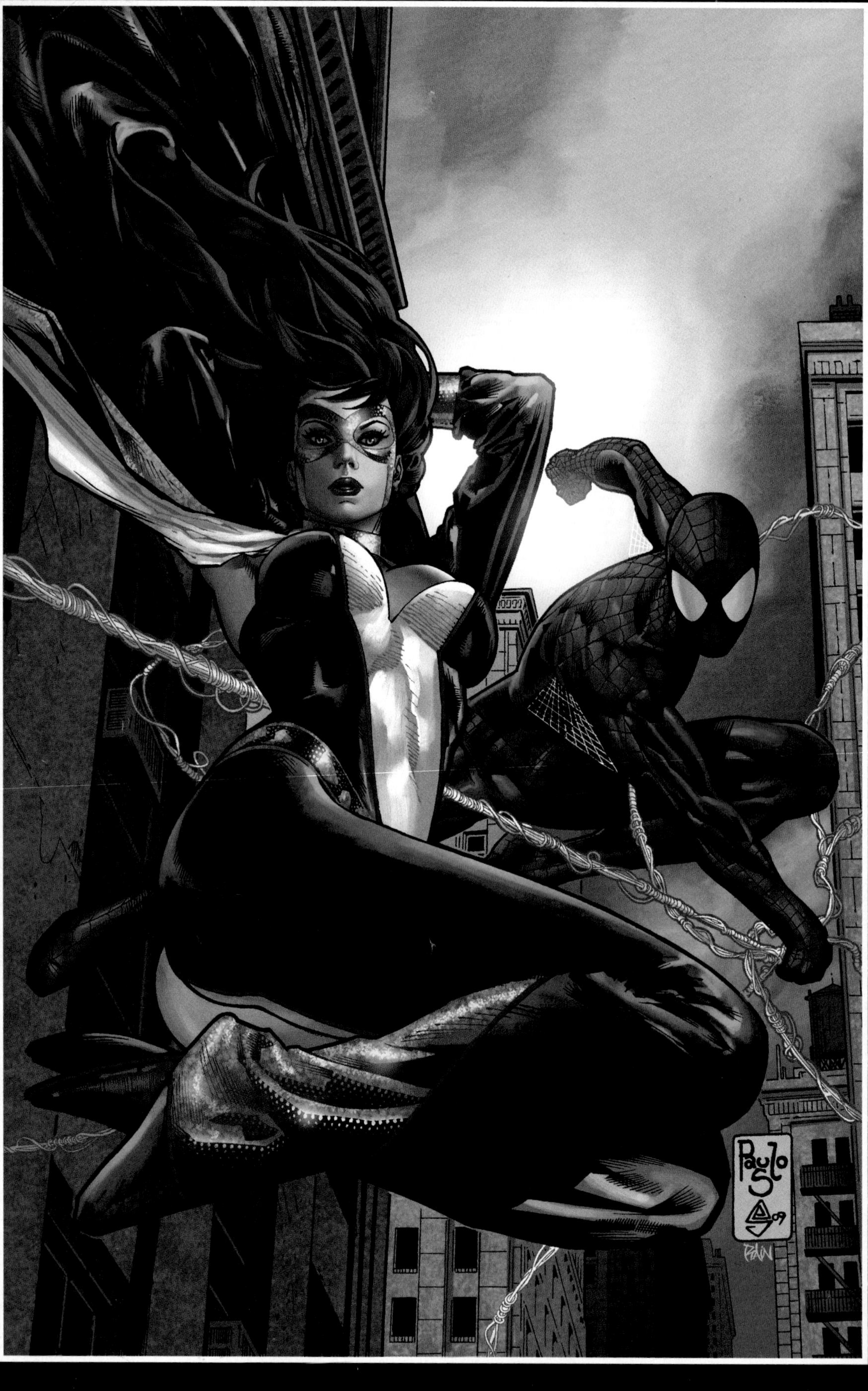

AMAZING SPIDER-MAN FAMILY #6: "EXIT INTERVIEW"

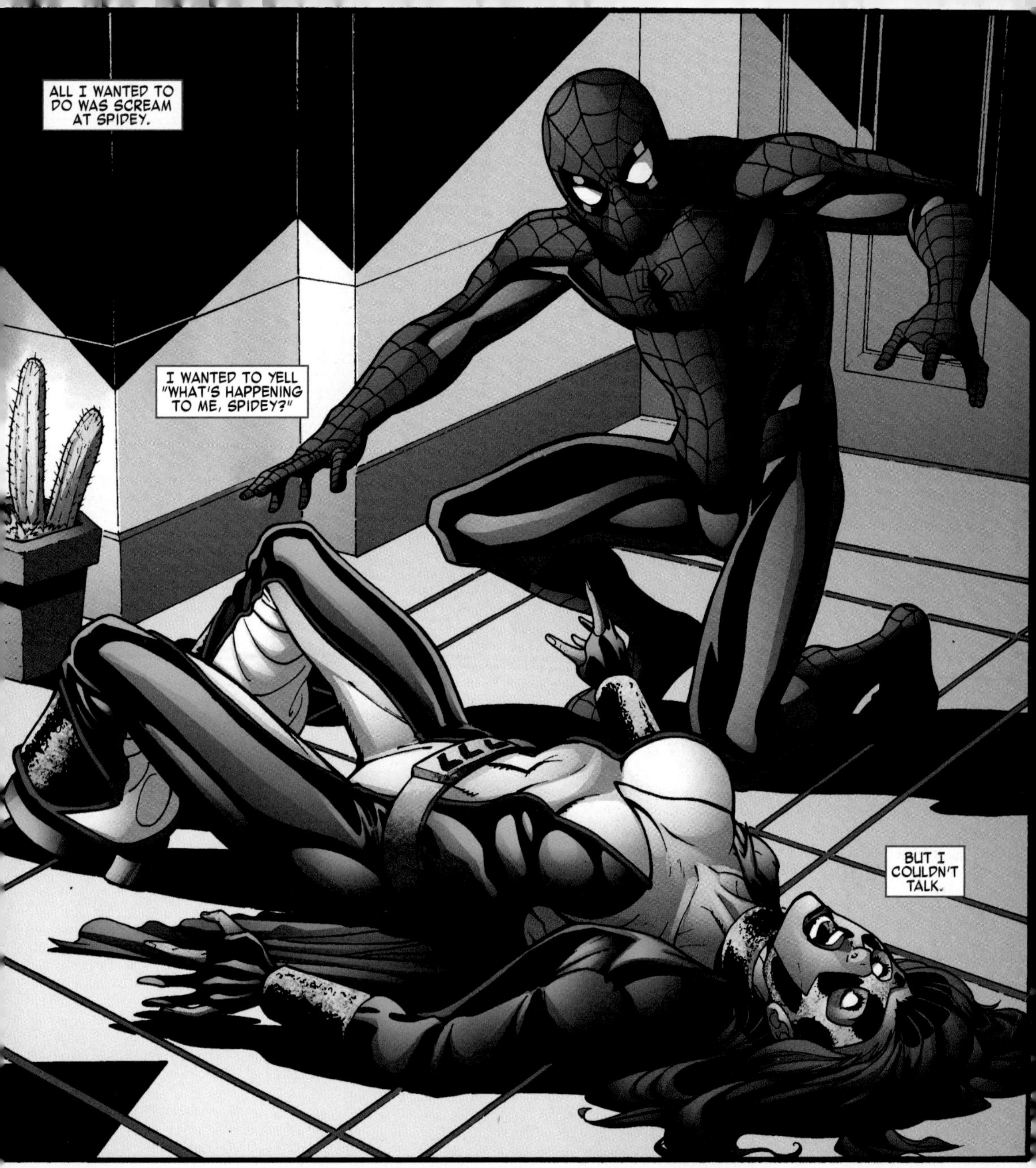
ALL I WANTED TO DO WAS SCREAM AT SPIDEY.
I WANTED TO YELL "WHAT'S HAPPENING TO ME, SPIDEY?"
BUT I COULDN'T TALK.

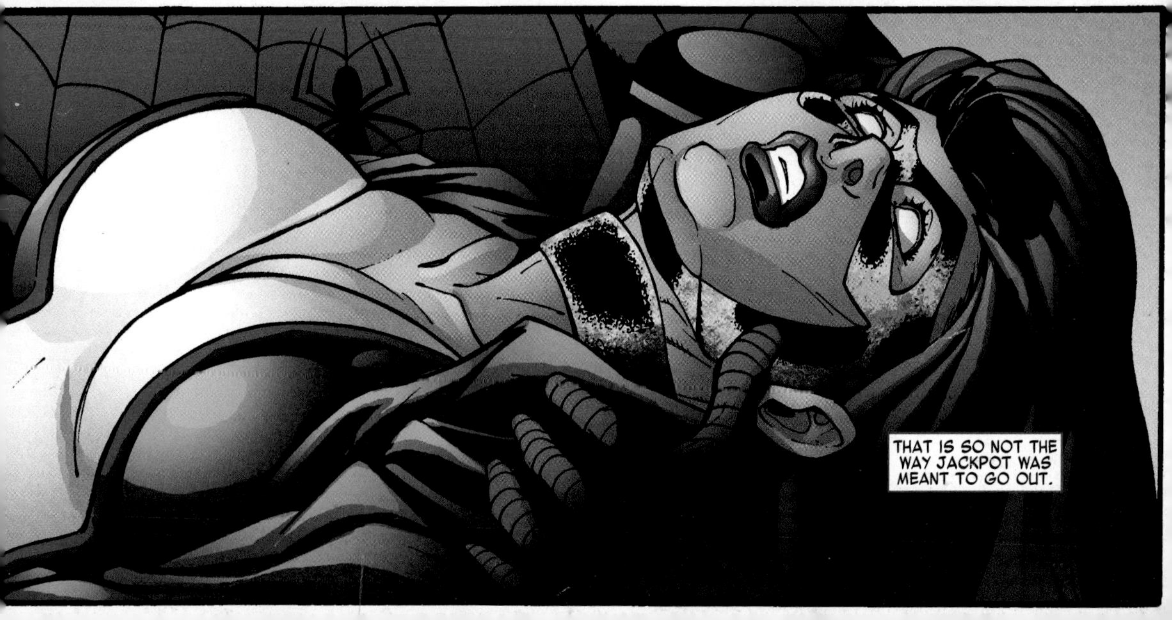
THAT IS SO NOT THE WAY JACKPOT WAS MEANT TO GO OUT.

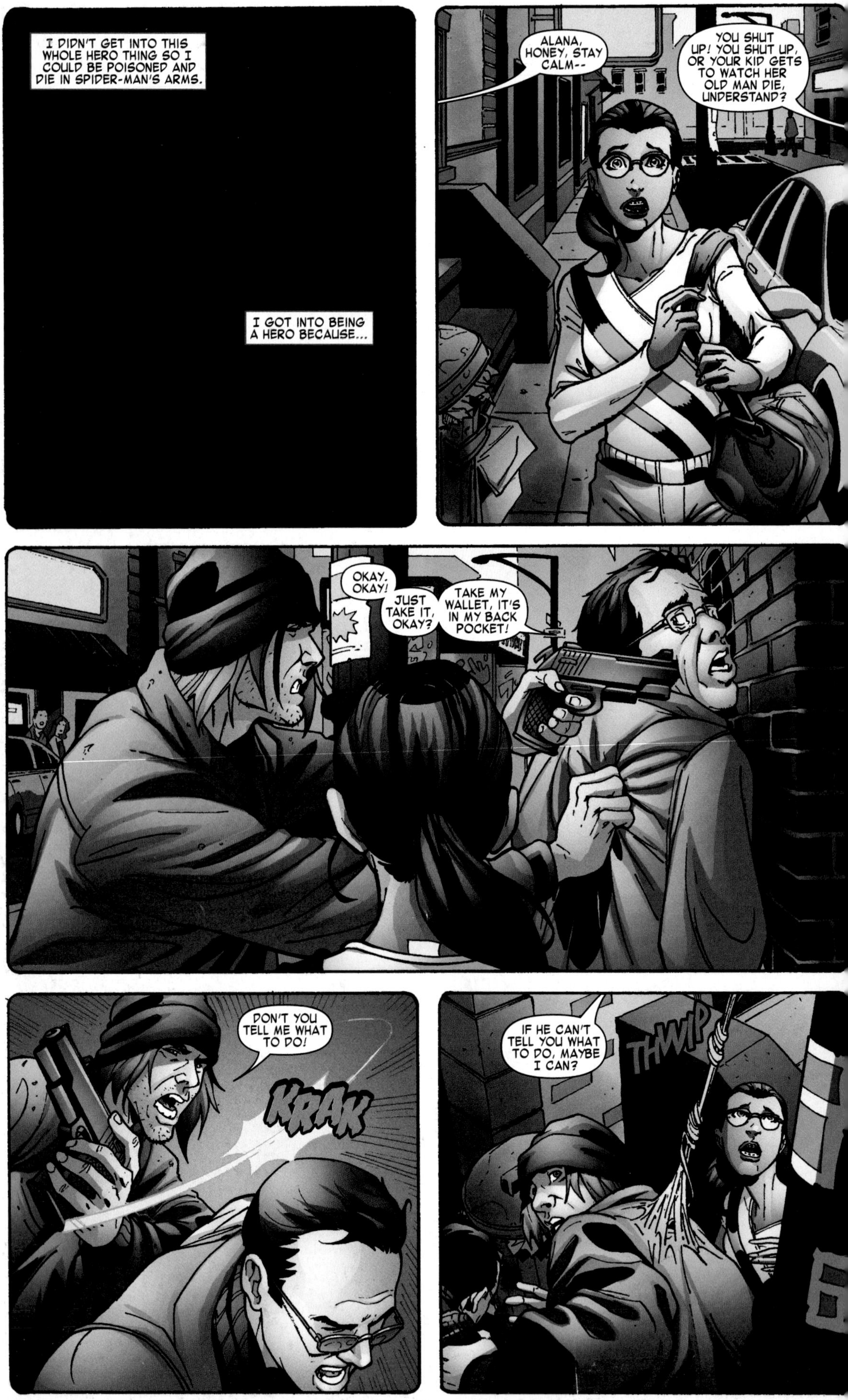
I DIDN'T GET INTO THIS WHOLE HERO THING SO I COULD BE POISONED AND DIE IN SPIDER-MAN'S ARMS.
I GOT INTO BEING A HERO BECAUSE...
ALANA, HONEY, STAY CALM--
YOU SHUT UP! YOU SHUT UP, OR YOUR KID GETS TO WATCH HER OLD MAN DIE, UNDERSTAND?
OKAY. OKAY!
JUST TAKE IT, OKAY?
TAKE MY WALLET, IT'S IN MY BACK POCKET!
DON'T YOU TELL ME WHAT TO DO!
KRAK
IF HE CAN'T TELL YOU WHAT TO DO, MAYBE I CAN?
THWIP

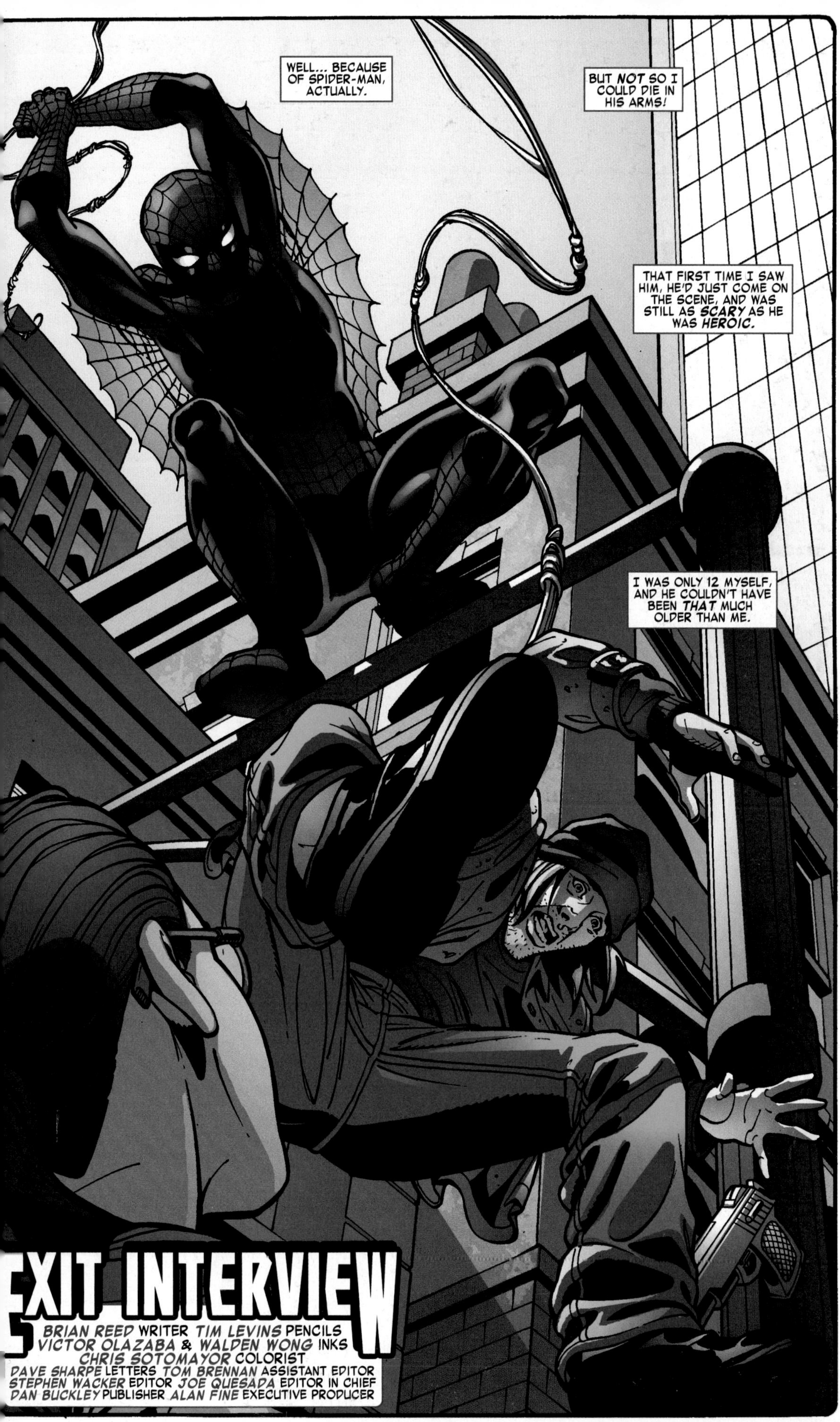

WELL... BECAUSE OF SPIDER-MAN, ACTUALLY.
BUT NOT SO I COULD DIE IN HIS ARMS!
THAT FIRST TIME I SAW HIM, HE'D JUST COME ON THE SCENE, AND WAS STILL AS SCARY AS HE WAS HEROIC.
I WAS ONLY 12 MYSELF, AND HE COULDN'T HAVE BEEN THAT MUCH OLDER THAN ME.
EXIT INTERVIEW
BRIAN REED WRITER TIM LEVINS PENCILS
VICTOR OLAZABA & WALDEN WONG INKS
CHRIS SOTOMAYOR COLORIST
DAVE SHARPE LETTERS TOM BRENNAN ASSISTANT EDITOR
STEPHEN WACKER EDITOR JOE QUESADA EDITOR IN CHIEF
DAN BUCKLEY PUBLISHER ALAN FINE EXECUTIVE PRODUCER

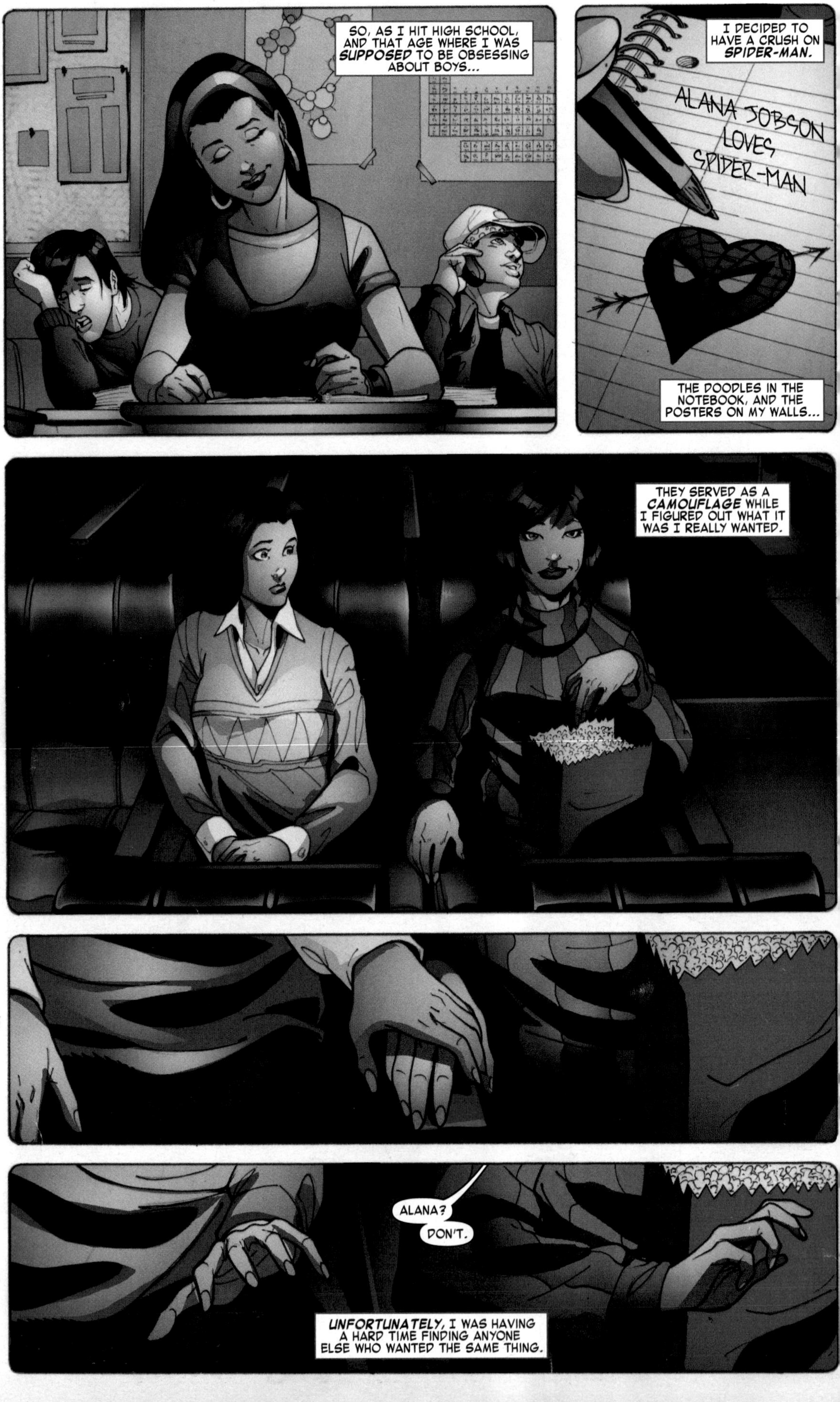
SO, AS I HIT HIGH SCHOOL, AND THAT AGE WHERE I WAS SUPPOSED TO BE OBSESSING ABOUT BOYS...
I DECIDED TO HAVE A CRUSH ON SPIDER-MAN.
ALANA JOBSON LOVES SPIDER-MAN
THE DOODLES IN THE NOTEBOOK, AND THE POSTERS ON MY WALLS...
THEY SERVED AS A CAMOUFLAGE WHILE I FIGURED OUT WHAT IT WAS I REALLY WANTED.
ALANA?
DON'T.
UNFORTUNATELY, I WAS HAVING A HARD TIME FINDING ANYONE ELSE WHO WANTED THE SAME THING.

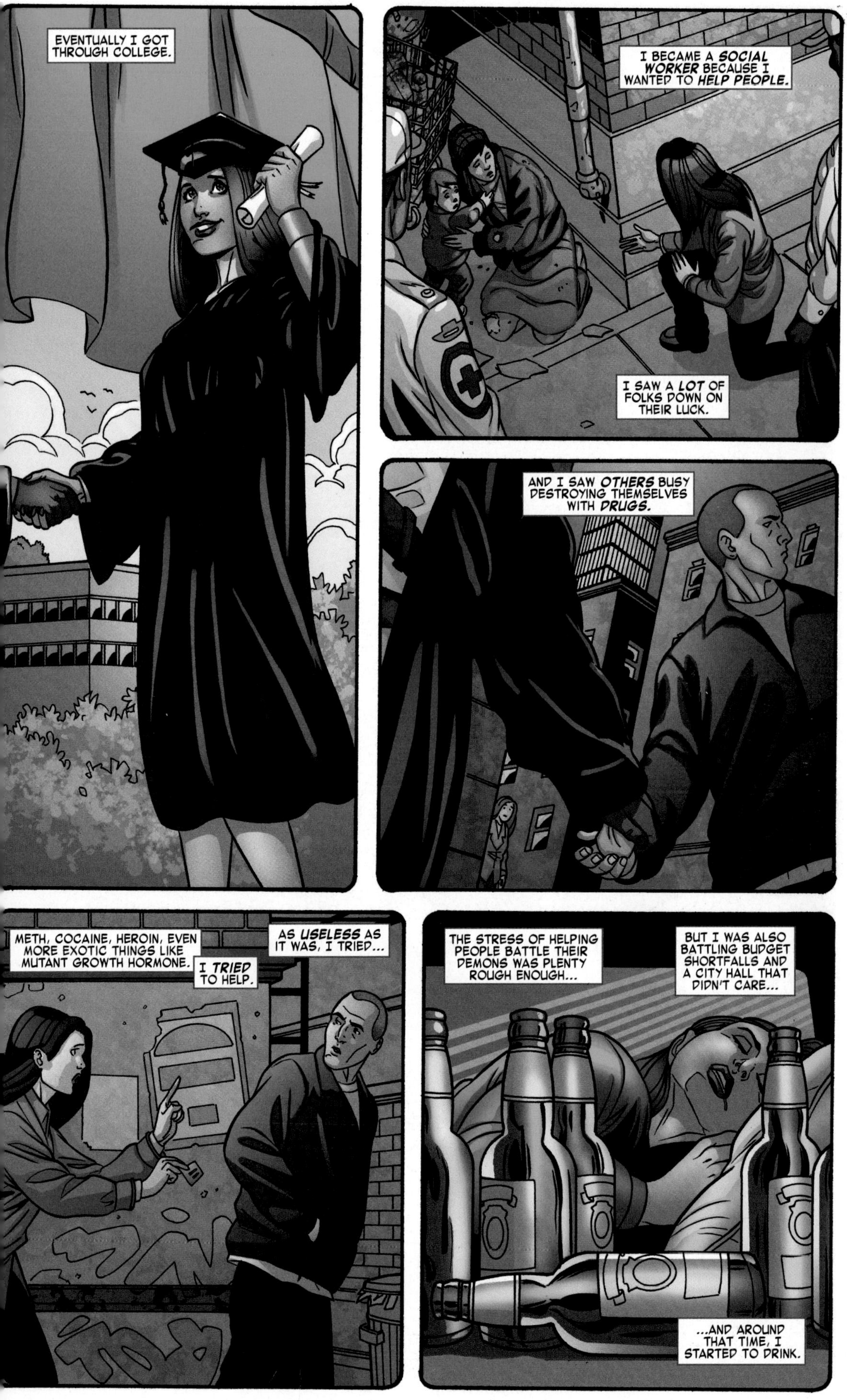
EVENTUALLY I GOT THROUGH COLLEGE.
I BECAME A SOCIAL WORKER BECAUSE I WANTED TO HELP PEOPLE.
I SAW A LOT OF FOLKS DOWN ON THEIR LUCK.
AND I SAW OTHERS BUSY DESTROYING THEMSELVES WITH DRUGS.
METH, COCAINE, HEROIN, EVEN MORE EXOTIC THINGS LIKE MUTANT GROWTH HORMONE.
I TRIED TO HELP.
AS USELESS AS IT WAS, I TRIED...
THE STRESS OF HELPING PEOPLE BATTLE THEIR DEMONS WAS PLENTY ROUGH ENOUGH...
BUT I WAS ALSO BATTLING BUDGET SHORTFALLS AND A CITY HALL THAT DIDN'T CARE...
...AND AROUND THAT TIME, I STARTED TO DRINK.

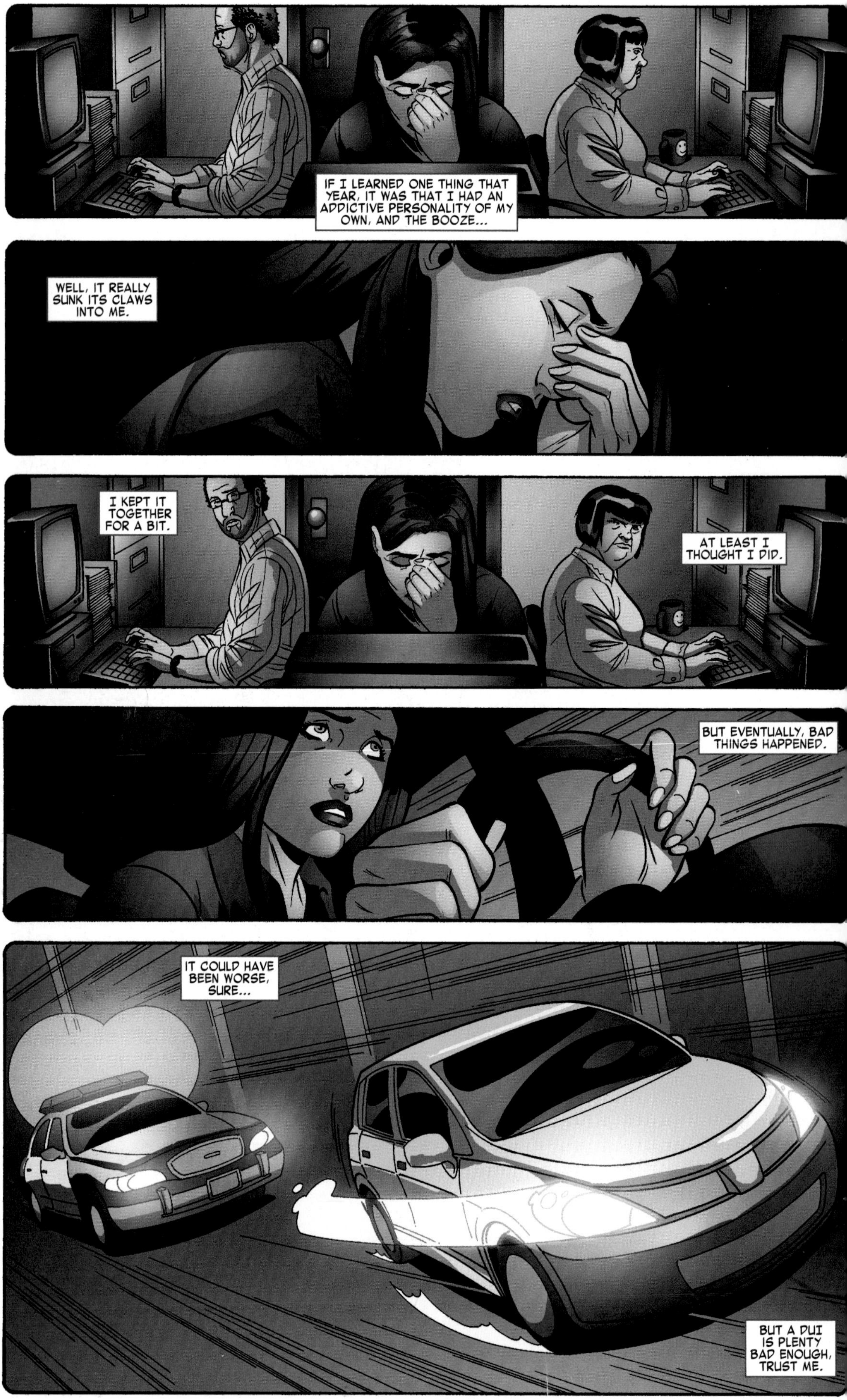
IF I LEARNED ONE THING THAT YEAR, IT WAS THAT I HAD AN ADDICTIVE PERSONALITY OF MY OWN, AND THE BOOZE...
WELL, IT REALLY SUNK ITS CLAWS INTO ME.
I KEPT IT TOGETHER FOR A BIT.
AT LEAST I THOUGHT I DID.
BUT EVENTUALLY, BAD THINGS HAPPENED.
IT COULD HAVE BEEN WORSE, SURE...
BUT A DUI IS PLENTY BAD ENOUGH, TRUST ME.

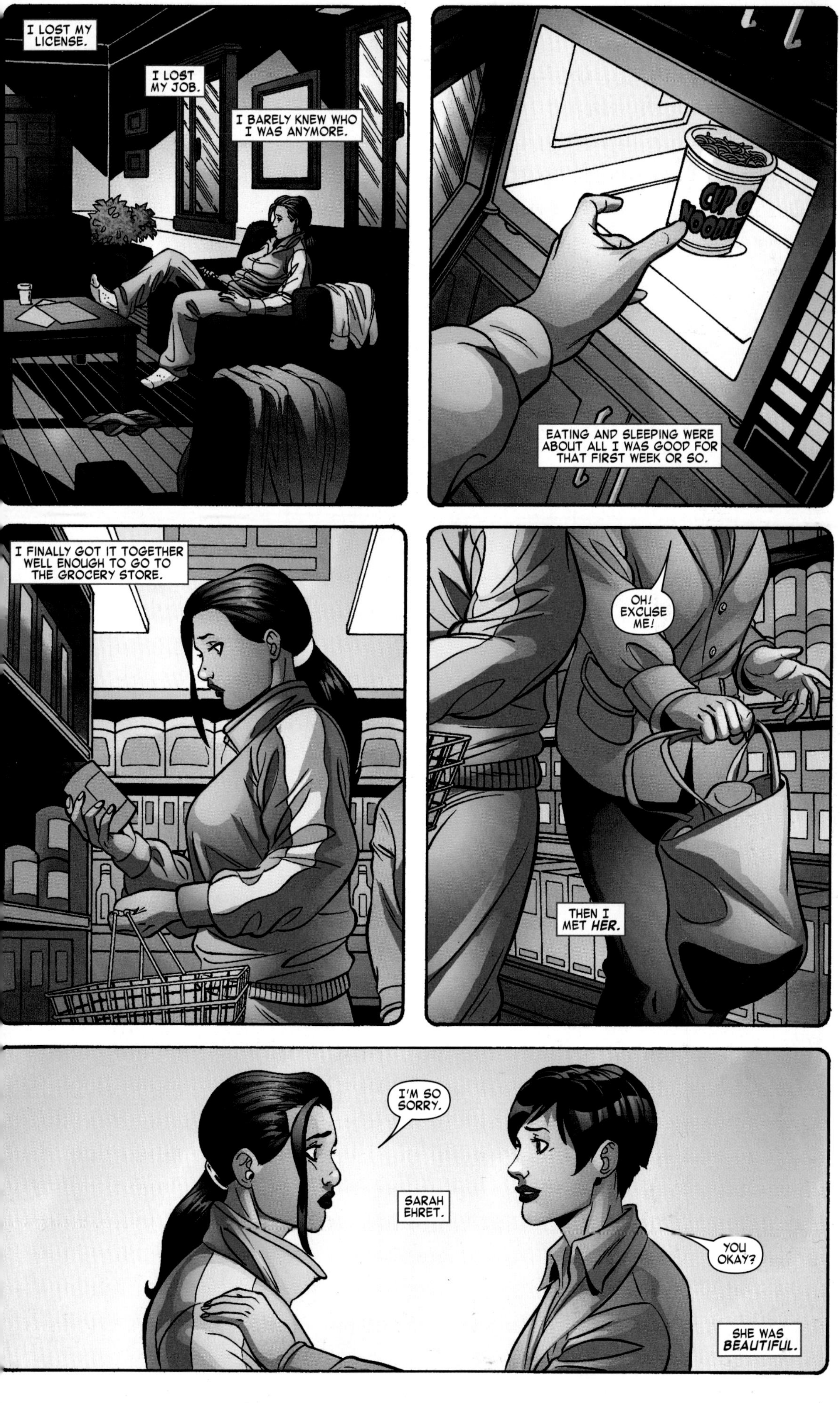

I LOST MY LICENSE.
I LOST MY JOB.
I BARELY KNEW WHO I WAS ANYMORE.
EATING AND SLEEPING WERE ABOUT ALL I WAS GOOD FOR THAT FIRST WEEK OR SO.
I FINALLY GOT IT TOGETHER WELL ENOUGH TO GO TO THE GROCERY STORE.
OH! EXCUSE ME!
THEN I MET *HER*.
I'M SO SORRY.
SARAH EHRET.
YOU OKAY?
SHE WAS *BEAUTIFUL*.

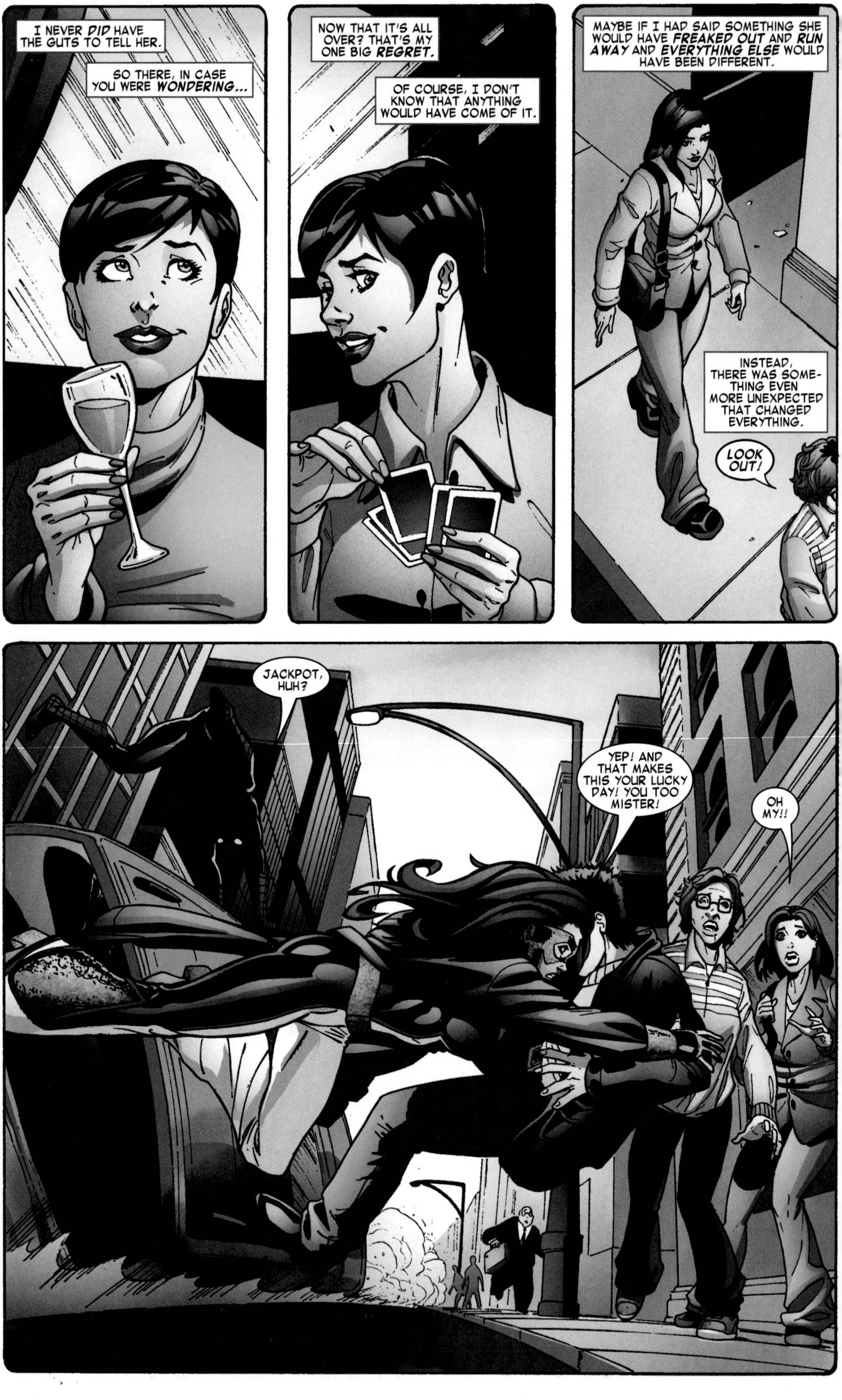
I NEVER DID HAVE THE GUTS TO TELL HER.
SO THERE, IN CASE YOU WERE WONDERING...
NOW THAT IT'S ALL OVER? THAT'S MY ONE BIG REGRET.
OF COURSE, I DON'T KNOW THAT ANYTHING WOULD HAVE COME OF IT.
MAYBE IF I HAD SAID SOMETHING SHE WOULD HAVE FREAKED OUT AND RUN AWAY AND EVERYTHING ELSE WOULD HAVE BEEN DIFFERENT.
INSTEAD, THERE WAS SOMETHING EVEN MORE UNEXPECTED THAT CHANGED EVERYTHING.
LOOK OUT!
JACKPOT, HUH?
YEP! AND THAT MAKES THIS YOUR LUCKY DAY! YOU TOO MISTER!
OH MY!!

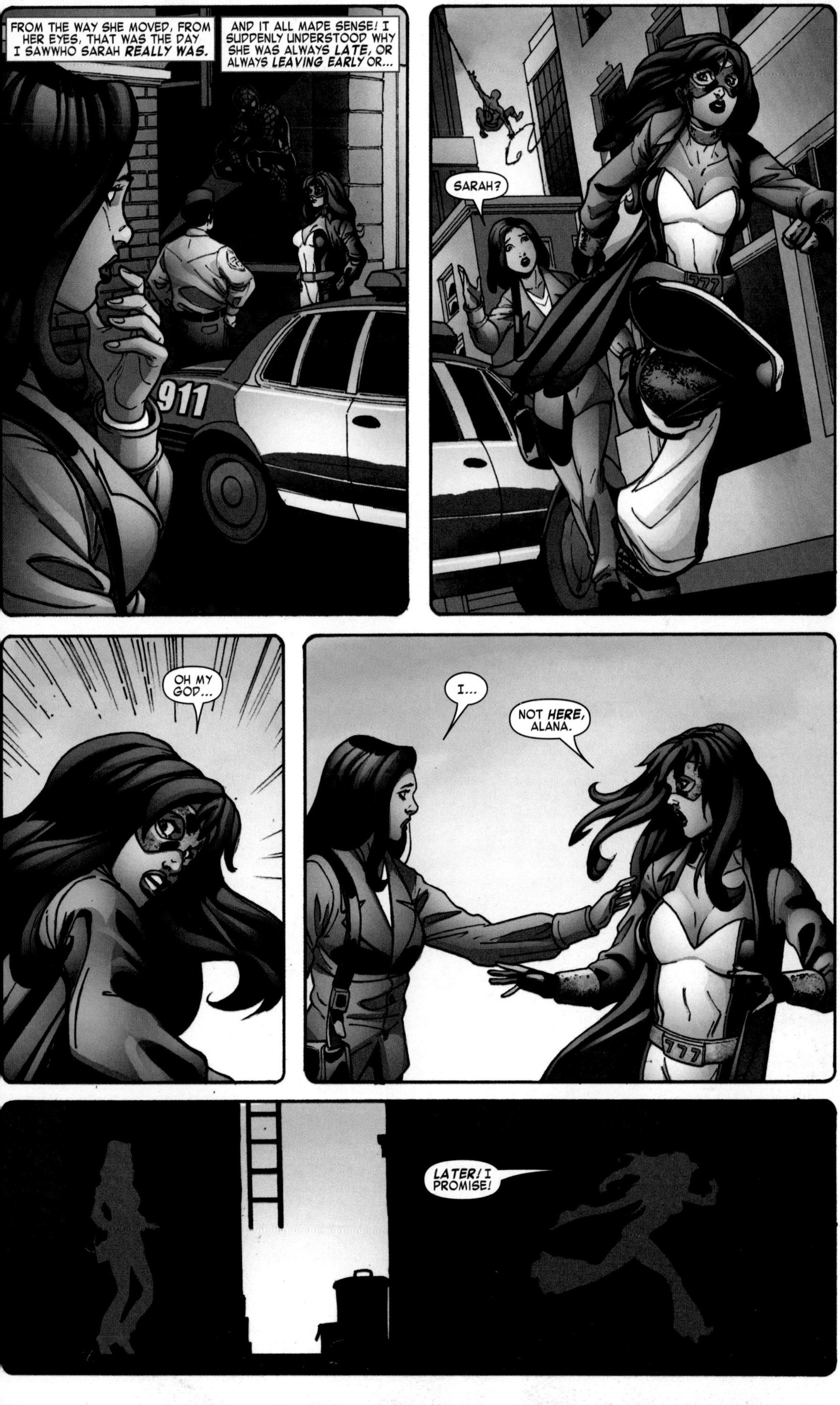
FROM THE WAY SHE MOVED, FROM HER EYES, THAT WAS THE DAY I SAWWHO SARAH REALLY WAS.
AND IT ALL MADE SENSE! I SUDDENLY UNDERSTOOD WHY SHE WAS ALWAYS LATE, OR ALWAYS LEAVING EARLY OR...
911
SARAH?
OH MY GOD...
I...
NOT HERE, ALANA.
LATER! I PROMISE!

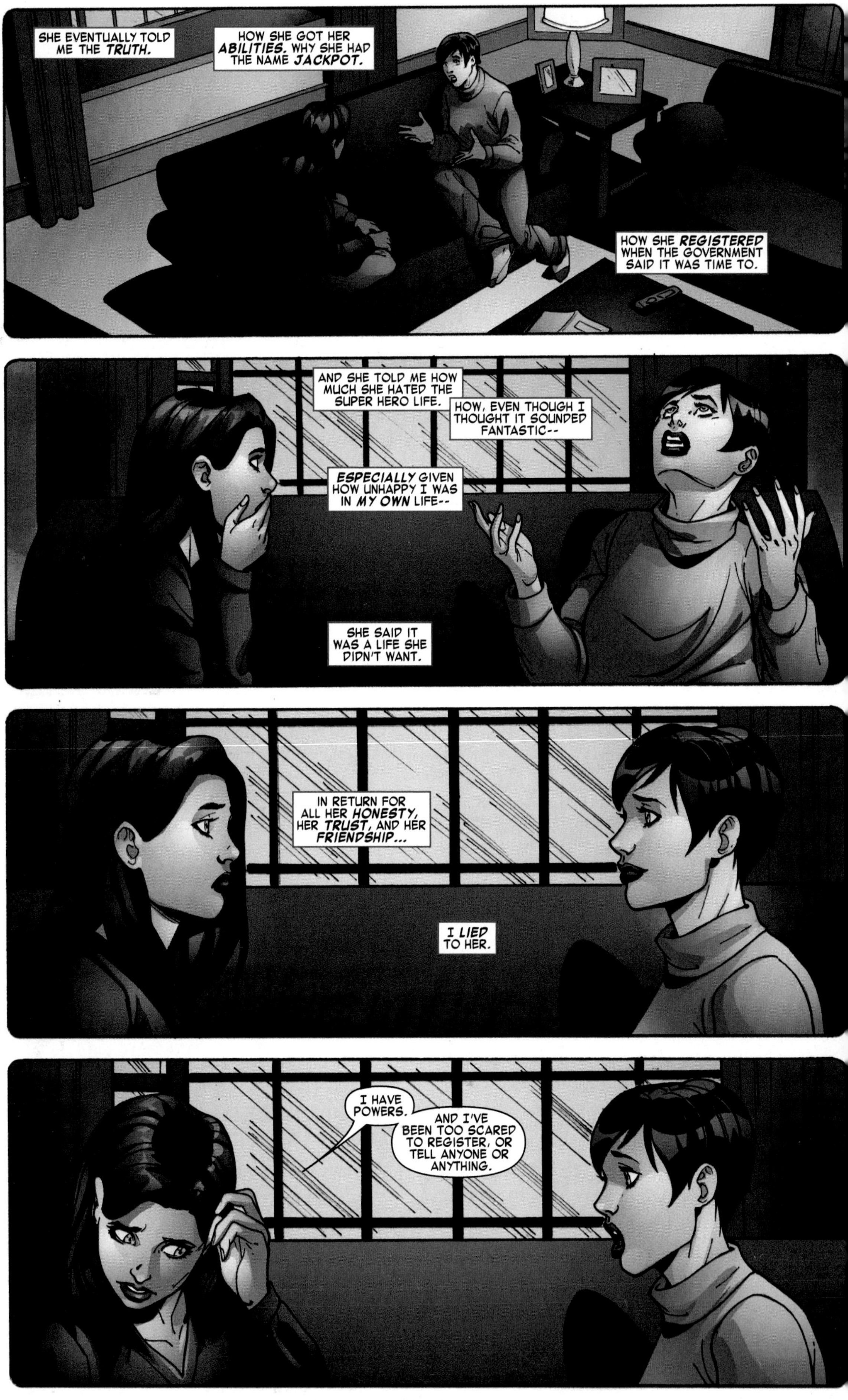

SHE EVENTUALLY TOLD ME THE TRUTH.
HOW SHE GOT HER ABILITIES. WHY SHE HAD THE NAME JACKPOT.
HOW SHE REGISTERED WHEN THE GOVERNMENT SAID IT WAS TIME TO.
AND SHE TOLD ME HOW MUCH SHE HATED THE SUPER HERO LIFE.
HOW, EVEN THOUGH I THOUGHT IT SOUNDED FANTASTIC--
ESPECIALLY GIVEN HOW UNHAPPY I WAS IN MY OWN LIFE--
SHE SAID IT WAS A LIFE SHE DIDN'T WANT.
IN RETURN FOR ALL HER HONESTY, HER TRUST, AND HER FRIENDSHIP...
I LIED TO HER.
I HAVE POWERS.
AND I'VE BEEN TOO SCARED TO REGISTER, OR TELL ANYONE OR ANYTHING.

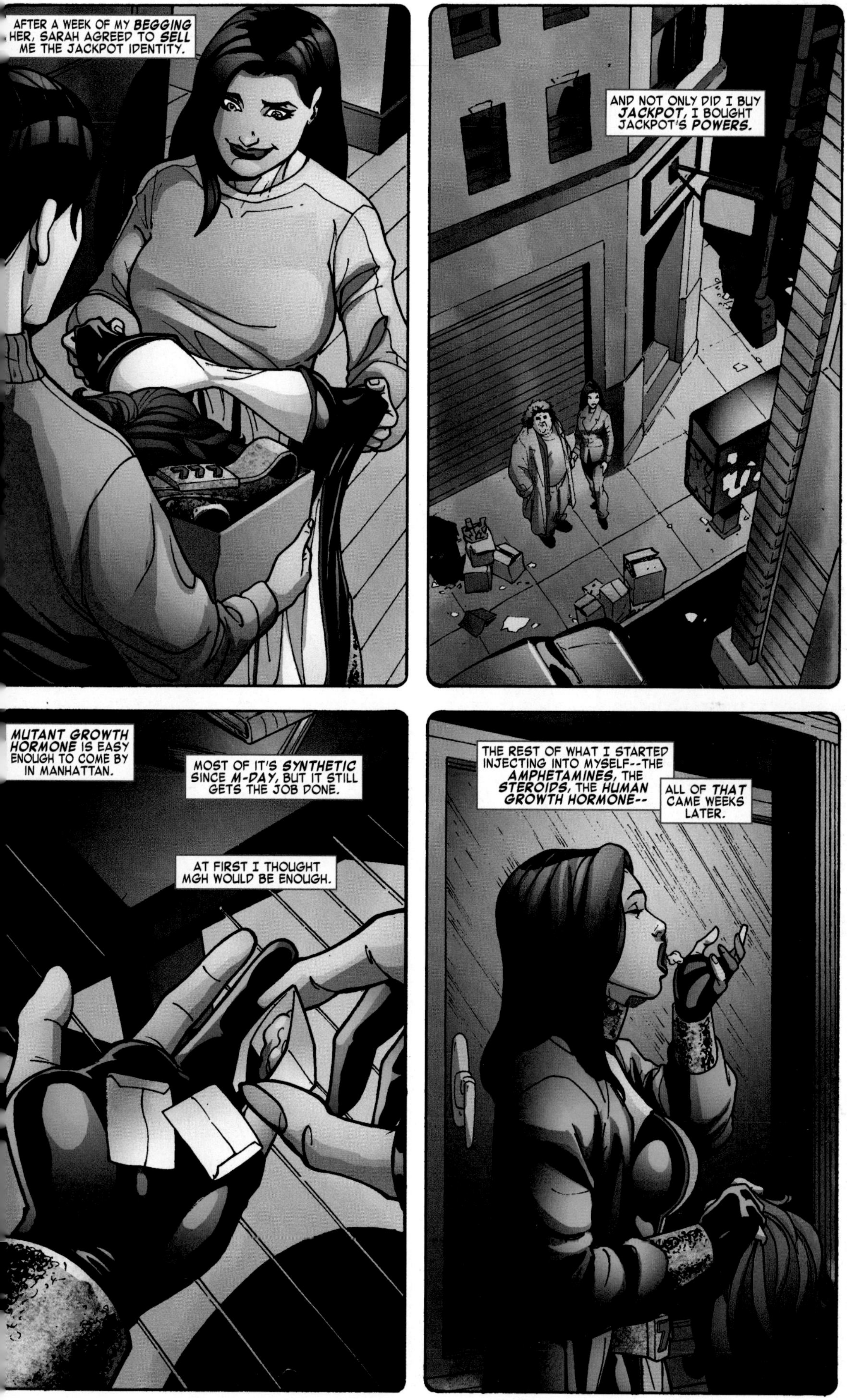
AFTER A WEEK OF MY BEGGING HER, SARAH AGREED TO SELL ME THE JACKPOT IDENTITY.
AND NOT ONLY DID I BUY JACKPOT, I BOUGHT JACKPOT'S POWERS.
MUTANT GROWTH HORMONE IS EASY ENOUGH TO COME BY IN MANHATTAN.
MOST OF IT'S SYNTHETIC SINCE M-DAY, BUT IT STILL GETS THE JOB DONE.
AT FIRST I THOUGHT MGH WOULD BE ENOUGH.
THE REST OF WHAT I STARTED INJECTING INTO MYSELF--THE AMPHETAMINES, THE STEROIDS, THE HUMAN GROWTH HORMONE--
ALL OF THAT CAME WEEKS LATER.

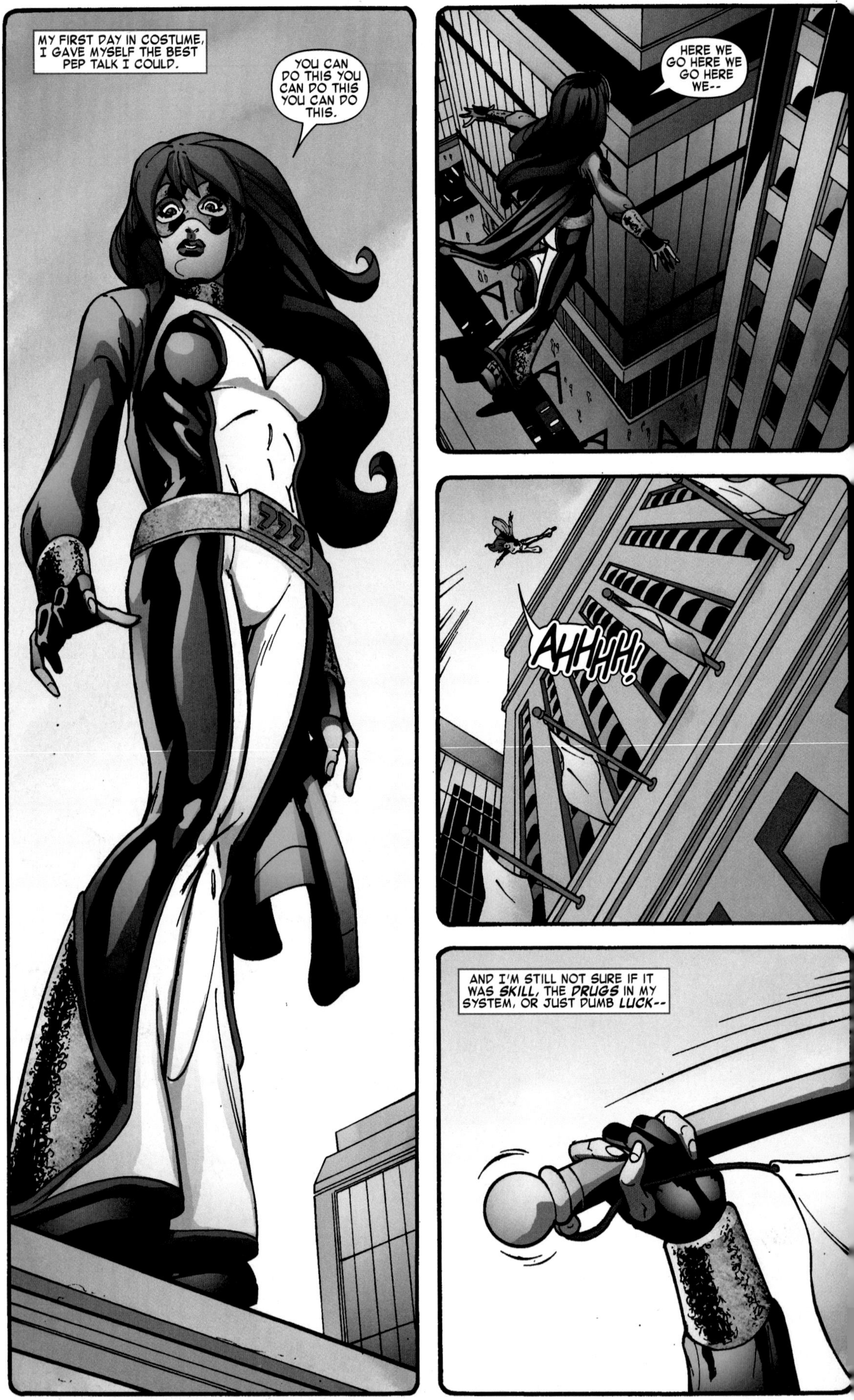
MY FIRST DAY IN COSTUME, I GAVE MYSELF THE BEST PEP TALK I COULD.
YOU CAN DO THIS YOU CAN DO THIS YOU CAN DO THIS.
HERE WE GO HERE WE GO HERE WE--
AHHHH!
AND I'M STILL NOT SURE IF IT WAS SKILL, THE DRUGS IN MY SYSTEM, OR JUST DUMB LUCK--

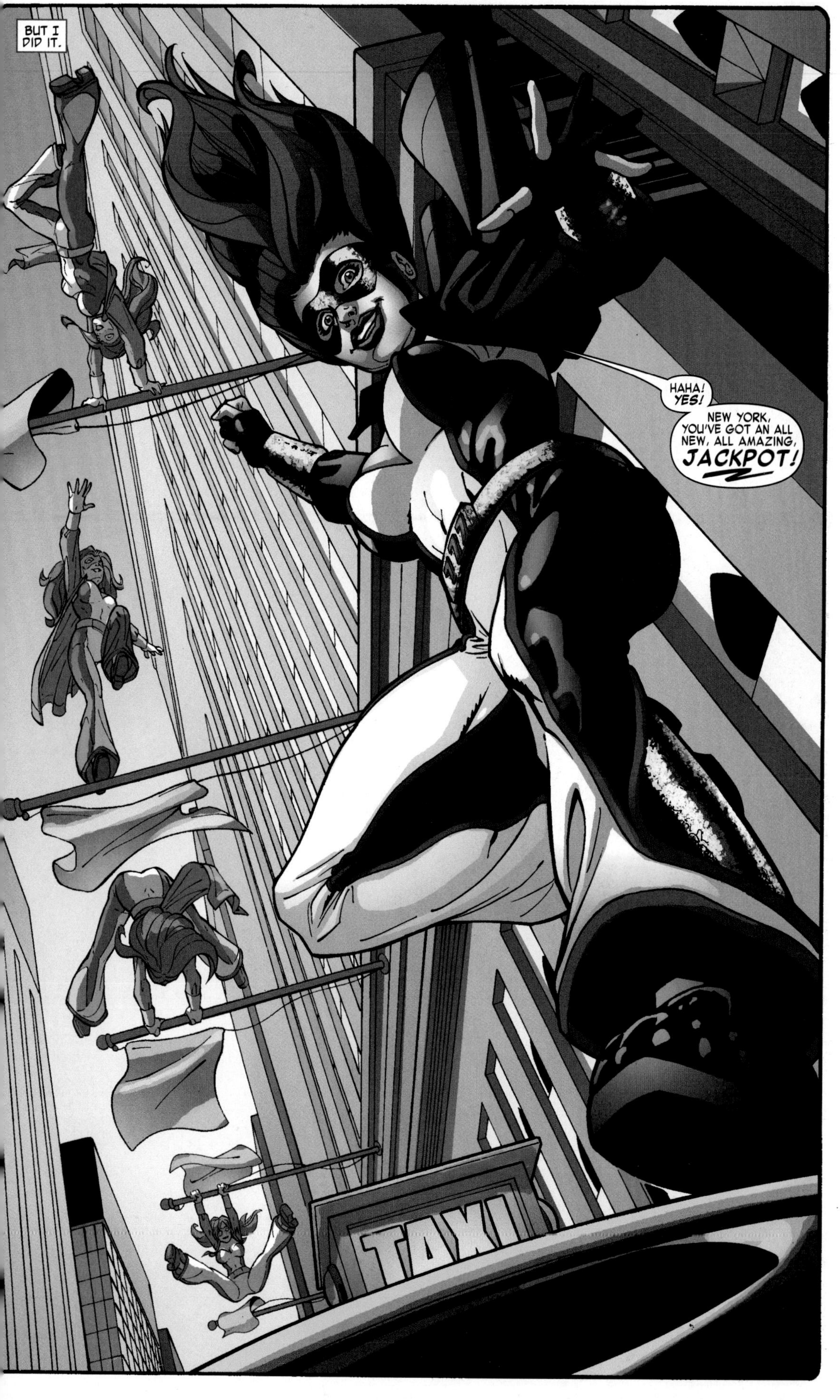

BUT I DID IT.
HAHA! YES!
NEW YORK, YOU'VE GOT AN ALL NEW, ALL AMAZING, JACKPOT!
TAXI

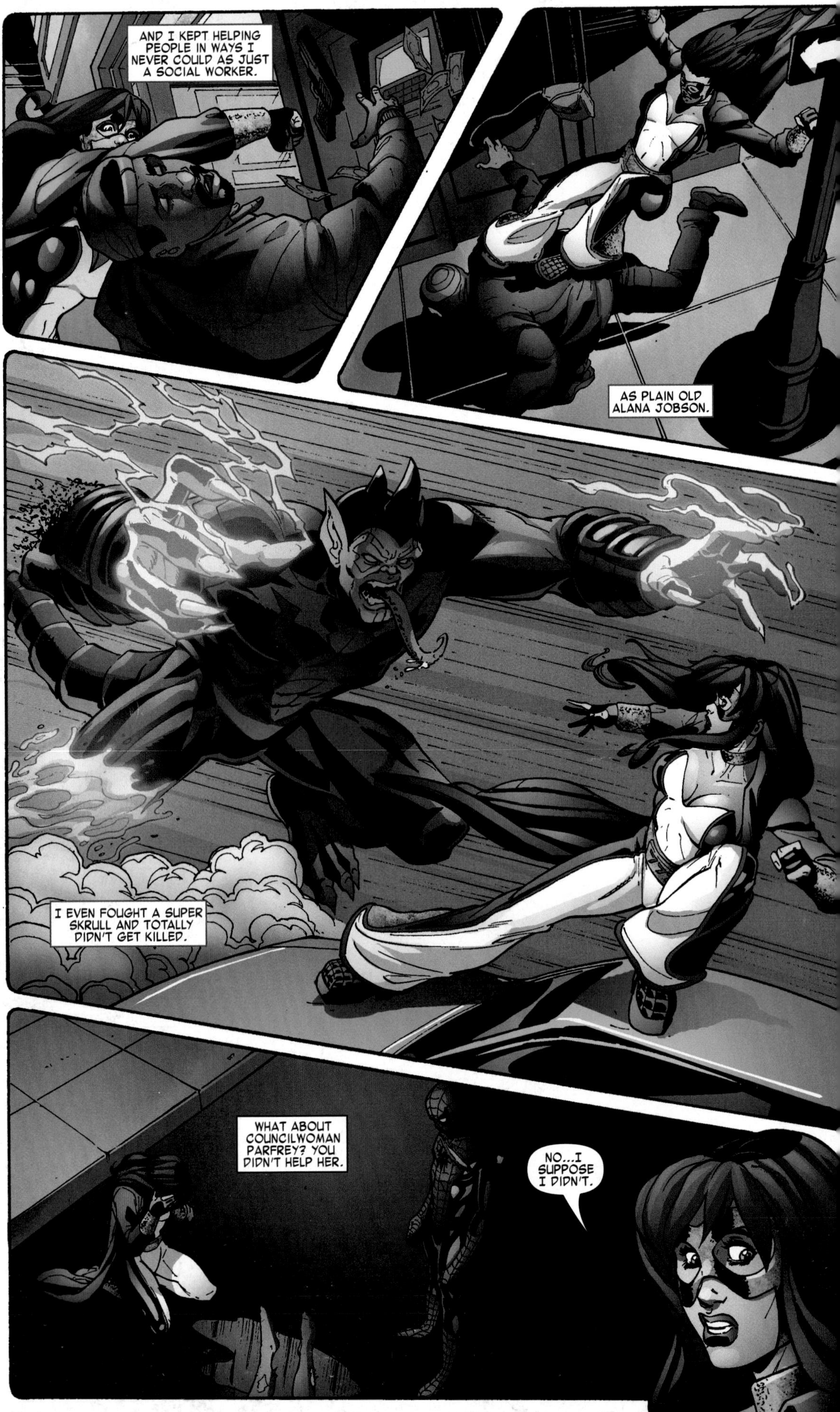
AND I KEPT HELPING PEOPLE IN WAYS I NEVER COULD AS JUST A SOCIAL WORKER.
AS PLAIN OLD ALANA JOBSON.
I EVEN FOUGHT A SUPER SKRULL AND TOTALLY DIDN'T GET KILLED.
WHAT ABOUT COUNCILWOMAN PARFREY? YOU DIDN'T HELP HER.
NO...I SUPPOSE I DIDN'T.

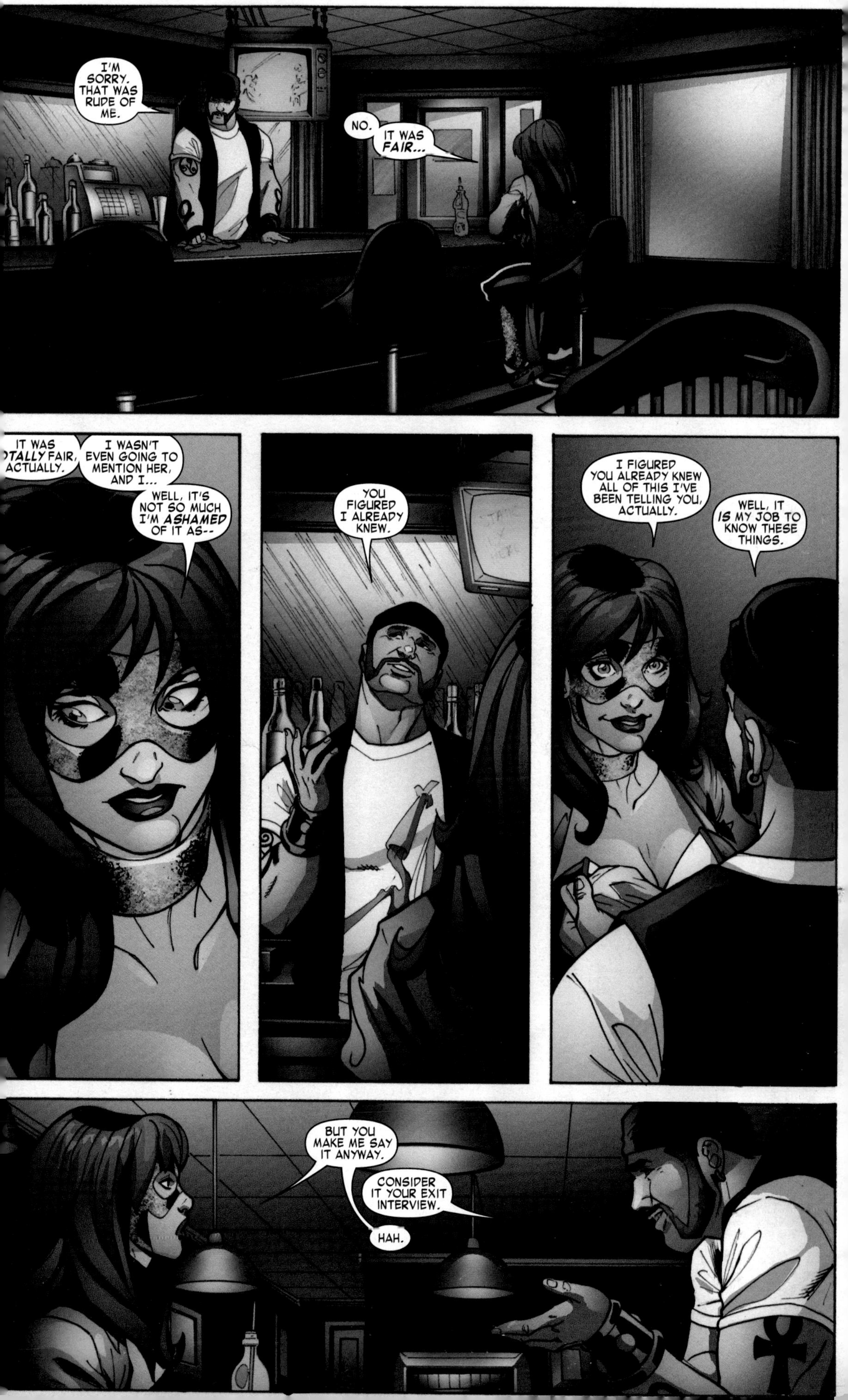
I'M SORRY. THAT WAS RUDE OF ME.
NO. IT WAS FAIR...
IT WAS TOTALLY FAIR, ACTUALLY.
I WASN'T EVEN GOING TO MENTION HER, AND I...
WELL, IT'S NOT SO MUCH I'M ASHAMED OF IT AS--
YOU FIGURED I ALREADY KNEW.
I FIGURED YOU ALREADY KNEW ALL OF THIS I'VE BEEN TELLING YOU, ACTUALLY.
WELL, IT IS MY JOB TO KNOW THESE THINGS.
BUT YOU MAKE ME SAY IT ANYWAY.
CONSIDER IT YOUR EXIT INTERVIEW.
HAH.

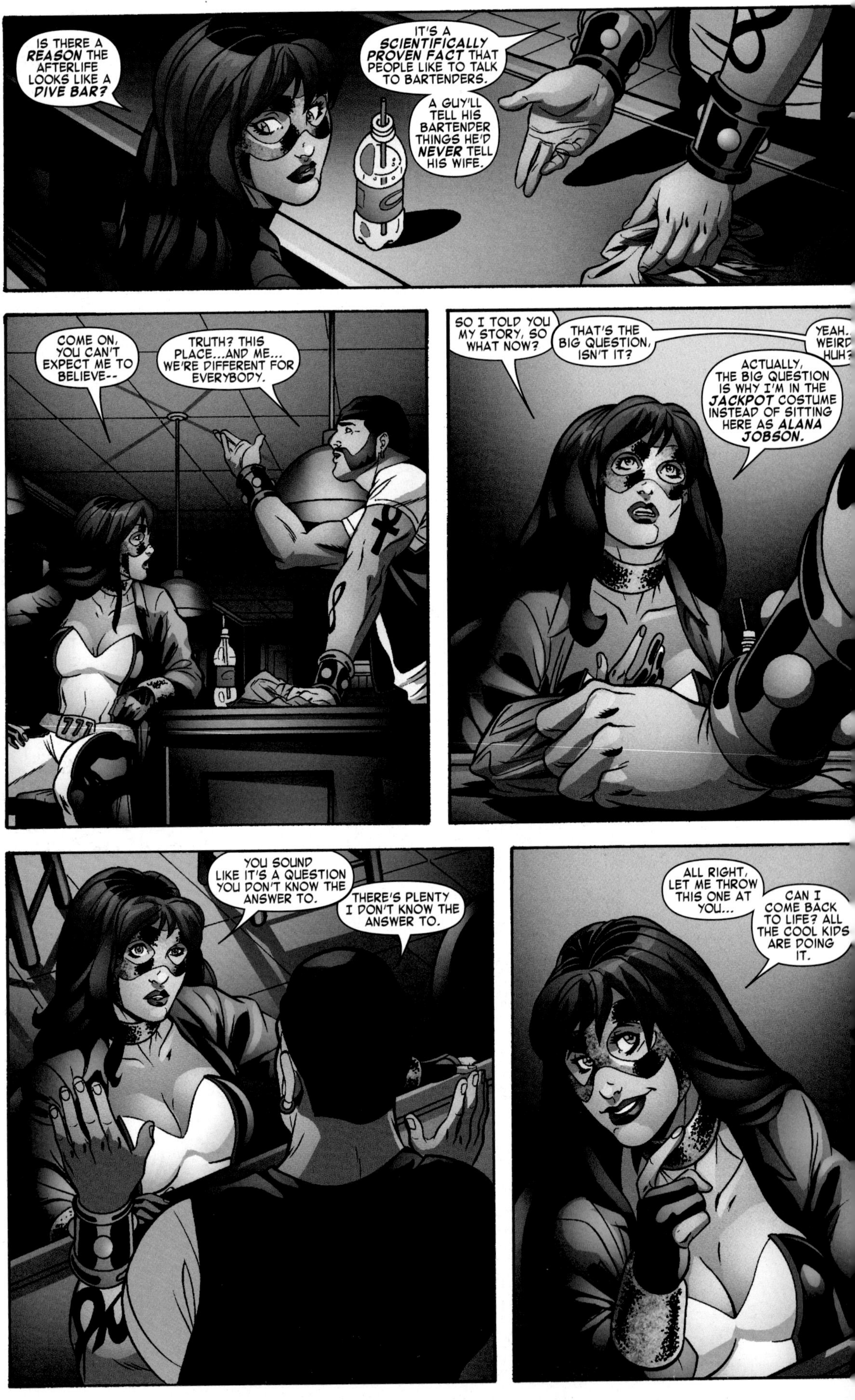
IS THERE A REASON THE AFTERLIFE LOOKS LIKE A DIVE BAR?
IT'S A SCIENTIFICALLY PROVEN FACT THAT PEOPLE LIKE TO TALK TO BARTENDERS.
A GUY'LL TELL HIS BARTENDER THINGS HE'D NEVER TELL HIS WIFE.
COME ON, YOU CAN'T EXPECT ME TO BELIEVE--
TRUTH? THIS PLACE...AND ME... WE'RE DIFFERENT FOR EVERYBODY.
777
SO I TOLD YOU MY STORY, SO WHAT NOW?
THAT'S THE BIG QUESTION, ISN'T IT?
YEAH. WEIRD HUH?
ACTUALLY, THE BIG QUESTION IS WHY I'M IN THE JACKPOT COSTUME INSTEAD OF SITTING HERE AS ALANA JOBSON.
YOU SOUND LIKE IT'S A QUESTION YOU DON'T KNOW THE ANSWER TO.
THERE'S PLENTY I DON'T KNOW THE ANSWER TO.
ALL RIGHT, LET ME THROW THIS ONE AT YOU...
CAN I COME BACK TO LIFE? ALL THE COOL KIDS ARE DOING IT.

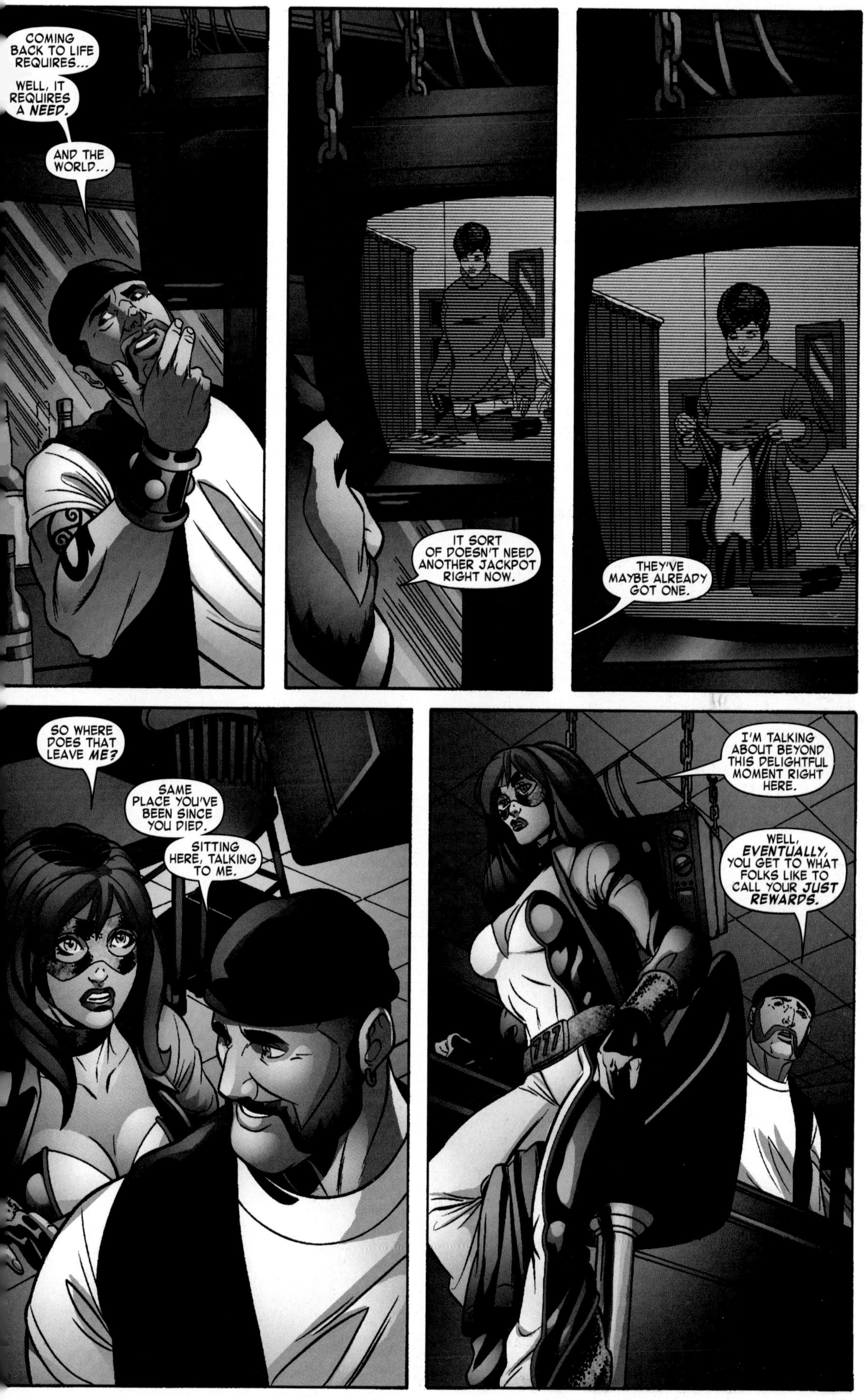
COMING BACK TO LIFE REQUIRES...
WELL, IT REQUIRES A NEED.
AND THE WORLD...
IT SORT OF DOESN'T NEED ANOTHER JACKPOT RIGHT NOW.
THEY'VE MAYBE ALREADY GOT ONE.
SO WHERE DOES THAT LEAVE ME?
SAME PLACE YOU'VE BEEN SINCE YOU DIED.
SITTING HERE, TALKING TO ME.
I'M TALKING ABOUT BEYOND THIS DELIGHTFUL MOMENT RIGHT HERE.
WELL, EVENTUALLY, YOU GET TO WHAT FOLKS LIKE TO CALL YOUR JUST REWARDS.

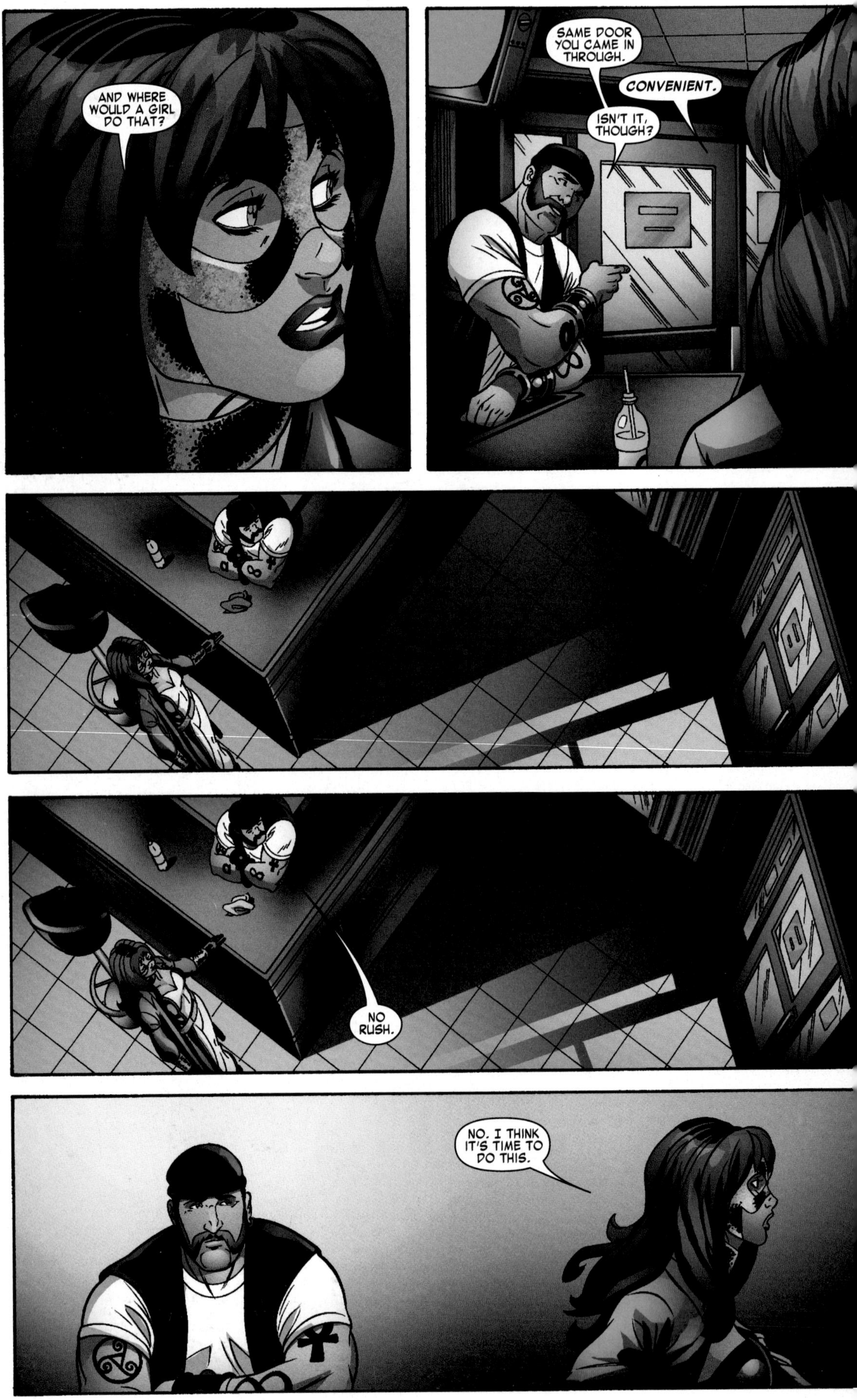
AND WHERE WOULD A GIRL DO THAT?
SAME DOOR YOU CAME IN THROUGH.
CONVENIENT.
ISN'T IT, THOUGH?
NO RUSH.
NO. I THINK IT'S TIME TO DO THIS.

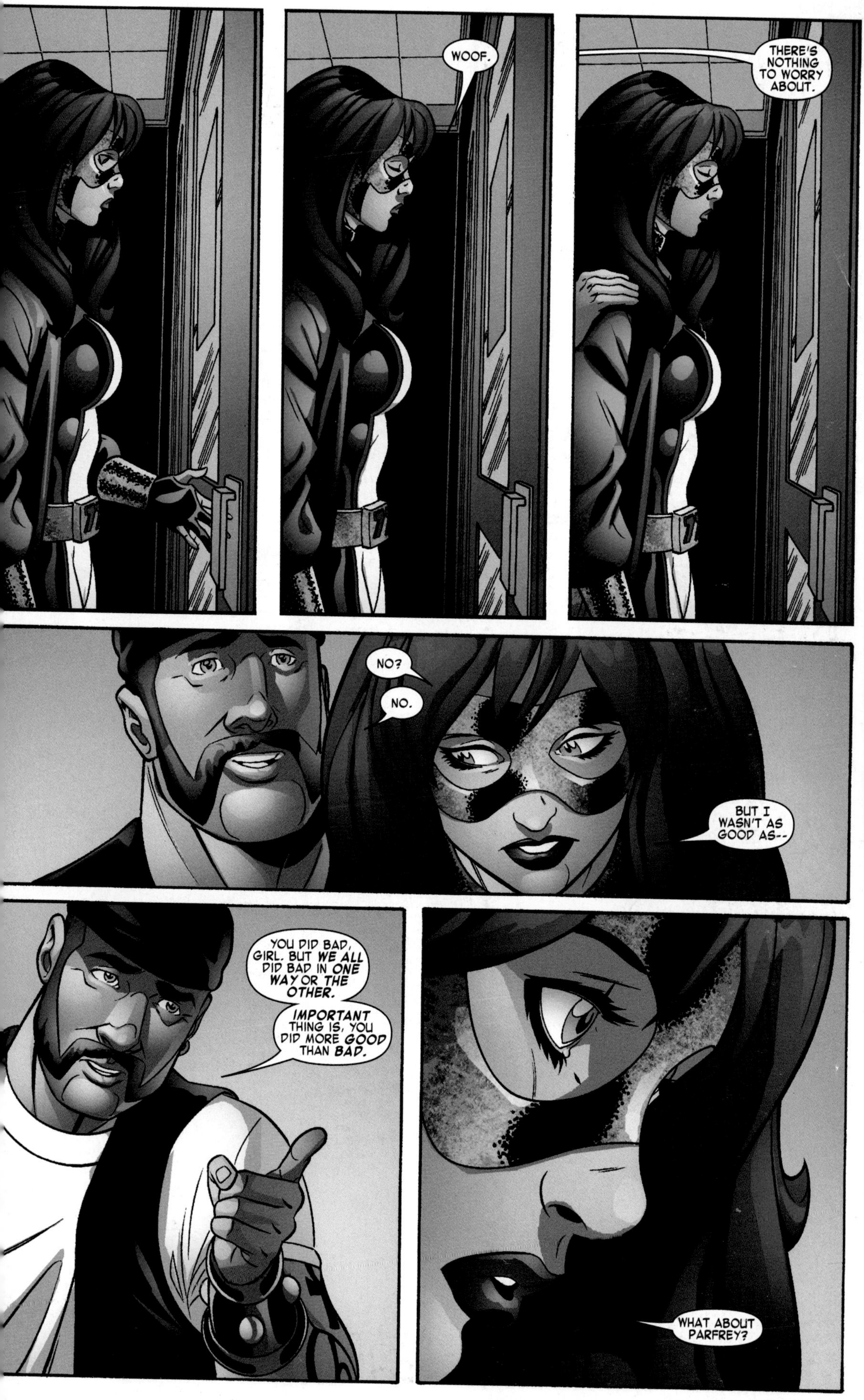
WOOF.
THERE'S NOTHING TO WORRY ABOUT.
NO?
NO.
BUT I WASN'T AS GOOD AS--
YOU DID BAD, GIRL. BUT WE ALL DID BAD IN ONE WAY OR THE OTHER.
IMPORTANT THING IS, YOU DID MORE GOOD THAN BAD.
WHAT ABOUT PARFREY?

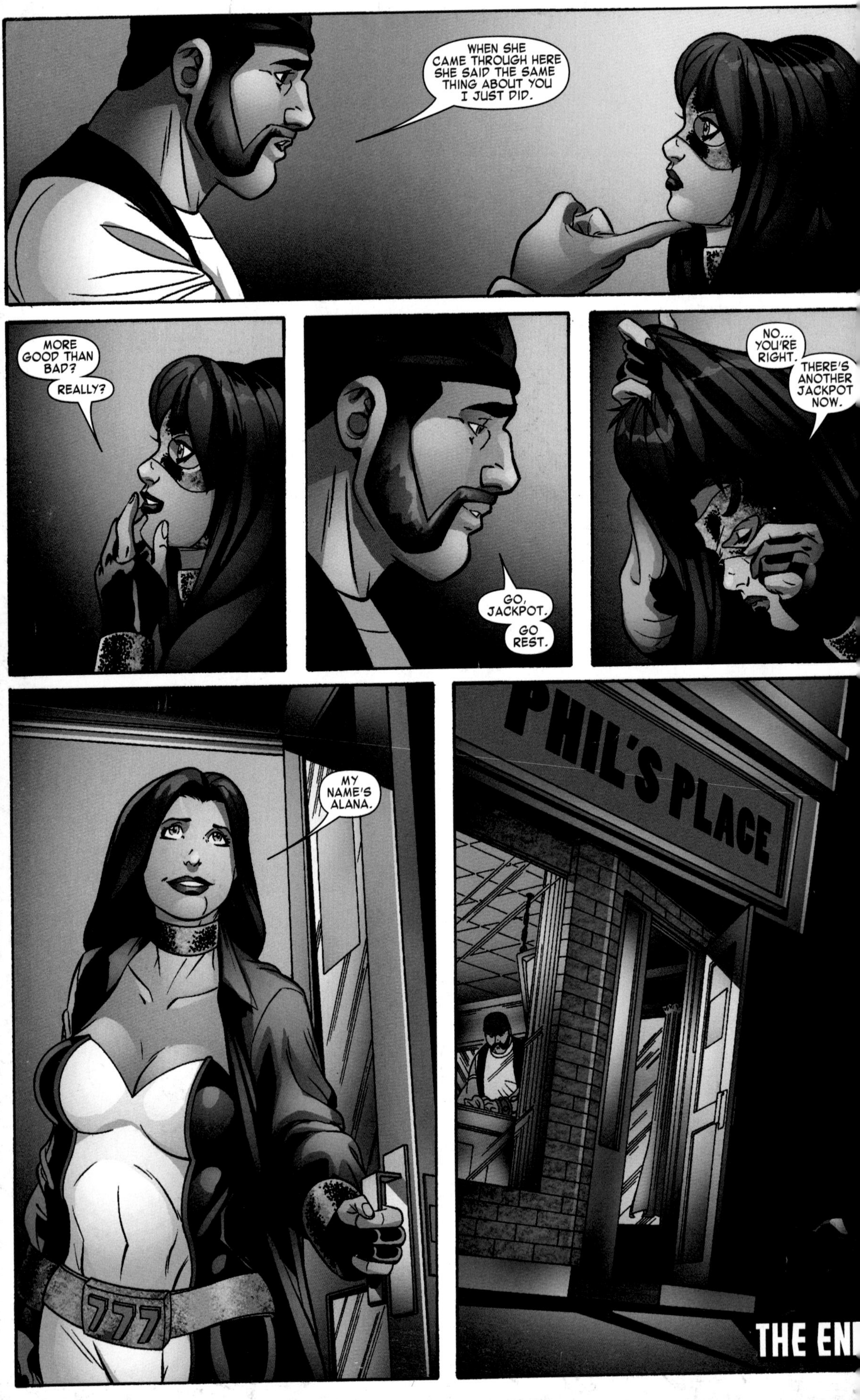
WHEN SHE CAME THROUGH HERE SHE SAID THE SAME THING ABOUT YOU I JUST DID.
MORE GOOD THAN BAD?
REALLY?
GO, JACKPOT.
GO REST.
NO... YOU'RE RIGHT.
THERE'S ANOTHER JACKPOT NOW.
MY NAME'S ALANA.
777
PHIL'S PLACE
THE END

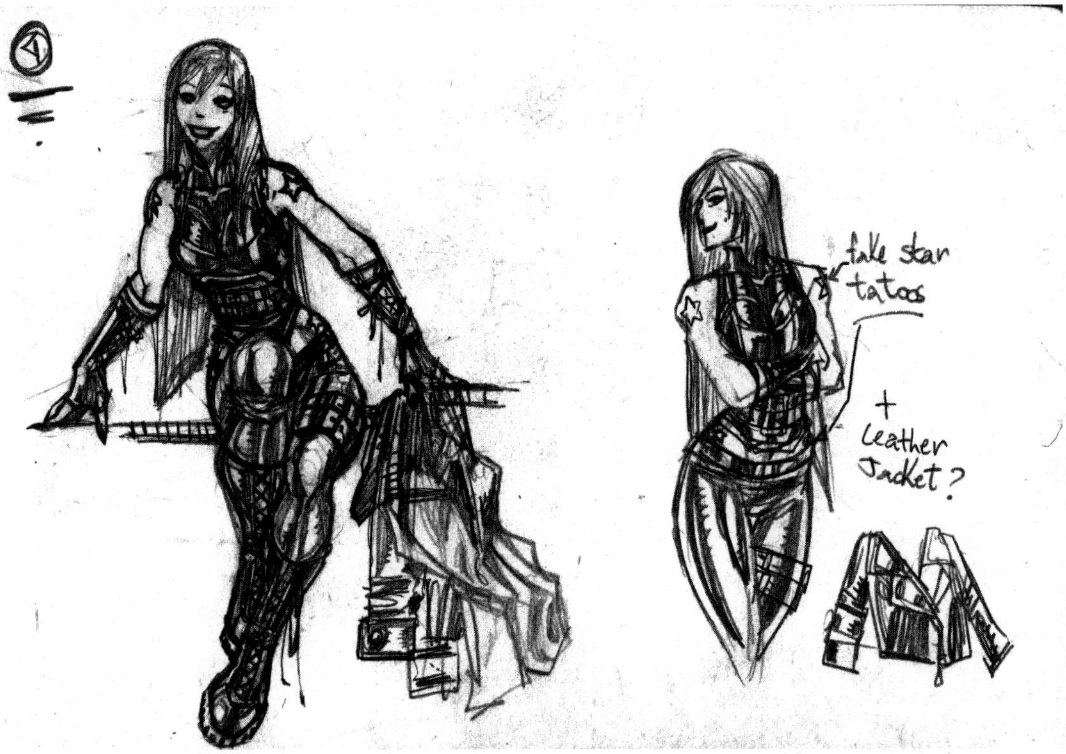
fake star
tatoos
+
Leather
Jacket?

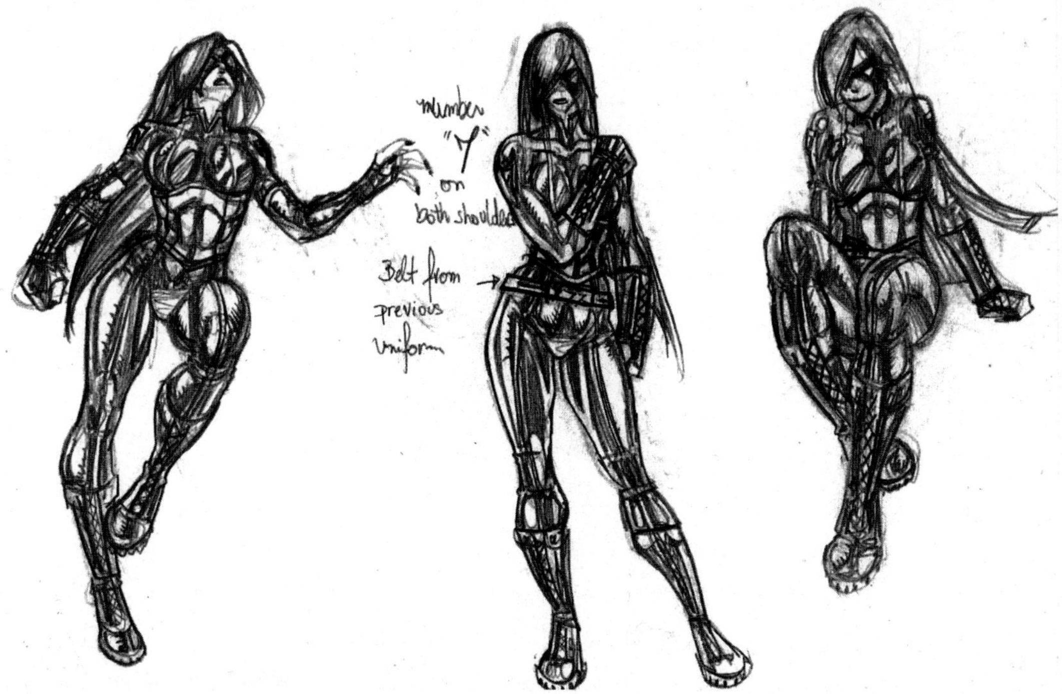
number
"4"
on
both shoulders
Belt from
previous
Uniform

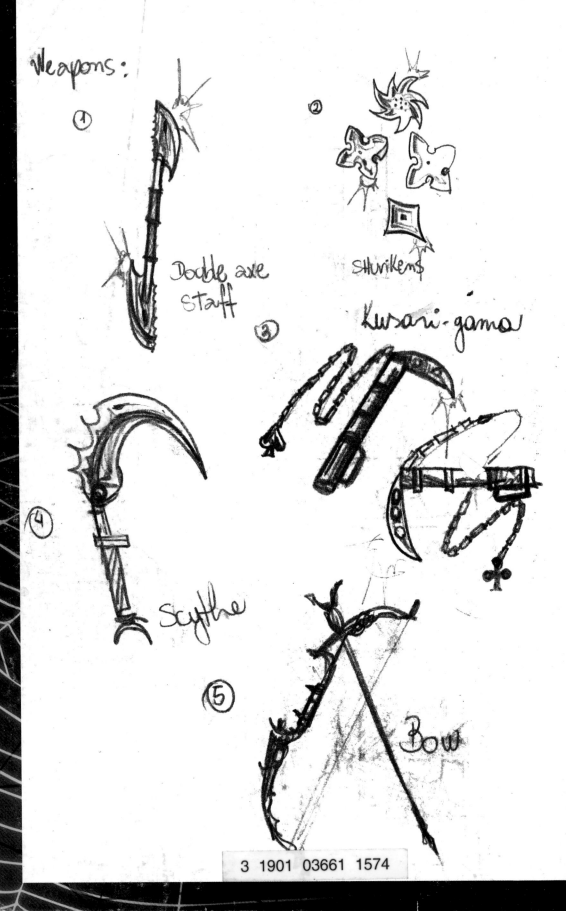

Weapons:

① Double axe staff

② Shurikens

③ Kusari-gama

④ Scythe

⑤ Bow